REVOLUTIONS IN SOUND

WARNER BROS. RECORDS

THE FIRST FIFTY YEARS

BY WARREN ZANES

CHRONICLE BOOKS
SAN FRANCISCO

Library of Congress Cataloging-in-Publication Data is available.

ISBN: 978-0-8118-6628-6

Manufactured in China

Designed by Ryan Corey, SMOG Design, Inc.

10 9 8 7 6 5 4 3 2 1

Chronicle Books LLC
680 Second Street
San Francisco, California 94107

www.chroniclebooks.com

CONTENTS

THE FIRST NAME IN ENTERTAINMENT

WARNER BROS RECORDS

THE FIRST NAME IN SOUND THE FIRST NAME IN SOUND
THE FIRST NAME IN SOUND THE FIRST NAME IN SOUND
THE FIRST NAME IN SOUND THE FIRST NAME IN SOUND
THE FIRST NAME IN SOUND THE FIRST NAME IN SOUND
THE FIRST NAME IN SOUND THE FIRST NAME IN SOUND
THE FIRST NAME IN SOUND THE FIRST NAME IN SOUND
THE FIRST NAME IN SOUND THE FIRST NAME IN SOUND
THE FIRST NAME IN SOUND THE FIRST NAME IN SOUND
THE FIRST NAME IN SOUND THE FIRST NAME IN SOUND
THE FIRST NAME IN SOUND THE FIRST NAME IN SOUND
THE FIRST NAME IN SOUND THE FIRST NAME IN SOUND
THE FIRST NAME IN SOUND THE FIRST NAME IN SOUND
THE FIRST NAME IN SOUND THE FIRST NAME IN SOUND
THE FIRST NAME IN SOUND THE FIRST NAME IN SOUND
THE FIRST NAME IN SOUND THE FIRST NAME IN SOUND

INTRODUCTION

It's easy to project something like *inevitability* onto a label as storied as Warner Bros. Records. What makes the company interesting, however, is that it emerged not decisively but awkwardly, stumbling out of the gates rather than galloping confidently toward its own realization. Because of its tentative beginnings, Warner Bros. Records could have been little more than a footnote in the larger narrative of American popular music. If the best product you've got is "Kookie, Kookie (Lend Me Your Comb)," there's no reason to assume that Jimi Hendrix, Randy Newman, Joni Mitchell, Prince, Neil Young, and Madonna are on the way.

Take this fact: Jack Warner once introduced Bob Newhart as "the man who saved Warner Bros. Records." Such a remark points to the wonderfully strange and still rather obscure beginnings of the company. Here is a label that didn't know what it was but took the steps *and* the missteps required to get where it was going, to invent its way into being. Through intuition, luck, impulse, guesswork, good sense, eccentricity, grand foolishness, and, yes, *vision*, Warner Bros. Records became Warner Bros. Records. Though a few characters loom large throughout this book, even the heroes of the story cannot take full credit for the rich history that unfolded. The cast is enormous, much larger than what is represented in these pages. In the sixty-plus interviews I conducted with artists and executives, Warner Bros. Records was described as a "menagerie" as many times as it was described as a "family." But in all cases it was remembered with warmth . . . and, in the majority, *awe*. Something unplanned took place in Burbank, and the right people were there to recognize it, cultivate it, derive from it a philosophy and a business practice, and, most critically, keep the machine running. Rarely do art and commerce get on as they have at Warner Bros. Records.

In many respects, this book is a collection of conversations with some of the people who put the fuel in, who worked for and recorded for Warner Bros. Records. Many of the interviews I conducted took place after my children were in bed, when, sitting in the partial darkness of my home office, I could really be taken for a trip. The person on the other end of the telephone line might be Lou Dennis, Randy Newman, Carl Scott, Tom Petty, Liz Rosenberg, Bob Krasnow, Wayne Coyne, Diarmuid Quinn, Ice-T, Paul Simon, Tom Biery, Ry Cooder, Petula Clark, or any other among the remarkable cast. The conversations transported me. If popular music culture is thick with storytellers, I had a direct line to some of the best. Their stories were not always consistent one to the next, but that—as is the case with any oral history project—is part of the pleasure. The search is not for facts but for the depth of feeling attached to individual memories. And my subjects' memories took me all over the place, into warehouses with indie record distributors, into studios where a teenage Prince was cutting demos, into offices where Ice-T's "Cop Killer" was being debated, into bathrooms, boardrooms, and alleyways. If a *fraction* of the passion my interview subjects shared with me comes across in these pages, it will be enough. Their love for the subject at hand, Warner Bros. Records and its music, drove this project. I was lucky to have had the conversations.

If I've mentioned a few of the principals involved, no individual is more central to this story than Mo Ostin. More than anyone, he created the *environment* that allowed what happened at Warner Bros. Records to happen. Many of my interviewees used that very word, "environment," as they attempted to describe what made Warner Bros. Records different. Yes, A&R came first. Therein lies the key to the label's approach. But as Mo Ostin and his team went about finding the many ways in which to actualize that priority, a culture emerged, a culture that involved a remarkable degree of employee empowerment—if you believed in an act, you could champion them, tout them, and, sometimes, break them. The deliberate manner in which Ostin eventually named Lenny Waronker the president of Warner Bros. Records is one of the most conspicuous gestures revealing Ostin's creative business strategy. As a producer, what Waronker did was find ways to create a context that maximized the creativity of his artists. As a record company president, he kept doing

that, *creating a context that maximized creativity*. And that's what Ostin wanted of him. Likely Mo Ostin wouldn't have stuck with this approach, or with Lenny, if it hadn't led to sales. But—and here's where the story gets really good—it did.

In the short time during which my former band, the Del Fuegos, was on the Warner Bros. Records roster, arriving there through affiliate label Slash Records, the staff included Mo Ostin and Lenny Waronker, but it also had people like Jeff Ayeroff, Michael Ostin, Russ Thyret, Steven Baker, Lou Dennis, Georgia Bergman, and others. Artists on the label at the time included Prince, ZZ Top, the Replacements, Madonna, Randy Travis. I remember driving out to Burbank for the first time, our managers concerned that we'd behave like jackasses once we were in the building. But, frankly, there was too much there to respect. Unbeknownst to our managers, we had our limits. It was Los Angeles: We had plenty of other places to behave like jackasses. We viewed the office as magical. We met John Fogerty in the hallway. Georgia Bergman put us on the phone with the great Stones' biographer Stanley Booth. Steven Baker told us about John Cale producing the Modern Lovers for the label. And, upon our request not his, Lenny Waronker scheduled a meeting with us—because we just wanted to be able to say we'd done it. In putting things together for this book, I've returned to the hallways at Warner Bros. Records, if only through the words of others, and it has been a joy. My old band loved that place, simply because people there talked almost exclusively about music. And that's just what I returned to. I wish time and space allowed me to get to everyone I wanted to, but the fifty years I was covering were fifty very good years. I couldn't get to it all. Not even close. But my aim was not to be comprehensive so much as it was to capture the spirit of a unique business approach that made art its priority.

I end with this: Given the remarkable amount of time we've recently dedicated to long, increasingly dull conversations about the state of the music business, about the uncertainty that looms—why can't we stop ourselves?—there's value in recalling what made the industry work once upon a time. If at first glance it seems that the business past offers little to the present, it's worth remembering that uncertainty is where a label like Warners began. *Return to the Machine Shop!* That's the imperative that I draw from the story of Warner Bros. Records. In that machine shop, a hand-me-down building on the Warner Bros. movie lot, a modest staff inadvertently arrived at a philosophy that for decades propelled the company: *If we make this about the music, we'll be okay.* If as a philosophy that sounds easy, it isn't. But the truth it carries is durable. And it does apply. If this book says nothing else, it says, "This happened." And even if the next music industry is going to be unlike anything we've seen before, the Warner Bros. Records lesson will again apply. It always will.

ITS BETTER IN BURBANK

THE ENSEMBLE
(INTERVIEWED FEBRUARY–MAY, 2008)

There is no disentangling the music of Warner Bros. Records from the people at the company who brought it into the world. Whether they worked in A&R, sales and marketing, art direction, radio promotion, creative services, artist relations, business affairs, publicity, or elsewhere 'in the building," many were the people and many were the departments that found innovative ways to connect the music with its audience. In putting together *Revolutions in Sound*, I made every effort to get the voices of the company onto these pages. While I could never talk to everyone who played a role, I did speak with many, all of whom are listed below. Some worked for the label for more than three decades, others for a shorter time. A few started in the mailroom and moved through the ranks, the spirit of the company in their bones. Others began their careers in regional offices or came to Warner Bros. Records through the affiliate labels that meant so much to the company's roster over the decades. All of them brought something to the party. All of them, at some point, fell in love with music and found a way to do something about it. Their voices speak throughout the book.

CRAIG AARONSO

JEFF AYEROFF

STEVEN BAKER

GEORGIA BERGM

DAVID BERMAN

TOM BIERY

BOB BIGGS

JIMMY BOWEN

STAN CORNYN

LOU DENNIS

Future Home of Warner Bros. Pictures Back Lot, early 1900s

CHAPTER ONE
BREAKING GROUND

AT A 1965 FRIAR'S CLUB DINNER HONORING JACK WARNER, FRANK SINATRA PRAISED THE WARNER SIBLINGS FOR SHOWING THE WORLD "THE TRUE MEANING OF BROTHERHOOD." AS SINATRA EXPLAINED, THEIR KNOWLEDGE OF THE CONCEPT CAME TO THEM NATURALLY— AFTER ALL, "THEY WERE BROTHERS AND THEY WERE HOODS."

WARNER BROTHERHOOD

Like most good comedy, Sinatra's brand of humor worked in part because of its uncomfortable proximity to the truth. Jack Warner was a good movie executive. He knew how to move amongst the stars, always tan, always laughing when the cameras turned his way. But when business demanded it of him, he could take it to the streets. In fact, by the time he founded Warner Bros. Records, there were no brothers in Warner Bros. Blood had lost out to business. Through cunning and a willingness to force his way through the thicket of Warner family ties, Warner got himself into the seat of power and his brothers off the lot. In the pages of *Vanity Fair* the moment is described less gently: "Jack had fucked his brothers but good." It was a maneuver Shakespearean in its proportions. Afterwards, the Warner boys would never speak again. This was the Jack Warner who, in 1957, wanted a record label. **Stan Cornyn:** "Everybody seemed to call him 'Chief'. He was always well-shaved. I think he had his own barber downstairs. When you walked into his office you'd go down some steps, and then there's that desk: seven to eight feet wide and up on a pedestal—so Jack Warner was always a little higher than anybody else in the room."

As with most matters in the entertainment business, Warner's interest in starting a record company came down to money. He was more than a little displeased when one of his contracted actors, Tab Hunter, scored a major hit for Dot Records. Hunter's "Young Love" went to number one in 1957. A second version, recorded by Sonny James, was at number four. You couldn't escape the song. From Warner's perspective, his company had raised Tab Hunter's visibility, groomed the young star, and Dot came in from behind to make the money on him.

Making matters worse, on a promotional tour for the Warner Bros. film *The Spirit of St. Louis*, Tab Hunter spent more time talking about his hit song with Dot Records than he did the failing movie he made with Warner Bros. In his own defense, the actor elaborated: "Everyone knew the plane landed safely . . . so they kept saying, 'Tell us about your new record'." *The Spirit of St. Louis*, directed by Billy Wilder at a cost of six million dollars, was considered a major loss. Needless to say, there were layers to Jack Warner's embarrassment.

And so, for all the wrong reasons, Warner Bros. Records was born. It was March of 1958. The company's address: 3701 Warner Boulevard, Burbank, California, a former machine shop on the Warner Bros. movie lot. Life in that building would never be a matter of great significance to Jack Warner, so long as money was being made. In the biographies written about him, Warner Bros. Records is typically left unmentioned. Warner's initial concern, Tab Hunter, though quickly signed to the new company, would never score another big hit. It may have looked simple when Dot Records sent "Young Love" to the top of the charts, but the birth of Warner Bros. Records was not going to be without labor pains.

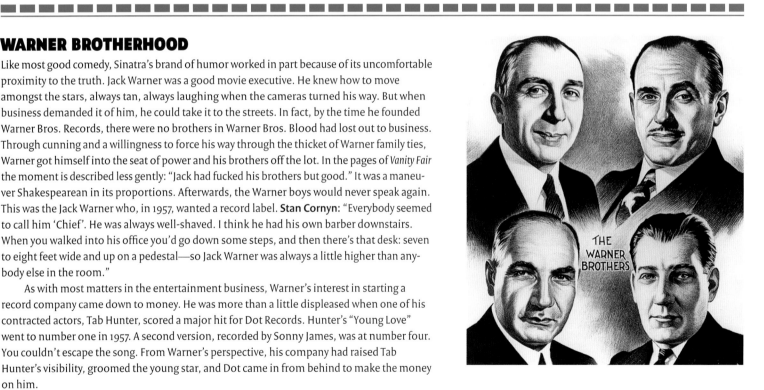

↑ The four Warner brothers circa 1930, clockwise from top left: Harry, Jack, Sam, Albert.

← Ingrid Bergman sheds a tear on the cover of the first Warner Bros. LP, the soundtrack to *For Whom the Bell Tolls*, featuring the Warner Bros. Studio Orchestra conducted by Ray Heindorf, 1958.

Opening spread: A 27-year-old Jack Warner breaking ground for the Warner Bros. Sunset lot in Hollywood, 1919.

↑ A Brunswick release from the period in which it was owned by Warner
Bros. Studios, circa 1931. No matter the talent involved—in this case Bing
Crosby—the Brunswick experience left the company wary of the record
business.

↑↑ A dust sleeve used in the first LP releases, featuring Warner Bros.'
motion picture studios lot. Used from 1958–1960.

↗ Tab Hunter's self-titled LP debut from 1958. It was Hunter on whom Jack
Warner pinned his hopes for the label.

→↗ Jim Conkling, the first president of Warner Bros. Records. The furrowed
brow would stay with him for most of the two-year period during which he
led the company.

→→ A brochure announcing the world premiere of Warner Bros. Records,
The First Name in Sound, September 1958.

OLD WOUNDS

To understand fully the launch of Warner Bros. Records, it's worth considering the prehistory
of that event. Warner Bros. Records wasn't the Warner family's first foray into the music business. In 1930 the company bought Brunswick Records for eight million dollars. Brunswick
had released songs from *The Jazz Singer*, starring Al Jolson and historically significant as the first
feature-length "talkie," a film employing synchronized dialogue. While the film's success had
helped to secure the movie company's future, the soundtrack did similar work for Brunswick.
A few years later the Warner Bros. purchase of Brunswick brought the two companies' interests together. Included in the deal were Brunswick's record-pressing plant, the Vocalion label,
and a number of other ventures in which Brunswick had a hand, including radios, bowling
balls, and billiard tables. Not wanting to be in the recreation business, Warner Bros. sold off
everything except the record-pressing machines and the record labels. But, over time, what
originally looked like a smart move became a source of shame. The company would have been
better off if they'd held onto the bowling balls.

Brunswick's track record before the Warner Bros. purchase included a number of high
points. The label had signed a young Bing Crosby, handled Jolson's recordings, and released
Cab Calloway's classic, "Minnie the Moocher." But the Depression battered the record industry.
Rather than await a change in fortunes, Warner Bros. got out, selling Brunswick for a major
loss to American Record Company. For those Warner Bros. film executives still around a quarter century later, the Brunswick deal was reason enough to stay out of the record business—
still. But, at the end of the day, it wasn't going to be their names on the label and it wasn't going
to be their decision.

THE INDUSTRY IN 1958

Bob Krasnow: "The music business was going through a huge transition." Since the 1930s,
the landscape of the recording industry had transformed. Among the changes that could be wit-
nessed in 1958 were those brought about by the rise of rock & roll, a music belonging to
post-War America and one of its native creatures, the teenager. Perhaps most significantly,
when rock & roll first hit, the major labels kept their distance, waiting for this new phenomenon to pass. That gesture, born both of contempt and, possibly, ineptitude, gave the culture
of indie labels a shot of adrenaline. Off on the margins, things heated up.

In the first years of rock & roll, entrepreneurship took many forms, visionaries and
madmen mixing freely—often indistinguishably and to great effect. Labels like Atlantic, Imperial,
King, Specialty, Red Bird, Modern, Sun, Chess, Roulette, and so many more operated with little
regard for the comparatively sterile culture of the major labels. It was a Wild West of sorts. And
in the immediate absence of laws, invention became a reflex. This spirit of invention wasn't,
of course, just in the business—you could hear it in the music. There was something vital going

on. Art and commerce had a good thing going. There was no Elvis Presley without Sam Phillips. It was a remarkably productive exchange that would affect the industry for years to come.

But if the indie scene was vibrant, populated with characters—strange, wonderful, sometimes awful characters—that's not where Warner Bros. launched its first efforts. **Seymour Stein:** "You couldn't compare Warner Bros. Records to anything good. They were horrible. I looked at every Imperial label, every Vee-Jay label, every Specialty label, every Chess and Checker . . . I never looked at Warner Bros. because the bulk of their early releases were crap." But as others have pointed out, there's little reason to expect that a company like Warner Bros. might have slipped into the world of the indies and gotten off on the good foot. They were, after all, a publicly traded company, far from the margins that housed the finest among the rock & roll labels. **Bob Krasnow:** "Even if Warner Bros. Records had wanted to start in the margins, they probably wouldn't have understood where the margins were." In the history of important American record companies, the Warner Bros. story is not one in which greatness haunted the company from the beginning. As Krasnow suggests, it's not that Warner Bros. wasn't invited to the party, they simply didn't know that one was taking place.

To be fair, if Warner Bros. Records followed any example, it only made sense that it would be that of the other movie companies with music interests, including MGM and Paramount. And those labels operated in a different sphere than did Sun Records or Atlantic. Warner Bros. Records was not entering into the music business from a single, rented room in a rough part of town—the company was situated on the lot of a major movie company, the company known for *Casablanca*. If they didn't act like an indie, it was for obvious reasons. **Joe Smith:** "The Chess brothers and Vee-Jay: Those people owned their labels and could do anything they wanted. Warners was part of a big corporation on the New York Stock Exchange and had to be careful with what they did." And careful they were. So careful that few would know they were there at all.

ESTABLISHING AN IDENTITY

Jack Warner wanted two obvious things for his company: strong leadership and, without too much of a delay, financial autonomy. In his thinking, the former would bring about the latter. Recommended to him was Jim Conkling, a veteran of the recording industry. Conkling presented Warner Bros. executives with a business plan that looked sensible, and, in the process, he got the offer to become the first president of Warner Bros. Records.

There was a solid rationale behind the selection. **Stan Cornyn:** "Jim was from the big school of the majors. That's what he was used to." Conkling had worked for both Capitol and Columbia Records. He had founded the Recording Industry Association of America (RIAA), an increasingly powerful advocacy organization for the music business. He played an important role in the birth of the National Academy of Recording Arts and Sciences (NARAS), the organization that gave out Grammy Awards. Finally, he was the man who had come up with the idea of "record clubs," a virtual profit machine that sent thousands of records to club members, whether they really wanted them or not. But despite his deep background and the company's visibility, Conkling was starting from scratch. **Jim Conkling:** "Here I was supposed to be starting a first-class record company. I had no secretary. I had no file cabinet . . . . In fact,

WORLD PREMIERE WARNER BROS. RECORDS

the first name in sound

the only things in the office besides the desk and chair were one lead pencil and a yellow pad of paper. That was it. That was Warner Bros. Records, Incorporated."

Conkling's first decision would be the most meaningful: On what musical area would the label focus its efforts? Though Tab Hunter would be among the first artists signed to the Warner Bros. roster, Conkling decided to go in what seemed a safe direction: the adult pop market. Rather than emphasize singles, Conkling made the LP a Warner Bros. priority. The decision to do so was not arbitrary. During Conkling's tenure as the president of Columbia, he played a key role in establishing the LP as a format for popular music. In what some called the "battle of the speeds," Columbia and RCA fought for 33 1/3 rpm and 45 rpm respectively. Conkling went so far as to work with publishers in order to bring royalty rates down, making the long player a fiscal possibility. Perhaps his heart was still in that battle. Given the connection between the young audience of the day and the singles format, it's no surprise that Conkling's interest in the album led Warner Bros. away from the youth market and straight into the arms of an equally unmoved adult mainstream consumer. **Bob Merlis:** "It was an album-oriented company from the beginning. They had these *conceptual* albums."

Artists like Ira Ironstrings and Buddy Cole—not coincidentally, *both* brothers-in-law to Conkling—released album after album in this "conceptual" vein. *Music for People with $3.98 (Plus Tax If Any)* by Ira Ironstrings, Cole's *Have Organ, Will Swing, Sousa in Stereo* by the Warner Bros. Military Band, *Waltzing Down Broadway* by Warren Barker, Irving Taylor's *Terribly Sophisticated Songs*. This selection, however small in relation to the enormous output of Warner Bros. Records' first years, captures the spirit of Warner Bros. Records in that era. **Lou Dennis:** "I was a disc jockey from 1953 until 1962 in Lewiston, Maine, and Waterbury, Connecticut. We started the whole rock & roll movement. Joe Smith was in Boston, and he was big time. I was in tertiary markets. I was playing the race records that would become rock & roll. Of course, I saw the Warner Bros. releases, Joe 'Fingers' Carr and so forth. I thought, 'What the hell is this?'"

Amidst the first year's many releases, there were surprisingly few soundtracks connected to Warner Bros. films. For whatever reason, Warner Bros. Records, different from MGM, was not quick to find a creative connection to its parent company. The releases seemed to hover in some odd space of the mainstream wherein they remained hidden from view and safe from the loud clang of the cash register.

THE VITAPHONIC ANSWER!

Technology had been good to Jack Warner. The so-called Vitaphone process had been part of Warner Bros. movie-making culture since 1926 when the silent film *Don Juan*, starring John Barrymore, would include a sound element, though not yet dialogue. If only as a name, "Vitaphone" would be used again in relation to Warner Bros. animation and yet again with

↑ The original Warner Bros. Records logo illustrated how closely it was allied with its motion picture studio, 1958.

↗ *Vitaphonic Stereo: Extra Sensory Perception in Sound.* Released in 1959, this album reveals the degree to which the company promoted "Hi-Fi" sounds in its first years. Who needs artists when you've got Vitaphonic Stereo!

the record company. Warner, together with Conkling, felt that technology could impact the fortunes of the new record company. In a 1958 letter to stockholders, Warner made his case, explaining that the music business had "more than doubled in size since 1955" and the "advent of stereophonic records for the home is expected to increase the market further." And so Vitaphonic Hi-Fi and Vitaphonic Stereo records were released, touted to distributors. **Stan Cornyn:** "Jim Conkling would turn to people he knew and say, 'There's no square dancing in stereo album.' So there it was, we'd see something like *Square Dance in Stereo*. I do suppose stereo was somewhat novel in those days, certainly in Wyoming." For years this technological angle would be promoted. By 1959 Warner Bros. would even release an album simply entitled *Vitaphonic Stereo*, as if that calling card was enough in itself, with no mention of the artists in the title. **Joe Smith:** "Support for the Vitaphonic idea came from Conkling, and after that, from Mike Maitland [Conkling's successor]. I remember when we took it out on the road to play for our distributors. To me, it sounded like the old records. So I would have the guy jack up the volume, and I'd say, 'Woo, that sounds a lot different!'"

Efrem Zimbalist, Jr.

Roger Smith

Edward "Kookie" Byrnes

Emphasizing adult pop albums and new technologies, shipping tremendous amounts of product without the support of airplay, Warner Bros. Records hobbled its first year. Tab Hunter's single, "Jealous Heart" only made it to number 62 on the *Billboard* charts in 1958. Still, it was the one Warner Bros. single that did make the charts that year. Rather than establish an A&R philosophy and go after new talent, they attempted to look within the Warner Bros. ranks for artists who might help to establish the recording division and sell a few copies in the process. And, frankly, it was still a better idea than to drift aimlessly in the adult pop area.

Stan Cornyn: "Conkling's other source for recordings came from across the street at the television studios." In late 1958, Warner Bros. television had a hit with *77 Sunset Strip*, an hour long, LA-based private detective series. *77 Sunset Strip* starred Efrem Zimbalist, Jr., Roger Smith, and Edd Byrnes, whose character, "Kookie," had his own hip vocabulary and greased hair that he always seemed to be combing. Kookie wasn't a private eye like the characters Zimbalist and Smith played. Instead, he was the parking attendant at Dino's Lodge. However, he quickly became *77 Sunset Strip*'s biggest attraction, especially with young people who yearned to be as smooth as Kookie. During the show Byrnes would talk "Kookie talk." He was the "ginchiest" (coolest) actor on the show, attracting a tremendous fan base as he "stabled the horses" (parked the cars) to earn a "Washington" (a dollar) or two. As a result, Kookie got more than two thousand fan letters a week for the next year.

Jim Conkling and his head of A&R, George Avakian, decided to sign Edd "Kookie" Byrnes to a recording contract. Despite his limitations as a singer, Byrnes went into the studio and cut a song called "Kookie, Kookie (Lend Me Your Comb)." To support him, Warner Bros. used yet another in-house teen personality, Connie Stevens. On record, Stevens begged, "Kookie, Kookie, lend me your comb," and implored the parking lot attendant to "stop combing your hair and kiss me. You're the maximum utmost."

"Kookie, Kookie (Lend Me Your Comb)" went to the number four slot on *Billboard*'s pop charts in 1959. It was Warner Bros. Records' first big hit single. **Lou Dennis:** "As a deejay, I could play 'Kookie, Kookie (Lend Me Your Comb)', but not the other stuff. My job was to get to the young people in town, so we played music that actually appealed to them." The follow-up album, *77 Sunset Strip*, went to number three on the album charts. With little time for subtle maneuvers, Conkling kept at it. "Kookie" Byrnes quickly went back into the studio and recorded "Like I Love You," which peaked at number forty-two. And then it was fellow actor Roger Smith's turn; he recorded "Beach Time." Smith, however, wasn't in possession of the Kookie magic; the single didn't make the Top Forty, stalling at number sixty-two. Conkling and Avakian tried to score another Warner Bros. hit single, this time with Connie Stevens, who now had a part on the *77 Sunset Strip* copy series, *Hawaiian Eye*, as well as more from Tab Hunter, but to no avail. Warner Bros. even had Clint Walker, the new star of the TV series *Cheyenne*, record an album of sacred music. Now they were really reaching.

HOW (NOT) TO SUCCEED IN BUSINESS

Conkling and Avakian enjoyed a moment of success with "Kookie, Kookie (Lend Me Your Comb)." Without that reprieve, the label's troubled beginnings might have led to a quick finish. But, at the same time, the single might have made it to the coveted number one position on the charts had Warner Bros. taken full advantage of its considerable if fleeting popularity. If Warners' A&R instincts were weak, their promotional efforts were even less developed.

Still a deejay up in Boston at that point, Joe Smith didn't think much of "Kookie, Kookie (Lend Me Your Comb)." But his teen radio audience liked the song, so he played it. Assuming that any label would welcome promotional help from a key radio station in a major market, Smith promised his friend, Cardinal Cushing of Boston, the leader of the city's large Catholic community, that he could get Kookie Byrnes to appear at a major Catholic Youth Organization (CYO) event. He set it up.

⬆ Trying to understand the teenage market: Granny appears in an ad for "Kookie" Byrnes' second single, "Like I Love You," 1959.

⬆⬆ The stars of *77 Sunset Strip* from the back cover of the hit LP named after the series.

FIRST NAME IN SOUND

Vitaphonic High Fidelity, the optimum in quality sound reproduction,
is an expression of the meticulous care and engineering skill
that go into the making of all Warner Bros. records.

A new recording is about to begin! The conductor carefully makes final preparations before the sound is recorded on tape.

The sound from the studio is carried to magnetic tape recorders which reproduce sound impressions on tape.

Music from the tapes are re-recorded on acetate discs. Fine microgrooves are cut in the lacquer master, and studiously inspected by microscope.

A newly recorded acetate disc is given a thin coating of silver and immersed in a plating tank to make a metal master. A metal mother, and later a stamper will be made.

The stamper is mounted in an automatic hydraulic press, labels are affixed and a hot "biscuit" inserted to produce the finished recording.

Careful visual inspection of each record for molding defects in the manufacturing process is a prime requisite.

Records are packed for shipping to record stores throughout the country.

A satisfied customer has purchased the recording from your neighborhood music dealer.

WARNER BROS. RECORDS, INC.

Vitaphonic High Fidelity . . . *the first name in sound!*

Joe Smith: "They stiffed me. I didn't believe a record company could be as stupid as Warner Bros. I had Byrnes making an appearance at Fenway Park, with people like Cardinal Cushing and Senator Jack Kennedy involved in the event, and they couldn't get him up to Boston. We were all waiting for Byrnes to appear and the Cardinal leans over and says to me, 'So, what about this here creep with the comb. Is he gonna show?' Well, he never did. I just couldn't believe it."

So angered was Smith by Warner Bros. Records' "complete lack of professionalism," that he fired off a letter to the label's brass, condemning the company and vowing never again to deal with its music or artists. **Joe Smith:** "I didn't think the label would make it. Nobody there seemed to know anything about the music business. They all just seemed to exist in a world that wasn't even close to reality. It was just a pitiful situation. Anybody who worked for that company was in the wrong place."

That's just what Jack Warner and the rest of the Warner Bros.' film and studio executives began to think about the fledgling record company. When 1959's fourth quarter numbers came in, there was, putting it gently, concern. A year into the music business venture, Warner Bros. Records was already in debt. More than three million dollars in debt, with nothing to show for it except "Kookie, Kookie (Lend Me Your Comb)" and one hit album, *77 Sunset Strip*, which only happened because of its connection to a hit TV series. The ghost of Brunswick Records began to walk the halls at the company. From where Jack Warner stood, it looked as if the only smart thing to do was to kill the label while the losses weren't completely debilitating. Conkling urged patience; Warner's advisors pulled in the opposite direction. **Joe Smith:** "They wanted to shut down that company."

For the moment, Conkling was allowed to carry on. Company finances, however, were under new scrutiny. Every move had to be approved through the New York offices of Warner Bros. movie division. Herman Starr, a formidable money manager, pulled the reins on Jim Conkling. And life in the machine shop in Burbank changed. **Stan Cornyn:** "I was having the time of my life. I reported to Joel Friedman and was writing liner notes, some of them terrible and a couple getting good. One day—I think it was on a Friday—Joel's secretary said, 'Can you come see Joel?' I walked twenty feet down the hall, and he said, 'I have some bad news.' Soon, I woke up to the fact that all down the hallway people were putting things in boxes. The company really shrank."

↗ From the studio to the store: The Vitaphonic record-making process is pictured on a 1958 Warner Bros. dust sleeve.

➜ The idyllic "Palm Tree" label was inspired by art from a 1920s orange crate.

WARNER BROS.' FIRST 15 LP RELEASES

MO OSTIN ON WARNER BROS. RECORDS

I was in shock when I was selected to run Reprise. I really wasn't qualified. I had so much to learn, and probably the weakest area for me—though it later turned out to be a very strong area—was that of A&R. I learned along the way and grew into that job. But it was never some lifelong goal of mine to be in the music business. It all happened by accident. Lenny [Waronker] knew what he wanted from the very beginning. I, on the other hand, just happened to get a record company position as my first job out of UCLA. As it turned out, it so engaged me that it became my life. The fact that I was able to accomplish as much as I did, and that we were able to build a company of the kind that Warner Bros. became, *that* surprises me even to this day. Every time I look back on the fifty years of my career I'm somewhat in awe of all that transpired. It was an amazing experience.

Because of my work at Verve with Norman Granz, Frank Sinatra's lawyer, Mickey Rudin, suggested me as a person who might run the label Sinatra wanted to start. I met with Frank's manager, after which I was supposed to meet with Frank himself. So, I went to meet Sinatra on the old Columbia lot, the Gower Studios. He was filming *The Devil at Four O'Clock* with Spencer Tracy. Mervyn LeRoy was the director. And as I walked on the set, Sinatra was engaged in a horrific argument with Mervyn LeRoy, I mean a real scream fest. Here I was with my future in his hands, getting ready to meet with Frank Sinatra to get his approval, and I face him in this sort of rage. It scared the hell out of me. But I walked into his dressing room, which was right there on the soundstage, and when he was through with what he was doing with LeRoy, he came in. I just didn't know what to expect, and my heart was pounding. And the guy just did some turnaround. He couldn't have been more excited, couldn't have been more enthusiastic, and couldn't have been more supportive. First thing he said was, "What are we going to do about A&R? Who are we going to sign?" That's what was uppermost on his mind. It was all about the music. That's the way he was. That mindset obviously influenced me.

Frank Sinatra's basic philosophy was to create a company in which the artist was the highest priority. He wanted to have a better creative environment for

the artist *and* a better economic environment for the artist. In fact, one of the first things he said to me when I met him was, "I want to build a better mouse-trap." His overall philosophy, forgetting about the kind of music he may have been involved in, was to have this high artist orientation. In fact, he might have been one of the first to let the artists own their own master tapes. Being an artist himself, he had natural sympathies that dictated our approach.

When we started Reprise, Sinatra forbade us to sign rock acts. He was very anti-rock. His kind of music was threatened by the emerging rock idiom. Finally, he saw that if we stayed the course, signing what I would call adult-oriented artists, there was no way we could compete. I was able to convince Frank that for us to survive we would have to get into the rock field. Once he allowed us to open doors in that direction we were able to do things that made us contemporary and capable of adapting to the changes of the music business. From then on we did everything we could to work within those changes.

When I came to Warner Bros. through the Reprise deal, the label was nowhere near as fragile as it was in the Jim Conkling years. In the first few years they made a whole host of errors and spent a tremendous amount of money. They ran before they could walk, doing things they were not yet mature enough to do as a label, such as starting their own distribution system before they had the product to distribute. When Mike Maitland came in, he had the benefit of a few roster additions that came at the tail end of Conkling's time: namely Bob Newhart and the Everly Brothers. Then they got Peter, Paul & Mary—and the company started getting themselves on track. But, really, we started out as a little independent label, not much different from what Verve was.

Over the years there were many signings that were important as signings but, on another level, a handful that were especially important with regards to solidifying the *identity* of the label. The Hendrix signing, for instance, was among the most important. Having Hendrix on our roster told our audience something about *who we were* as a company. I can't pretend I knew then how important Hendrix would be, but I had a strong sense for him as an artist, for his sound and his look. Joni Mitchell was another incredibly important signing, I think. She was brought to my attention by Andy Wickham, an A&R man of ours I met at Monterey. We thought she'd be great for us, but we had no way to find her. She had recently left her husband. We made all kinds of inquiries as to where she was, but nothing turned up. Out of the blue, I got a call from a guy named Irwin Winkler, a movie producer. I was the only person in the music business he knew all that well, so he called to tell me about this girl his music guys had signed. He said they were very excited about her, that he couldn't tell me anything about her music but that he knew they wanted a $25,000 advance. I asked who it was, and he told me it was Joni Mitchell. Another happy accident. The Kinks! They were incredibly important for the label. They were the first formidable rock band we signed once the ban was lifted—meaning once Sinatra allowed us to go after rock acts. They were absolutely amazing. We felt strongly about Ray Davies as a songwriter. "You Really Got Me" was huge for us and then it was followed by some six hit singles in a row. That was a transformation of our image. Neil Young was another very important artist for us.

If Warners should be remembered for something, I would say it should be remembered for its basic philosophy. It was a company about artists, a company that believed in freedom and creative control for the artist. The aim was to allow the artist to evolve and develop, in an environment of complete support. The highest priority was the music. I think we put together a roster that was so impressive that we were the envy of most every company out there. That may be an immodest thing to say, but when you look at what we had, whether Prince or Madonna or the Chili Peppers or Green Day, we had the best record company in those great days of the record business. Despite the changes in the industry, I think there's plenty to learn about the music business by looking back on that. It's unfortunate that circumstances have changed, that the economics have put enormous pressure on the people running record companies. But there's still something in that old idea, *always music first.*

↑ The Smart Set, 1958.
↗↘ Mary Kaye and her Trio, circa 1960.
↘↘ Buddy Cole, circa 1960.
↘ Connie Stevens, 1958.
↗ George Greeley, 1959.
© Chico Hamilton, circa 1960.

LENNY WARONKER ON WARNER BROS. RECORDS

When I shifted from being a record producer to being a record company president, and realized that my vocabulary was completely different from any other executive in the company—because I just didn't have it when it came to business affairs—I was initially concerned. But I also saw that, when it came to matters of the business in the strict sense of business, I had Mo, the best.

I think Mo's goal was to bring in somebody who was musical and could, as president, deal with the creative community. When Joe Smith left, that position remained open, nobody got it. Mo never said that he wanted me to be in there—he intimated it, through loose, abstract conversations about me being a creative kind of executive—but, really, he waited for me, until I said to him that maybe I should do something else because I'd hit the wall when it came to producing. The time was right. I didn't see myself being in the studio forever.

When I took this new position, about which we'd spoken only in a very general way up to that point, Mo told me not to worry about the business, that I'd get it. We had a fifteen-minute conversation on the topic. Then, as I was leaving his office, I said, "Well, what does this actually mean? Is there a title?" He said, "Yeah. You'll be president." I walked out. And then I walked back in, saying, "Wait a minute. We'd better talk about this." So we set up a time the next day.

The following day I arrived at his office with a yellow legal pad, pencils and so forth, trying to be presidential. Then there was dead silence for what felt like thirty minutes. It was probably thirty seconds. Mo looked at me and said, "Just go do."

I didn't understand that for a while. It took me a long time to figure out that I was not going to be a conventional record company president. It wasn't in the cards to do otherwise. But, also, if I could invent—not even invent, really, because it's just who I was—a way to use my native language as a producer, it would give us a better context for how we work records. Now there would be somebody in there who could talk to artists about the process of making records, understanding what people go through.

In so many ways, dealing with artists was the same thing as being a producer. It was all about listening and suggesting and staying the hell out of the way at the same time. And often my suggestion to an artist might not be the right suggestion, but it would focus an artist's mind enough so that they could make whatever situation we're dealing with their own . . . and then it works out even better. Sometimes there's nothing to say at all—most times, because the artists are so good. It came out in an A&R meeting one time that if we had to tell our artists what to do, then we had the wrong artists.

I knew when I was making a record like Van Dyke Parks' *Song Cycle*, or the early Ry Cooder records, or Randy Newman's . . . I knew that these were guys who, following Mo's thinking, deserved to have their records put out. They were really good. I didn't have the understanding or the capacity to know just what making those records would mean, but certainly there was a sense of importance around them. Those recordings showed that there was a musicality within the label. But I also believed—and this is an idea I learned from my father—that if you're doing something good, good things follow. Artists would come to the label because of those records. The creative community recognizes when something is going on musically, whether it's selling or not.

It really made sense when James Taylor called me and said he wanted me to produce him. He did that because of Randy Newman and Ry Cooder. He wanted to make a record with the kind of sensibility he heard in their recordings. So, yes, we could afford to do records like Ry's and Randy's because we had other things hitting commercially, some of which came our way because of Ry and Randy. Much later, during the R.E.M. drama—and, for me, it *was* a drama trying to recruit them—I saw that Peter [Buck] and the others knew everything I had done as a producer and that the label had done, and it was causing them to lean toward Warners. That was like an affirmation of a Warners philosophy that grew up in the late 1960s and continued on from there. If it's good and it doesn't sell, you can't get hurt. I used to say that all the time: We can't get hurt doing this.

77 SUNSET STRIP

Capitalizing on the popularity of the TV series by the same name, Warner Bros. Records rushed into the recording studio to make *77 Sunset Strip*, an album that celebrated the music of the very successful private eye series. Warren Barker, who had written music for 20th Century Fox, Columbia, and MGM prior to this, was named musical director. With Warner Bros. behind him, Barker hired top LA session players to cut Mack David and Jerry Livingston–penned tracks like "77 Sunset Strip Cha Cha," "Swingin' on the Strip," "Blue Night on the Strip," and the title song, "77 Sunset Strip." To those originals he added smart interpretations of the Rodgers and Hart number "You Took Advantage of Me" and Cole Porter's "I Get a Kick Out of You." The track listing was rounded out by a number called "Kookie's Caper," which paid tribute to Edd "Kookie" Byrnes, the show's teen hero. In a case of the low man on the totem pole attracting the widest audience, Byrnes played a parking lot attendant on the show, albeit a parking lot attendant who aspired to work as a private eye.

As *77 Sunset Strip*'s original liner notes put it, "Music is an integral part of *77 Sunset Strip*, and that it has contributed much to the outstanding success of the new Warner Bros./ABC-TV show is axiomatic. The light touch of comedy, interesting

characters, and music which reflects the pulse of the glamorous Sunset Strip bind the show together each week." The music has a cool to it. Barker emphasized jazz-flavored lounge tracks and blues-tinted mood pieces that gave the recording a hip, seductive quality. The series' theme song was modified for the album; a longer version, punctuated by a saxophone section, hinted at sultry jazz and a smooth R&B feel.

While the album made the top ten, a single of 1959 not on the LP, "Kookie, Kookie (Lend Me Your Comb)," would take the TV show's music in a different direction and, in turn, get Warner Bros. its first hit record. All this success led to Edd "Kookie" Byrnes leaving the show in a dispute. But the parking lot attendant who wanted to be a private eye would return to the show—and in a case of life imitating art, or at least life imitating television, Byrnes renegotiated to come back to the program not as a parking lot attendant but as a genuine private eye. Teenage America now had the hero it deserved. Warren Barker would go on to create the soundtrack for the Warner Bros. TV show *Hawaiian Eye*, in addition to recording his own album, *Warren Barker Is In!* As the cover of that album declared: "Kookie is IN! Obscure folksongs are OUT." Perhaps.

CHAPTER TWO
TAKING FLIGHT

IN 1960, TWO YEARS AFTER THE COMPANY'S BIRTH AND IN THE WAKE OF A STEADY STREAM OF DISAPPOINTING SALES AND QUESTIONABLE RELEASES, THINGS AT WARNER BROS. RECORDS BEGAN TO CHANGE.

MILLION-DOLLAR BASH

Why? The reasons are multiple. From one angle, change was imperative, and it seems Conkling finally recognized that. From another angle, how many records can you put out before something sticks? As Nick Tosches suggests, "In the course of not knowing what was what, the company had also mistakenly released some interesting if unnoticed records." But no label would survive, and certainly not flourish, with bombardment as the sales strategy. The history of Warner Bros. Records would unfold in relation to the conscious decisions made in that critical window of time when Jack Warner was losing his patience with the record business. As Jack Warner said to Joe Smith upon Smith's arrival at Warner Bros. Records: "We're terrible. And whose name do you think is on that label?"

What Conkling and Avakian did was both bold and desperate: They signed a few established acts that had scored hits for other labels. One of them was Bill Haley. **Joe Smith:** "When they signed Bill Haley to the label they were about five years too late. The bloom was off that rose." The other act was the Everly Brothers. **Stan Cornyn:** "The Everlys were very much alive then." The price for the act with life still left in the body? A million dollars over ten years. It was an enormous amount of money for a label in dubious financial shape. Somehow, Conkling managed to convince the fiscal watchdogs in New York that it all made sense. It was a move that meant life on the second floor at 3701 Warner Boulevard could, at least for the moment, carry on.

To some recording industry insiders, the Everly Brothers signing, like that of Bill Haley, was ill advised. In a business in which timing was everything and careers short, it seemed that Warners was paying top dollar for an act that may not have many more hits to deliver. On the other hand, it was true that the Everly Brothers were certified pop stars. Don and Phil Everly had their first hit in 1957 with "Bye Bye Love," which went to number two on the pop charts. Released on the Cadence label, the single featured the brothers' close harmonies and a rich acoustic texture that fell somewhere between the sound of Nashville and the pop sheen of New York and Los Angeles. The song's spare production, which cleared room for the harmonies that were at the heart of it all, was perfectly suited to radio, where it found a wide audience in the teenage market. "Bye Bye Love" was followed by "Wake Up Little Susie," "All I Have to Do Is Dream," and "Bird Dog," all of which went to number one. Few acts, teen pop or otherwise, sold like the Everly Brothers in the late 1950s.

When Conkling found out that Don and Phil Everly's contract was up at Cadence, he began to make moves to bring the duo to Warner Bros. If the young label didn't have the kind of track record that might attract an established act, Conkling knew that he did have one thing that would work in his favor: The Everly Brothers really wanted to try their hand at movies, and they thought Warners could help make that happen. They'd seen Elvis Presley make the jump to films and thought perhaps they could do the same.

When Conkling and Warner Bros. offered the Everly Brothers that decade-long, $100,000 per year contract, the brothers agreed. With that, Warner Bros. Records went from nearly folding to having on its roster one of the biggest names in pop music. How Conkling was able to convince Herman Starr, the Warner Bros. executive most intent on seeing the company get out of the music business—and the person most responsible for extricating Warner Bros. from the Brunswick Records mess years before—remains a bit of a mystery.

Among those grateful for the addition to a suffering roster was Joe Smith, who, several months after Conkling signed the Everly Brothers, would leave his job as a Boston disc jockey and head to California to join the label as its chief promotions man. **Joe Smith:** "At the time, there was no one at the company who really had a good sense about what was going on in the

↑ Laughing all the way to the bank, a 1960 ad from *Billboard* announcing the Everly Brothers' latest hit, now on Warner Bros. Records. Their contract was purported to be the biggest in history.

← The cover shot from 1960's *A Date with the Everly Brothers*. The album featured "Cathy's Clown," a cover of Little Richard's "Lucille," four Boudleaux and Felice Bryant songs, and Boudleaux Bryant's self-penned classic "Love Hurts." Opening spread: Peter, Paul & Mary hit the stage in 1964.

THIS WEEK	ONE WEEK AGO	TWO WEEKS AGO	THREE WEEKS AGO	TITLE Artist, Company Record No.	STEREO	WEEKS ON CHART
				⭐ STAR PERFORMERS showed the greatest upward progress on Hot 100 this week.		
				Ⓢ Indicates that 45 r.p.m. stereo single version is available.		
				Ⓢ Indicates that 33⅓ r.p.m. stereo single version is available.		
1	2	3	15	CATHY'S CLOWN . . . . Everly Brothers, Warner Bros. 5151	Ⓢ	6
2	1	1	1	STUCK ON YOU . . . . Elvis Presley, RCA Victor 7740	Ⓢ	8
3	5	13	42	GOOD TIMIN' . . . . Jimmie Jones, Cub 9067		6
4	3	2	2	GREENFIELDS . . . . Brothers Four, Columbia 41571	Ⓢ	14
5	4	4	6	NIGHT . . . . Jackie Wilson, Brunswick 55166		10
6	6	5	3	SIXTEEN REASONS . . . . Connie Stevens, Warner Bros. 5137		17
7	8	8	7	CRADLE OF LOVE . . . . Johnny Preston, Mercury 71598		9
8	10	21	37	HE'LL HAVE TO STAY . . . . Jeanne Black, Capitol 4368		4
9	7	10	8	LET THE LITTLE GIRL DANCE . . . . Billy Bland, Old Town 1076		15
10	12	23	34	PAPER ROSES . . . . Anita Bryant, Carlton 528	Ⓢ	7
11	17	30	59	BURNING BRIDGES . . . . Jack Scott, Top Rank 2041		6
12	16	27	33	LOVE YOU SO . . . . Rod Holden, Donna 1315		8
13	15	22	19	CHERRY PIE . . . . Skip and Flip, Brent 7010		8
14	13	9	11	STAIRWAY TO HEAVEN . . . . Neil Sedaka, RCA Victor 7709	Ⓢ	9
15	9	6	4	SINK THE BISMARCK . . . . Johnny Horton, Columbia 41568	Ⓢ	12
16	22	33	57	YOUNG EMOTIONS . . . . Ricky Nelson, Imperial 5663		5
17	11	7	5	THE OLD LAMPLIGHTER . . . . The Browns, RCA Victor 7700	Ⓢ	11
18	41	71	—	SWINGING SCHOOL . . . . Bobby Rydell, Cameo 175		3
19	14	11	14	WHITE SILVER SANDS . . . . Bill Black's Combo, Hi 2021		12
20	20	17	20	FAME AND FORTUNE . . . . Elvis Presley, RCA Victor 7740	Ⓢ	7

↑ The Everly Brothers give Warner Bros. Records its first number one hit, 1960.

↗ On the heels of its success with the Everly Brothers, Warner Bros. Records would top the album charts with an unknown accountant from Chicago. Bob Newhart shows 'em how to smoke, 1960.

music world. The Everlys were on the downside of their career when Conkling signed them. Signing them for that amount of money was ridiculous. But I was happy that the Everly Brothers had come aboard. At least Warner Bros. had an established act to work with. Without the Everly Brothers, all they'd be promoting would be TV stars trying to turn into pop music stars. And that wasn't working too well."

The Everly Brothers' first single for Warner Bros. was released in April, 1960. "Cathy's Clown," a somewhat melancholy, yet melodically infectious song pitched to a teen audience, soared up the charts. It was the satisfying result of a bold signing: a number one single for Warner Bros. Records—and this one wasn't cut by a TV personality. Here was a Warner Bros. hit recorded by one of the great pop acts of the rock & roll era. "Cathy's Clown" sold more than three million units.

THE (QUIET) KING OF COMEDY

The success of the Everly Brothers in 1960, which also included another Top Ten single, "So Sad," and a pair of hit albums, *It's Everly Time!* and *A Date with the Everly Brothers*, was not the only event that repositioned Warner Bros. Records that year. Connie Stevens reached number three with "Sixteen Reasons." But, more crucial to the long-term identity of Warner Bros. Records, amidst a batch of releases from artists including the Trapp Family Singers, Ira Ironstrings (again), Buddy Cole (again), Bill Haley, and too many others, there was a hidden victory that no one saw coming. Jim Conkling and George Avakian would be able to add to their accomplishment list an unlikely bit of A&R work that resulted in a number one record and three Grammy Awards: The signing of an unknown Chicago comedian, Bob Newhart. Taking a chance on Newhart was just that. But it was a chance very different from the monetary gamble that defined the Everly Brothers' deal. In fact, it would be hard to spend less on a number one album.

At the time of his signing, Newhart was an accountant with no comedy track record outside of Chicago. He lacked credentials and experience. If influenced by the likes of Jack Benny and George Burns, Newhart's style was something new, something odd. There were no traces in his work of the vaudeville spirit that still haunted American comedy. Though Spike Jones was a Warner Bros. artist, also signed well after his prime, Newhart represented another time and place altogether. Newhart was quiet, his intelligence apparent but never imposing. He

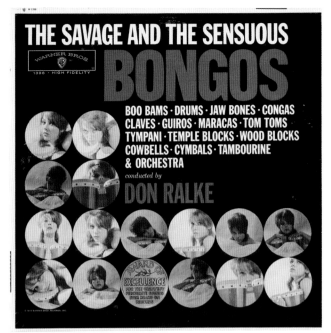

was the weird, introverted kid in class—all grown up. Despite that, when his first album, *The Button-Down Mind of Bob Newhart*, came out, the public's response validated Conkling and Avakian's instincts. Newhart's style somehow fit the times. **Stan Cornyn:** "Newhart and the Everlys—those two things rescued Warner Bros. Records. Newhart was very, very original, thoughtful, smart, good. He did sketch comedy monologues, which I don't think had been done much, if at all. Years later I was interviewed by the Library of Congress when that album was added to their registry of recordings." Newhart's album was named to the Library of Congress registry just after 1959 recordings by John Coltrane and Miles Davis.

It would be the first comedy record in recording history to assume the number one spot on the album charts. For Warner Bros. Records, the Newhart success was a reminder of the best possible A&R experience: when a gut-level belief in an unknown resulted in a hit. To this day Newhart cites his triple Grammy win of 1961 as the highpoint of his career. And even for a label that would define itself primarily through its music, this success was no less significant. As Jack Warner was happy to note on more than one occasion, Bob Newhart was the man who kept Warner Bros. Records afloat.

While releases continued to cover the spectrum, with titles such as *The Savage and the Sensuous Bongos* by Don Ralke, (the optimistically titled) *Together for the Last Time* by Joe "Fingers" Carr and Ira Ironstrings, and *How to Get the Most Out of Your Stereo* (Various Artists) clogging the channels, an aesthetic, likely only perceived in hindsight, was nonetheless emerging. The Newhart breakthrough was key in all of this. If in later years Warner/Reprise would be recognized by *Rolling Stone* as the realm of the "intellectuals," comedy played a role in establishing that sense of things. From Newhart to Tom Lehrer to Richard Pryor, Steve Martin, Steven Wright, and others, comedy signings would act as an implicit declaration of Warner Bros. Records more subversive side. Through its comedy recordings, Warner Bros. could signal its capacity to think outside the mainstream while still selling records, something Buddy Cole was not able to do for the label. **Lenny Waronker:** "Even though most of the Warner Bros. releases of that time weren't of interest, there was something of a mindset going on over there. From early on comedy was a tradition. And good comedy is one of the hardest things to do."

STOCK OPTIONS

After two years of limited success, in 1960 Jim Conkling and Warner Bros. Records seemed to have reversed their fortunes with some real successes. But in Conkling's case, it wasn't going to matter. It may have been a case of too little too late, but the man they called "Chief" decided that Conkling's time was over, and the reasoning, it has been said, had to do with more than the record company's financials. When Conkling decided to sell off his Warner Bros. studios stock, Jack Warner and other company executives chose to doubt his commitment to the record label. Just as the label's first president had managed to get the record company a taste of

↑ *Together for the Last Time*, Joe "Fingers" Carr and Ira Ironstrings, 1960.

↑↑ *The Savage and the Sensuous Bongos*, Don Ralke, 1960.

↖ Spike Jones, circa 1960. He was past his prime by the time he signed to the label—but he was still willing to use his head, if the money was right.

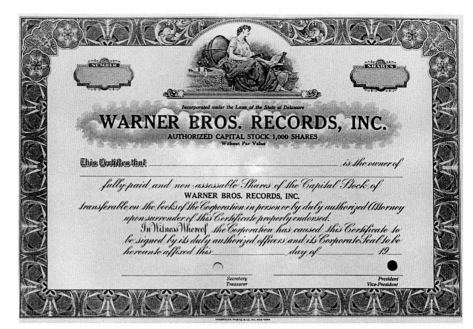

commercial and critical success, he was out. Likely the first two years cast a shadow. If from one angle Conkling had turned an often pathetic, even laughable record company into one with results to show, he had crossed the line when he dumped his Warner Bros. stock and pocketed a million dollars in the process. For Jack Warner, that one might have been personal. **Stan Cornyn:** "I don't know the whole story. I don't think Conkling's kids even know the whole story. I think they had made some decisions 'across the street,' as we used to say. The fact that Conkling's successor was hired before Conkling left suggests that this was about more than selling shares of Warner Bros. stock."

The new president, Mike Maitland, came from the same place as Conkling: Capitol Records. He was a natural salesman and a good judge of executive talent. He seemed like a man who could keep Warner Bros. Records on a path to regular profits. **Joe Smith:** "We had to change everything, and Maitland was a very good guy to lead the change. He was a likable man. He radiated some confidence. He'd been a big executive at Capitol for a lot of years. But we had to clean up the whole appearance of the company. If you go by the records you put out, this company sucked. Shortly after I came to the label I made a tour of the distributors, came back and told Mike Maitland, 'I can't stand this; I've got to get out of here. Our distributors hate us.' And why? Basically, because there were no hits."

Maitland also knew enough about the record business and his own abilities to allow Smith and the others he hired to do things their way. This would prove crucial to the label's turnaround. **Stan Cornyn:** "Mike Maitland did a number of wise things, I think. First of all, he recognized that he didn't have good instincts on what to sign. He turned to Joe and others." Despite the advance, Warner Bros. Records wasn't able to follow up its 1960 successes in 1961. Flexibility was going to be required as Warners continued the process of establishing an identity for itself. Maitland allowed Smith to buy up masters as one way of getting some singles into the pipeline; as a strategy, it was often the cheapest way to get product out without long-term commitment or recording costs. A more traditional signing, Bob Luman, a performer considered a country act but later inducted into the Rockabilly Hall of Fame, scored a number seven hit with "Let's Think About Living." The song came to him through Everly Brothers' manager Wesley Rose and was written by Felice and Boudleaux Bryant, the husband and wife team behind many of the Everlys' hits. For the label, the song meant plenty in the short term. But the A&R approach behind Luman's success was still scattershot, a considerable distance from what would begin to crystallize by the end of the decade.

The Everly Brothers continued to make records, but with each passing year their sales would diminish. Newhart released a successful follow-up, *Behind the Button-Down Mind*. The other product? The catalogue remained middle of the road, focused on adult popular music. The *Gone With the Wind* Soundtrack Re-Recording, featuring the Max Steiner score, was a success in some respects—but not one that would define the label. In 1962 Emilio Pericoli had a hit with "Al Di La." The Routers, with the song "Let's Go (Pony)," made it to number nineteen on the charts. In 1963 Jimmy Durante released his version of "September Song" and got part way up the charts. **Bob Krasnow:** "To say some of that early music was disposable would be kind." If the original rationale behind forming Warner Bros. Records had everything to do with making the most of what was happening in film and television, few were the examples of that scheme paying off. But in 1962, with the release of *The Music Man* soundtrack, there was, at least, one more example of records and movies coming together to reinforce one another. It would prove an exception.

↑ Joe Smith backstage at the Cow Palace in 1962. In a few short years, this same man would sign the Grateful Dead.

↑↑ Mike Maitland was named president of Warner Bros. Records in 1960. Looser than he looked, Maitland built the team that brought the company into a new era.

↗ The object of so much controversy for Jim Conkling, a Warner Bros. stock certificate.

PETER, PAUL AND MARY

WARNER BROS.
RECORDS

CLIMATE CHANGE

One force that emerged in that time, which pushed Warner Bros. Records toward the door leading to the 1960s cultural revolution, was folk music. Through this music and in that moment, Warner Bros. would begin to claim its ground. **Joe Smith:** "We went along with kind of middle of the road music. But when Mike Maitland came in, he gave all of us an open shot to sign whatever we thought would turn it around. For me, finding new talent was simply a matter of survival. One of those acts was Peter, Paul & Mary." It would prove a turning point.

Managed by Albert Grossman, best known as Bob Dylan's manager, Peter, Paul & Mary fit somewhere between the collegiate folk of the Kingston Trio and the coming world that Dylan would help to define. Grossman, with a background in booking folk clubs, proved a formidable manager. **Carl Scott:** "Only a fool would not smile back at Albert Grossman." Rather than ask for a big advance, Grossman asked for a higher percentage on the "back end," a move that would finally make his act (and Grossman) a lot of money. **Bob Krasnow:** " Albert Grossman was the godfather. I loved that man."

Joe Smith solidified his reputation. The trio's self-titled record was released in early spring, 1962. **Joe Smith:** "I knew folk music was really happening on college campuses, so I loaded up the group and all the records that would fit in a van and headed for the schools that made up the Big Ten in the Midwest—Michigan State in Lansing, Michigan in Ann Arbor, Ohio State in Columbus, Ohio, and others. I'd find out where the center of the campus was and put up a big sign that said: 'Warner Bros. Records Presents Peter, Paul & Mary' and have them start playing. Pretty soon a crowd would gather around us, and it was easy to see that the students really liked the music. I sold their album right out of the back of the van."

Peter, Paul & Mary made it to the top of the album charts that spring. The album also spawned a pair of Top Forty singles, "The Lemon Tree" and a cover of Pete Seeger's "If I Had a Hammer." **Lenny Waronker:** "That was really big, a classic record at the time. It's nothing I would gravitate

↟ Getting Peter, Paul & Mary into the stores, the new display, 1964.

↟↟ Reading aloud on the road, Mary Travers, Peter Yarrow, and Noel Paul Stookey, 1963.

to now, but I certainly did then." Suddenly, the group was playing to sold-out audiences on college campuses and in concert halls around the country. Their string of successes was just beginning, however. *Moving*, their 1963 follow-up to *Peter, Paul & Mary*, contained the hit "Puff (The Magic Dragon)," a huge single written by Peter Yarrow that pushed the album to the number two slot on the pop charts.

Albert Grossman gave the group two Dylan songs for its third album, *In the Wind*. Grossman figured that if the world heard about the genius of Bob Dylan through Peter, Paul & Mary, he'd be helping the cause of two of his acts at the same time. He gave the group "Don't Think Twice, It's Alright," one of the best songs on *The Freewheelin' Bob Dylan*, and "Blowin' in the Wind." The latter quickly went to number two on the singles charts, while *Moving* made it to number one on the album charts. Peter, Paul & Mary was the hottest singing group in the country and suddenly the music world was also paying attention to the artist who wrote the single. Albert Grossman's strategy had worked—as was often the case—and he couldn't have been more satisfied. **Joe Smith:** "The success of Peter, Paul & Mary happened at the perfect time. Their success meant success for Warner Bros. Their credibility gave us credibility. For the first time, we were riding high, and it felt pretty damn good."

WARNER BRUDDAHS

Warner Bros. approached the early 1960s folk boom from another angle with Allan Sherman. Recording parodies of traditional songs, Sherman released *My Son, the Folk Singer*. For some reason, America responded. The record went to number one on the album charts. Knowing a good thing when they earned it, Warner Bros. quickly got Sherman back into the recording studio and cut *My Son, the Celebrity*, which also went to number one—and then *My Son, the Nut*, yet another number one album. A hit single from the latter album, "Hello Muddah, Hello Fadduh," immortalized the summer camps that so many in the listening audience attended in their youth. It touched a nerve, and for that reason it could be heard on radio stations across the land in 1963. **Stan Cornyn:** "When he was hot, he was *red hot* for us. I even remember they ran out of album jackets down at Music City and would sell records in inner sleeves to people who just had to have them."

Maitland and Smith guessed that, unlike Bob Newhart, who had quietly become one of America's most popular comedians and continued to release hit albums, Sherman's run couldn't go forever. But the label had just signed an African-American comedian named Bill Cosby. They felt like this was something that might last. With *Bill Cosby Is a Very Funny Fellow, Right!*, they continued to build the label on a strong base of comedy records.

Warner Bros. Records ended 1963 firmly in the black. Likely Jack Warner felt better. Though 1963 would see the release of such recordings as *Swedish Polkas and Hambos*, at least that wasn't the whole story. The days were numbered in which the last remnants of Jim Conkling's adult pop label would dog Warner Bros. Records. **Joe Smith:** "We had this phenomenon with Allan Sherman, so we were in business. We had records on the charts, people talking about them, selling them. But did that define us? I'd say it didn't. It kept us alive. When we broke out of that with the Dead and Jimi Hendrix and some rock & roll artists, that was the real story."

➤ For a few years running, Allan Sherman was the unlikely hero of the pop charts. Here Sherman strikes a pose during the photo sessions for *My Son, the Nut*, 1963.

➤ Bill Cosby was discovered by Carl Reiner and recorded his 1963 Warner Bros. Records debut at The Bitter End in Greenwich Village. His presence on the label, and his quick success, cemented the company's reputation in comedy.

↑ Mike Coolidge, Jack Warner, Allan Sherman, Mike Maitland, circa mid-1960s.
↗ Bob Luman, 1961.
↦↗ Marty Paich, 1959.
↦↦ Jimmy Durante, circa early 1960s.
↦ Tom Lehrer, mid-1960s.
© The Routers, early 1960s.

PHIL EVERLY ON THE WARNER BROS. YEARS

We met with Jack Warner when we signed. He could speak cockney, and Donald could do some of that, too. So the two of them talked a little cockney. It was kind of fun. We walked around the Warner Bros. lot, did a photo session, and dropped by where they were shooting a western, sponsored by Borax, that featured Ronald Reagan as host. Reagan was quite funny, of course, making jokes in between shots.

Warner Bros. approached us because the Everly Brothers had fulfilled their three-year contract with Cadence. And they offered the million-dollar contract. It was the largest contract a company had *ever* offered an act. But another part of the reason we signed with Warner Bros. had to do with our desire to bridge into the movies. Once we were with the label, we went to Warner Bros. acting school. We got apartments in Los Angeles, came in off the road, and took classes for three months. We had a pretty good time—the whole time! It was like a three-month vacation. I'm sure our hearts were in it, in a sense, but we were young—truth is, we were a bit more focused on the idea of being in one place for three months in a row. We'd been traveling so much for so long.

There was another thing that attracted us to Warner Bros., however, and that was Jim Conkling. We loved Jim. He was a great man. When we met him, we found him inspirational. It made us keen to go to the label. I know that some view his first releases with skepticism, but you can't judge a man like Jim Conkling by a list of songs. He probably did so many things that most folks will never know about. He was a real classy man. At that time I didn't know that the label was struggling to get something going. I don't know if I was just young and foolish, but I didn't sense that they were in any kind of trouble. Maybe because we had belief in ourselves, we knew all was well.

Mike Maitland, who followed Jim Conkling, was another great guy. They had a string of really good people. Joe Smith was another. We knew Joe back when he was a promoter, back in the very beginning. Everybody who wound up running that label had a lot of class. There was a style to Warner Bros. Records. They made good choices—frankly, I never saw them make a bad move. Everyone was always so pleasant. But, then again, people have a tendency to be pleasant if you're selling records. But I don't remember a bad moment in the whole song and dance.

"Cathy's Clown" was our first single for the label, which turned out to be a great one for us. That worked out very well, that beat was so unusual and brand-new. But part of what made things work was that Jim Conkling was always very keen on letting us do just what we wanted. He had a great respect for artists and knew how to guide and allow creativity. We would ask for something, and generally we'd get it. I remember we saw the movie *Tunes of Glory* and asked if they could get us the piper who played in the film. And they did. So we tried to work

out something with bagpipes . . . but never got it done. But you just had to suggest something, and they'd try to make it happen.

About a year after signing with Warners we split with Acuff-Rose, which meant that we could no longer get Bryant songs [material by Boudleaux and Felice Bryant, writers behind many early Everly hits]. That's when things really changed for us. Some projects came into being because we didn't have the time to find new material. One of my favorites from the Warners years, however, is "Cryin' in the Rain." It's the only song Carole King and Howie Greenfield wrote together. We had gone up to Don Kirshner's office looking for material—and that's what we found. Bottom line is that a good song is a good song. It's like driving a great car—you can't go wrong with that.

"Walk Right Back" was a Sonny Curtis song. Sonny wrote the theme song for *The Mary Tyler Moore Show*. I remember him playing the Mary Tyler Moore song live, and he'd introduce it by saying, "This is the song that allows me to drive a Buick." Sonny also wrote "I Fought the Law." Of course he was *also* in the Crickets—and after Buddy Holly died we played with the band, knew them quite well. By the time we cut "Walk Right Back," however, Sonny was in the army. It's funny, but when we heard the song it only had one verse. So J.I. [Allison, the Crickets' drummer] called Sonny and told him to write another verse, which he did. But by the time the second verse got to us, we'd already cut the track and it was coming out. You can hear it on there—just one verse. The first time Sonny heard it was on Radio Luxembourg when he was in Germany.

We also covered R&B songs on a number of albums. Ray Charles, Little Richard—but, of course, everybody listened to R&B then. We grew up listening to country, but rock & roll—what they call rock & roll, at least—was a combination of country and R&B. It's important to remember, though, that music didn't live in compartments back then. Hardly anybody remembers that songs like "Bye Bye Love," "Wake Up Little Susie," and "All I Have to Do Is Dream" were R&B hits, not just pop hits. Everyone was listening to everything. It's a shame that it has become more splintered since that time. Back then there wasn't a line between the different types of music. If you played a guitar, you played a guitar.

One of our last—maybe even our very last—Warner Bros. records was *Roots*. Lenny Waronker really set out to do something with that album. It was a very creative project. He'd heard the old Everly Family radio show tapes from the 1950s, which I think inspired the direction we took on that project. And, of course, he had a very talented bunch just standing around there with him. Randy Newman, Ry Cooder, and others. There was a lot of talent. I appreciated that he approached this with a first-rate sensibility. I just don't have one bad memory of that time.

WB Records Presents

♪ ♪

7 6

The MUSIC MAN

WARNER BROS.
PICTURES PRESENTS
MEREDITH WILLSON'S

WB **The MUSIC MAN**

WARNER BROS.
MEREDITH WILLSON'S

The MUSIC MAN

ROBERT PRESTON · SHIRLEY JONES
BUDDY HACKETT · HERMIONE GINGOLD · PAUL FORD
RAY HEINDORF · MORTON

Showing
Exclusively
AT HOLLYWOOD

Paramount
Theatre

Display window for *The Music Man*, 1962.

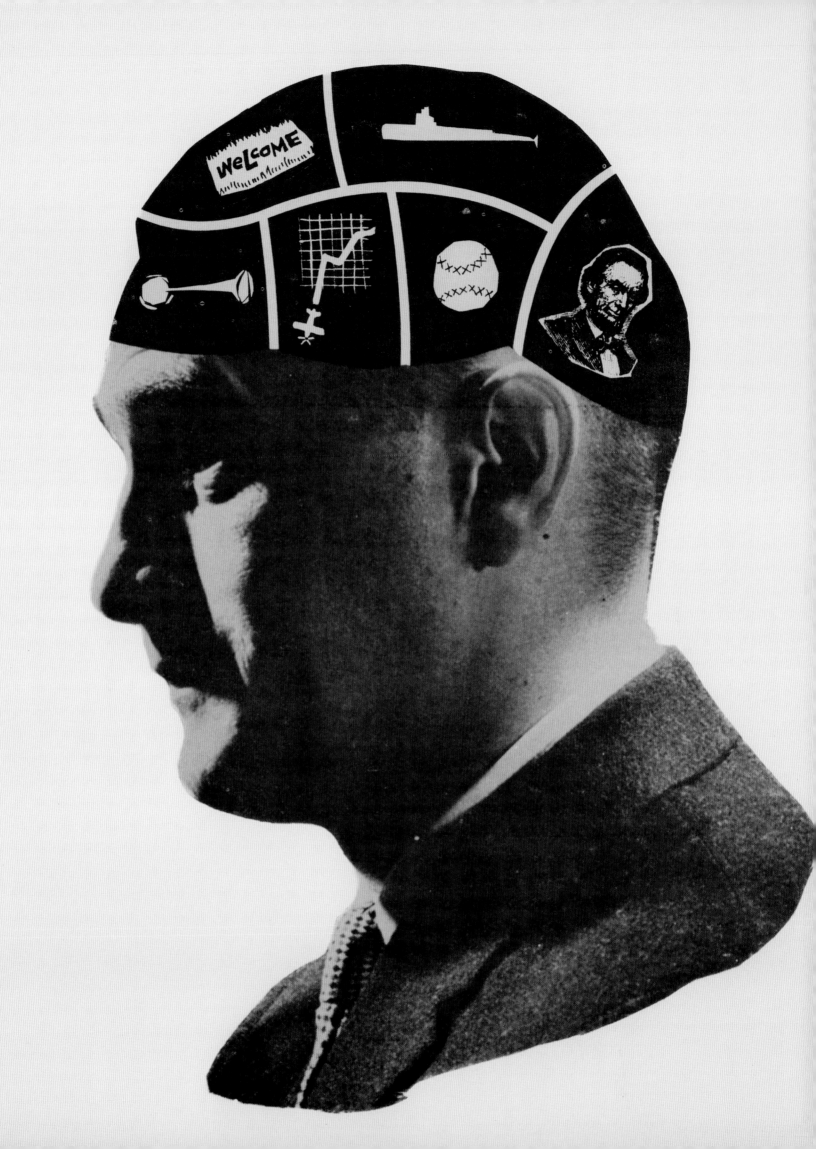

THE BUTTON-DOWN MIND OF
BOB NEWHART

I was in Chicago in the late 1950s, making a living as an accountant, and really not doing much of anything with comedy. I certainly didn't have a career to speak of. I'd been writing a few things, but I had no idea if any of it would lead to a break sometime down the road. Then a friend of mine, a disc jockey named Dan Sorkin, who knew the head of Warner Bros. Records—Jim Conkling—called him on my behalf. He told Conkling that he really ought to hear some of my material. So, most likely because Conkling didn't want to offend Dan, he suggested I get hold of a tape recorder and put my material on tape.

To my complete surprise Conkling liked what he heard. At the time, comedy records were just beginning to make a little noise. They didn't even have a category of their own. Instead, they were in the spoken word record bins. Mort Sahl had put out a record, so had Shelly Berman, and Mike [Nichols] and Elaine [May]. But there wasn't much else.

Anyway, probably because Warner Bros. didn't have too many artists on their roster, being so new, Conkling told me he wanted to do an album. "We'll record you live at a nightclub," he said. I told them that was a problem, since I'd never played a nightclub before. I had done some radio and local television in Chicago, but never a nightclub. Somehow they lined up an appearance in a club in Houston called The Tidelands. I was the opening act, and on February 12, 1960, I walked out on a nightclub stage for the first time, and I was absolutely terrified.

It wasn't long before I realized that I had only enough material for one side of an album. All I had was a skit on a submarine commander called "The Cruise

of the U.S.S. Codfish," another one called "Abe Lincoln vs. Madison Avenue," and a third, "The Driving Instructor." So, during the two weeks in Houston, I had to come up with a lot more material, which I did. I came up with "Nobody Will Ever Play Baseball" and "Merchandising the Wright Brothers." If the people around me thought it was funny, I'd include it during my act and use the audience's reaction to see if it was good enough to record. By the time George Avakian, the Warner Bros. A&R man, came down to Houston to record me, I had enough material to make the album.

Around April I contacted Warner Bros. to see when the album, which was called *The Button-Down Mind of Bob Newhart*, was going to be released, and they told me that every pressing of the record was being rushed to Minneapolis because the record was really breaking there. It was so hot that the local newspaper actually listed the times the disc jockeys would play tracks from the record. Almost overnight, I began getting calls to do national television, including *The Ed Sullivan Show*. My career just took off, thanks to that record. What amazed me even more was that *The Button-Down Mind* won three Grammys that year, including Album of the Year and Best New Artist.

A few months later I was at a dinner, and Jim Conkling and Jack Warner were both there to introduce me. Jack Warner, in a way only he could do it, said, "Ladies and Gentlemen, this is the man who saved Warner Bros. Records."

NOEL "PAUL" STOOKEY ON PETER, PAUL & MARY

Back then Warner Bros. Records was in a kind of Quonset hut. Mike Maitland was there. And the other artists were, maybe, Bob Newhart, the Everly Brothers, and ourselves. Allan Sherman came, I think, a year later. But there's something about your first kiss—and Warner Bros. was our first kiss. They had faith, right there at the beginning of the folk movement. They understood that there was a new kind of lyrical outreach and musical integrity that was coming. And, really, the label was about a year or two ahead of the curve.

Groups like the Weavers had hit earlier, but with material that was drawn pretty much from traditional folk music. Contemporary expression was not what that earlier phase was about. It was burgeoning toward the end of the Weavers' exposure, but that exposure was severely truncated by the McCarthy hearings and the black listings. When we came around, we did not have that battle—we had other dragons, such as the civil rights movement and the Vietnam war. But the Weavers were the core of what we learned from, though we had other great teachers like Josh White and Woody [Guthrie], the labor movement, gospel music.

The critical part of folk music's popularity was not so much stylistic, like working without echo or lush string arrangements, but in what it did through its lyrics—folk gave popular music permission to talk about something other than dating behavior. And that was the paradigm shift, still with us today, for which folk music was responsible in the early 1960s. We're still seeing the effects of that. Because of what folk music brought to the picture, popular music was given license to comment on all aspects of human experience.

Albert Grossman, our manager, was a great believer in the idea that you *earned* your place in the commercial market. Therefore he did not insist on large advances. For a young company like Warner Bros., which didn't have a huge

bankroll for an act that was not yet established, this was great. Albert believed in us, so he always went in for a low guarantee and a high percentage. The deal we struck with Warner Bros. was phenomenal for the time. We had total control of the product, from recording to graphics. We got to pick our own material. It wasn't a question of doing singles. And Albert asked for only enough money to make the record.

I remember the first time we walked those funky stairs into the second floor of the Quonset hut to meet the label's brass. Mike Maitland was built like a guard for the Pittsburgh Steelers. And he had a kindness that was tempered with a lot of strength, like it came from dealing with some tough issues. Sometimes I had the sense that Mike didn't know what the music was about—but he certainly knew who to employ. I'd say the major player in our history was Don Graham, a promotion guy from Warners. He was independent, but he broke "Lemon Tree," made us sweethearts of San Francisco. He was golden.

Mo was grandpa and Joe was like an uncle, like Mike Maitland's younger brother. Joe had a lot of energy, very ebullient, understood the music a bit more. Sharp and quick. Mo Ostin had slow wisdom, an overarching understanding of the music business. But throughout all of this there was something we came to recognize was unusual and individual in these people, and that was a genuine kindness toward their artists. You read about this occasionally. But it's not always there. It was for us.

I don't know too many artists who have been with the same record company for forty years—or many artists who have signed with the same company three times. Forty years later we went to the label and played in the cafeteria for everyone at Warners. But that's how it always was.

MARK COHEN ON ALLAN SHERMAN

When John Belushi's character in *Animal House* destroyed a folk guitar, he was onto something. The movie was set in 1962, a time when folk music of all kinds, not all of it worth remembering, was everywhere. In its more troubling manifestations, folk was being pawned off as authentic, and unintentionally funny performances were giving rise to something like a new genre. Someone had to take a stand, and someone did. That year, Allan Sherman kicked the schmaltz out of folk music.

Rotund, bespectacled, and clean-shaven, Sherman was the perfect unhip antidote to the overly earnest side of the folk era, and his debut album, *My Son, the Folk Singer*, became a national sensation with its Jewish parodies of folk standards. Out of the plaintive "Greensleeves"—which features a lovesick knight serenading a maiden—Sherman made "Sir Greenbaum's Madrigal." Greenbaum's heart is also breaking, but not for love. It's his lousy job that's killing him. "All day with the mighty sword/And the mighty steed/And the mighty lance./All day with that heavy shield/And a pair of aluminum pants." Not exactly the kind of talk heard at the Round Table. Did King Arthur kvetch? And Sherman caught fire with listeners when he twisted the soothing lullaby, "Frere Jacques," into the comic alarm clock, "Sarah Jackman."

Sarah Jackman, Sarah Jackman
How's by you, how's by you?
How's your brother Bernie?
He's a big attorney.
How's your sister Doris?
Still with William Morris.

Billboard magazine pegged Sherman's *Folk Singer* album as a winner only among Jewish audiences in New York and Los Angeles but had to eat its words when fans in Atlanta revealed a hunger for the parodies. Folks in the bible belt preferred the "Streets of Miami" to the "Streets of Laredo" and the "Ballad of Harry Lewis" to the "Battle Hymn of the Republic." Who knew? For over a century the "Battle Hymn" had thundered, "Mine eyes hath seen the glory/Of the coming of the Lord./He is trampling through the warehouse/Where the grapes of wrath are stored." Sherman kept the music's melodramatic character, but in place of the Lord he sang of the pointlessly heroic Harry Lewis, who died in a fire while working for garment manufacturer Irving Roth. Although the fire was raging, Harry, that schlemiel, "stood by his machine." His reward was that "He had the finest funeral/The union could afford." Sherman wrote him a lasting epitaph. "Oh, Harry Lewis perished in the service of his lord./He was trampling through the warehouse/Where the drapes of Roth are stored."

No one could blame *Billboard* for underestimating Sherman's appeal. Incredibly, *Folk Singer* kicked off one of the most spectacular winning streaks in American comedy, securing Warner Bros.' place as a leader in that area. In less than twelve months that album, and follow-up hits *My Son, the Celebrity* and *My Son, the Nut*, gave Sherman three gold albums and a Grammy for "Hello Muddah, Hello Fadduh." All three records applied the deflationary power of Jewish humor to folksongs, symphony pieces, and any recognizable tune Sherman could mangle without infringing a copyright. He packed the concerns of everyday life into tunes whose sacred status had made them stale and pretentious. Earnestness was exposed to ridicule, icons were cut down to size, and Allan Sherman made a fortune.

Sherman's parodies signaled that Americans were ready to end their quiet acceptance of established icons. For Warners, his recordings were part of a history that would include not just Bob Newhart but Tom Lehrer, Richard Pryor, Steve Martin, Steven Wright, Sam Kinison, Adam Sandler, and many more. For the comedy world, Sherman's work signaled the beginning of a golden age of Jewish-American humor that made the parody its favorite vehicle. In the movies alone one saw this in Woody Allen's *Take the Money and Run*, *Sleeper*, and *Play It Again, Sam*, and Mel Brooks' *Blazing Saddles*, *Young Frankenstein*, *High Anxiety*, *Spaceballs*, and *Men in Tights*—all Shermanesque parodies of established films or film genres that were overdue for a pie in the face. Belushi destroyed only one folk guitar. Sherman's parodies, on the other hand, were weapons of mass destruction.

CHAPTER THREE
SOUND DECISIONS

THE STORY OF WARNER BROS. RECORDS WOULD HAVE UNFOLDED, LIKELY UNRAVELED, IN A VERY DIFFERENT WAY WERE IT NOT FOR THE ENTRANCE OF FRANK SINATRA.

ENTER REPRISE

In 1963, Jack Warner, hot to land a movie deal with Frank Sinatra, agreed to purchase the singer's fledgling record label, Reprise, as a part Sinatra's contract as an actor. **Stan Cornyn:** "Sinatra had this label, which was not doing well. In some respects, it was founded on the same beliefs held by Jim Conkling. For instance, Sinatra wanted to record full albums on his artists. He was an artists' guy. That was an expensive approach. So, his moneyman, attorney Mickey Rudin, got Reprise put into the deal when Sinatra signed the movie contract."

Sinatra was a proven commercial commodity, to be sure. *Oceans 11*, the film that inspired Warner to go after Sinatra, had been a big hit. But, as a recording artist, the early 1960s weren't his best years. He made a couple of monumental albums for Capitol in the 1950s— *In the Wee Small Hours* and *Songs for Swingin' Lovers!*—but a slow period followed. Reprise was Sinatra's answer to his disgust with Capitol. As he let it be known, he hated the artistic limitations he believed Capitol Records imposed on him.

Reprise, as conceived by Sinatra, was a record company where artists had creative freedom and great music was the norm. He formed the label in 1960, and it quickly became the recording home for his friends and for artists he admired. With an idealized vision for what was possible, Sinatra set out to make sure that his artists would never again have to answer to a record company that didn't respect the music itself. In addition to Sinatra, the Reprise roster included Dean Martin and Sammy Davis, Jr., Jimmy Witherspoon and Barney Kessel, Duke Ellington, Rosemary Clooney and Ethel Merman. Martin and Sinatra sold records. Sinatra even brought home a couple of Album of the Year Grammy Awards for his efforts. Lou Monte cut an album called *Pepino the Italian Mouse and Other Italian Folk Songs* and had a hit with it. But, from a fiscal perspective, too few artists on the Reprise label were charting. Likely Mickey Rudin realized that Sinatra was better at making records than selling them. Jack Warner came knocking at precisely the right time.

Sinatra agreed to the deal, under the condition that he remain part owner of Reprise. **Mo Ostin:** "He and Mickey Rudin could appreciate that Reprise had long-term value and therefore still kept an ownership interest. They had an equity of one-third of Warner Bros. and one-third of Reprise, which turned out to be an incredible asset." In September 1963, the papers were signed, and suddenly Mike Maitland, who had been left out of the negotiations, had a new label to look after, which, unlike Warner Bros., was not making a profit. Not only was Warner Bros. Records now burdened with a label that possessed disappointing sales figures and an uneven roster, until it was in his hands Maitland didn't even know the deal was happening. But Jack Warner didn't care what Mike Maitland felt or wanted. Sinatra was now part of Warner Bros. Studios.

THE ACCOUNTANT

With Reprise came an executive named Mo Ostin. **Lou Dennis:** "Once you had worked with Mo Ostin, it was hard to work for other people." Shortly after Ostin graduated from UCLA with a degree in economics, he began his career in the music business with Norman Granz at Verve Records in 1953. Granz was a tastemaker, the man who, among other things, produced the celebrated series, "Jazz at the Philharmonic." **Mo Ostin:** "At the time, I really had no aspirations to be in the record business. My interest in music was as a fan. I liked jazz, the big bands, and the other music from the 1940s. But I had no musical literacy as far as playing music went or any special knack for finding talent. When I got the job at Verve, it was, at first, just that, a job. It paid the bills and fed my family."

Ostin did administrative work for Verve. Because Verve was a small record company, however, Ostin's responsibilities broadened over time. In a knowing move, Granz gave Ostin the title of "controller" to go along with his increasing responsibilities, what Ostin calls a

↑ Frank Sinatra, 1963.

← Warner Bros. Records staff in front of the original offices at 3701 Warner Boulevard—the former machine shop, circa 1966.

Top row: Lowell Frank, Phil Rose, Don Schmitzerle, Jimmy Hillard, Ed West, Jimmy Bowen, Dick Glasser, Sonny Burke, Ed Thrasher.

Bottom row: Stan Cornyn, Joel Friedman, Mike Maitland, Joe Smith, Lenny Waronker, Russ Regan, Gene Block.

Opening spread: Frank Sinatra in the studio, liking what he hears, circa 1963.

↑ No longer on Capitol Records, Frank Sinatra unveils his new Reprise label.
Do you think he gets his message across in this ad copy?

↑↑ Mo Ostin and Frank Sinatra, early 1960s. Sinatra's efforts to establish
Reprise as a safe haven for artists would have a lasting effect on Ostin.

"title with a purpose." Granz's idea was that Ostin's title would help him in dealing with indie record distributors, a notoriously brutish lot. Watching Granz deal with such artists as Ella Fitzgerald, Billie Holiday, Anita O'Day, Count Basie, Oscar Peterson, Coleman Hawkins, Charlie Parker, and Dizzy Gillespie, among numerous other jazz greats on the Verve roster, Ostin took note of the way Granz cultivated relationships with his artists, coaxing the best music out of them that he could. **Mo Ostin:** "I was exposed to virtually every aspect of running a record company—finance, contracts, international and domestic distribution—I did everything except find and handle the talent. Norman Granz reserved that part of the business for himself."

At the time, one of Verve's biggest fans was Frank Sinatra, who loved jazz and longed to own a jazz record label. Granz's view that artists should have the freedom to do what they wanted to do in the recording studio mirrored Sinatra's, so Sinatra instructed his lawyer, Mickey Rudin, to buy Verve. As it happened, Granz was interested in selling the label and moving to Europe. But when negotiations with Rudin bogged down, Granz sold Verve Records to MGM. Rudin, eager to placate Sinatra, suggested that Sinatra form his own label, a cheaper but far riskier proposition than buying a proven company. With the idea of Reprise thus established, Rudin remembered Verve's controller, Mo Ostin, as someone with integrity and intelligence. Ostin had little interest in working for MGM, and happened to be a fan of Frank Sinatra. It was a match. Ostin resigned his position with Verve to work directly with Sinatra and Rudin in their attempt to turn Reprise into a major record company. Sinatra was president of Reprise; Ostin was named vice president. When Reprise was sold to Warner Bros. Records, Mo Ostin went with it. **Stan Cornyn:** "Who is this? That was the general attitude at Warner Bros. when Mo arrived. But it worked."

Mike Maitland was instructed to get Reprise on the path to profit and create an environment in which Warner Bros. and Reprise could coexist artistically. Maitland and Ostin chopped away at the Reprise roster, letting go most of the acts on it, no matter how big they once were. **Stan Cornyn:** "Maitland handled the Reprise deal well, despite the fact that it caught him by surprise. I remember Mo and Mike sitting in Mike's office and going through the Reprise roster. And, yes, a lot of Reprise was dropped."

Now running two labels, Maitland decided to promote Joe Smith and make him head of Warner Bros., keeping Ostin as head of Reprise. Maitland himself would oversee Warner/Reprise, letting Ostin and Smith run their respective labels the way they saw fit. **Mo Ostin:** "Warner Bros. was an established name in entertainment, but Reprise wasn't. I knew that I had to establish its young identity. I fought for the separation between Warner Bros. and Reprise, so we were treated as individual operations. Warner Bros. and Reprise were competitive labels, and the competition made both labels stronger."

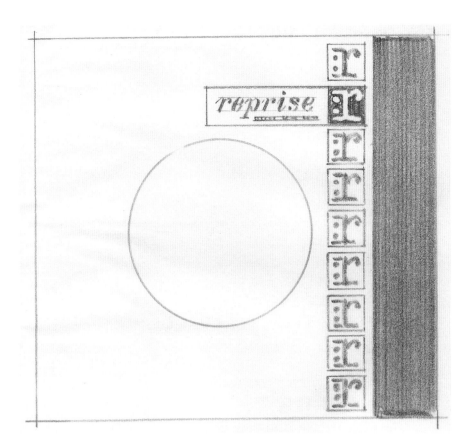

SINATRA'S RETURN

It helped Reprise that Sinatra, working with A&R man and producer Jimmy Bowen, would again chart major hits. Bowen joined Reprise in 1963 to make records and find new talent. He had been a disc jockey and led a rock & roll band called the Rhythm Orchids, but Bowen also had significant range as a producer. Bowen's first big break at Reprise came not with Sinatra, however, but with Reprise label mate Dean Martin. The track that made the difference was "Everybody Loves Somebody," a number one smash. The song had been written nearly fifteen years earlier by Martin's pianist at the time, Ken Lane. Martin's first version of the song was jazz-flavored. The second version had an orchestral arrangement and a chorus. The team at Reprise so liked the latter that in addition to releasing it as a single, the label made it the title track of Martin's next album.

Jimmy Bowen: "Dean Martin's success paid everyone's salary for a couple of years. We put out 'Everybody Loves Somebody,' and it seemed like nobody would want to hear a record like that at the time. But there was a disc jockey in Massachusetts and one in New Orleans, and they both liked the record enough to play it. And it just caught fire. We sold something like fifty thousand copies of the song the first week. Nobody could believe it. Dean Martin fooled everybody. He was doing three albums a year, at least two movies, and a television show, and everyone thought he was a drunk. That was just part of his thing. He had a great mind."

Sinatra called Bowen on the basis of Martin's success. And for the next few years they worked together, cutting songs that included "Strangers in the Night" in 1966. Having introduced Nancy Sinatra to Lee Hazlewood, Bowen would also co-produce with Hazlewood "Somethin' Stupid," a 1967 Frank and Nancy Sinatra duet that resulted in a big hit. Jimmy Bowen: "Sinatra was easy to work with so long as you had your act together. He didn't suffer fools. If the session was supposed to start at eight, I'd have the orchestra there at seven. I got all the mistakes out before he got to the studio, so when he walked in all he had to do was sing. We always had twenty or thirty people in the studio when Sinatra recorded. He liked to have a real audience there. I got as many beautiful women as I could find, had them sit on chairs, look pretty, and listen. He always got his best performances when he sang to an audience." As with Warner Bros., Reprise was stabilized by this string of hits. But the music that would define the label was still yet to come.

A PIECE OF ENGLAND

In 1964 the Beatles arrived, changing the landscape of popular music. Few in the record business saw it coming. Every record company, every musician and songwriter, every producer, every disc jockey, and every music fan, no matter their opinions of the situation, had to contend with the upheaval. In round one, the major American record companies missed the Beatles, the band signing its first US record deal with Vee-Jay, an indie out of Chicago. But Capitol Records moved in and signed the band before other labels could grasp the lasting significance of the moment.

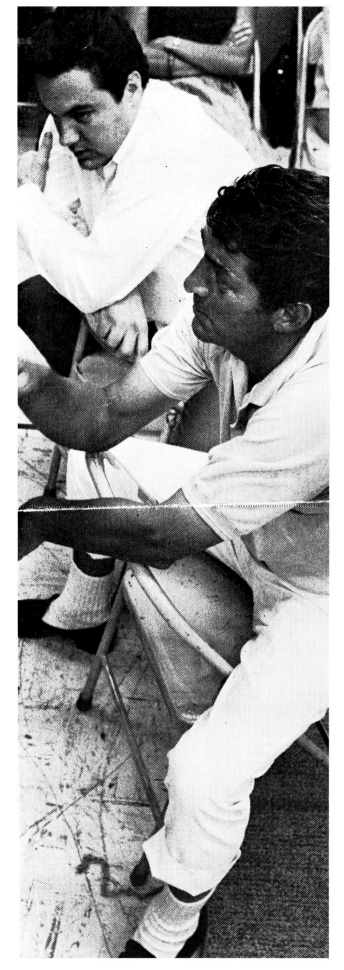

↑ Jimmy Bowen with Dean Martin in the studio, circa 1964. Bowen's background was in rock & roll and his career would later explode in Nashville, but at Reprise he produced important records for Frank Sinatra, Dean Martin, Sammy Davis, Jr., and others.

↖ An early sketch for what becomes the standard Reprise single sleeve.

Perhaps the fact that Warner Bros. Records hadn't yet embraced rock & roll in early 1964 was not surprising, given the recent success of its folk and comedy records. Peter, Paul & Mary had been one of the best-selling acts of 1963. Allan Sherman was right up there in sales with the folk trio. But the Beatles slowed America's interest in folk music. One year later, at the Newport Folk Festival in Rhode Island, Bob Dylan, affected by the changes, would perform with an electric guitar and a backing band. In the eyes of many, Dylan's embrace of rock meant one era in pop music had ended while another began. But Dean Martin was still selling. The shift was far from complete.

Joe Smith: "The Everly Brothers told me about the Beatles. They said that there was this band that wore their hair funny and all had the same suits but musically were absolutely amazing. Unfortunately, we couldn't really capitalize on all the excitement going on in England because Warner Bros. Records didn't have offices over there. We did business through an English label, Pye. But Pye couldn't compete with Decca and EMI, two of England's biggest record companies. We were a long way from being players in England in 1964."

Initiated by Reprise before the Sinatra deal, the arrangement with Pye was something that arrived with Mo Ostin. And in the year 1964, no matter Joe Smith's measured analyses, Pye did bring a few key acts into the picture. Particularly considering the fact that in 1964 the only Top Twenty hit at Warner Bros. proper was the Premieres' "Farmer John," the Pye relationship was crucial. Through Pye Joe Smith would find Petula Clark, an artist who would release several hits on Warner Bros. over the next several years. And, again through Pye, Mo Ostin would find the Kinks. **Mo Ostin:** "I wasn't aware of what was going on in England, early on. My music was the same music that Sinatra liked—jazz. Fortunately, at Reprise I was responsible to make international deals, but it wasn't until I started going overseas to Europe and England that I became aware of all these changes taking place. Once we realized the size and scope of all these musical changes, we started to pay attention." The Kinks' American hits, "You Really Got Me" and "All Day and All of the Night," together with later songs like "A Well Respected Man" and "Sunny Afternoon," would give Warner Bros. an important connection to the music coming out of England. With the Beatles arrived a new cultural moment that would ultimately provide the context for the emergence of Warner/Reprise as the gold standard for what a label should and could be.

SAN FRANCISCO

Bob Krasnow: "San Francisco was always San Francisco, something that's alien to the thinking of everyone else in the United States. It still is." In late 1965 and 1966, few outside the Bay Area really knew what was going on there. It was, at first, largely a local revolution. That changed when RCA signed the Jefferson Airplane to a contract and released the band's debut album *Jefferson Airplane Takes Off* in late 1966. Just after the Airplane joined RCA, Tom Donahue, a San Francisco disc jockey who knew Joe Smith from Smith's radio days, called his old friend to let him know that there was a lot more unsigned talent in San Francisco and that Warner Bros. ought to get in on the action before it was too late. One of the bands Donahue told Smith about was the Grateful Dead. **Carl Scott:** "I took Joe Smith over to meet the Grateful Dead, which was something Tom Donahue had set up. He went over with me, wearing his little blue suit that Warners executives wore, and we both agreed we wouldn't eat or drink anything while we were in the house because we wouldn't know what was in it."

Smith signed the Grateful Dead for $25,000, giving Warner Bros. an asset that would only reveal its importance over time. But it was a bold step away from the Conkling legacy and the mainstream A&R efforts that still dominated the label's roster. **Stan Cornyn:** "It was a new turn, and certainly healthier for the record company than trying to build a catalogue out of the word 'stereo' and polkas." As a transitional moment, the San Francisco adventure would take several of the executives out of their element, a field trip that would benefit the label. **Joe Smith:** "Truthfully, I hadn't a clue as to what the Grateful Dead were all about when I signed them in 1966. But I did realize that there was a buzz on the street about them and that I didn't need to fully understand them or even like their music in order to sell their records. The band had something like seven managers at the time. You never knew which one would show up at a meeting or pick up the phone. One night while I was there, my wife and I were having dinner in San Francisco at a restaurant called Ernie's, and Tom Donahue tracked me down to tell me that the Grateful Dead were finally ready to talk about getting a recording contract done. My wife and I went to the Avalon Ballroom and, wow, it was like walking into a Fellini movie. The music, the lights, the drugs, the people dancing, the overall craziness—it was just overwhelming. We watched and listened with our mouths open the whole time. When it was over, we did the deal. The Grateful Dead had its recording contract, and Warner Bros. had its first big hippie band."

↑ Tom Donahue, the man who sold Autumn Records to Warner Bros. Records. More than anyone else, Donahue launched free-form FM radio, a format that would be a natural home for Warner Bros. Records' increasingly eclectic roster.
↑↑ The Grateful Dead's first long player, 1966.
↖ Clocking in around two minutes, this first single of the Grateful Dead's "Dark Star" was a far cry from legendary live versions, some of which filled more than an hour. Seen here is the 45 picture sleeve from 1968.

AUTUMN HARVEST

Joe Smith was willing to bet heavily on San Francisco but, in this instance, found himself reigned in by Mike Maitland. **Joe Smith:** "After I signed the Dead, I came back to Mike Maitland and said, 'I can sign every act up there for $25,000 apiece.' I'm talking Janis Joplin and Country Joe and so forth. He said, 'Let's see how we make out with the Dead.' I told him that by that time it would be too late. Which is exactly what happened."

Perhaps to make up for what was missed, Smith went on to buy a small San Francisco indie label, Autumn Records, that was run by Tom Donahue and his partner, fellow San Francisco deejay Bobby Mitchell. For less than $15,000, Warner Bros. got a batch of Bay Area bands, including the Beau Brummels, the label's most successful act. While at Autumn, the Beau Brummels had two national hits, "Laugh, Laugh" and "Just a Little," which reached number eight on the pop charts in 1965. Both songs suggested that the Beau Brummels were touched more directly by what was coming out of England than by what was bubbling under in their own city. But with two successful singles to their credit, it seemed as if the Beau Brummels, with Warner Bros. marketing and distribution behind them, could break at an ever higher level. But it wasn't to be—in fact, the most significant part of the Autumn Records purchase was not the Beau Brummels but a few unknowns who surfaced because of the deal: Lenny Waronker, Carl Scott, and Ted Templeman. **Carl Scott:** "I worked for Tom Donahue and Bob Mitchell in San Francisco as their office manager. They also employed Sly Stone. We formed a publishing company, a production company that did shows at the Cow Palace, and a record label, Autumn Records. They eventually sold the label to Joe Smith at Warner Bros., who wanted the Beau Brummels. Out of that they got the Tikis, who would be renamed Harpers Bizarre. Lenny Waronker, Van Dyke Parks, and Randy Newman were all involved with Harpers."

Waronker was the son of Sy Waronker, founder of Liberty Records. In the summers during high school, Waronker worked for his father's company. After graduation in 1963, he signed on with Metric Publishing, an affiliate of Liberty Records, and started making demos for the company's songwriters. **Lenny Waronker:** "I'd ask writers to go into the studio with me to record songs, with hardly any budget to make the demos. Working with little or no money in the studio forced me to use my brain. I had to think through situations. I couldn't rely on money to get me through my problems. There simply wasn't any. It was 1965, I think, when I got a call from Mo. At the time, Warner Bros. was starting to do some really interesting things. I had always liked the Everly Brothers, the Peter, Paul & Mary records, and the company's comedy records were first-rate. I thought I'd get an opportunity to do what I really wanted to do, which was to produce records."

One of Waronker's first major assignments for Warner Bros. was to wade through the Autumn purchase and assess its worth. He identified the Beau Brummels, the Mojo Men, and the Tikis to be the best of the lot. But keeping the Tikis was less about the band's potential for making hit records and more about doing something new with its leader, Ted Templeman. **Lenny Waronker:** "Ted was open to anything. I talked to him about the possibility of putting

⬆ Lenny Waronker and Randy Newman in the studio recording with the newly acquired San Francisco band, the Beau Brummels.

⬆⬆ The Beau Brummels, 1966. Though they scored two hits prior to joining Warner Bros. Records, they would never recapture that chart success. As a catalyst, however, they brought together a group of individuals that would be crucial to Warner Bros. Records on both the creative and business sides.

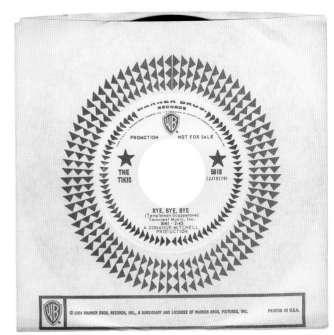

the Tikis behind him and starting fresh with something new, and he said, 'Sure.' I had heard a song on the radio by Simon & Garfunkel that I really liked called 'The Fifty-Ninth Street Bridge Song (Feelin' Groovy).' Since I was really hoping that as a producer I could make what I can only describe as artful pop music, I told Ted to listen to the song to see if he heard the same things in it that I did."

Harpers Bizarre was built around a warm, pop sensibility that looked to the Beach Boys as much as it did to artists from England and San Francisco. With Waronker producing, Harpers Bizarre cut a new version of "Fifty-Ninth Street Bridge Song," and the single shot up the charts in early 1967, peaking at number thirteen. With Waronker becoming a part of the Warner/Reprise team, the company's creative center began to form. From his position atop both labels, Mike Maitland didn't interfere with all that was crystallizing. **Joe Smith:** "We were finding artists to bring into the Warner/Reprise family, but we weren't dictating what they were going to do or how they were going to sound. We weren't acting like a lot of other record companies, but that wasn't a bad thing, not at all."

The bands that came from San Francisco were altogether different in character from the Marketts and the Routers, two Warner Bros. acts that had charted hits including "Out of Limits," "Let's Go (Pony)," and "Batman Theme." Based around session players, the latter bands were studio creations put together by Joe Saraceno. Saraceno made records cheap, could take anyone he wanted on the road as members of the bands (since they didn't really exist *as* bands), and had hits along the way. A producer's creation, the Marketts and the Routers could be charged with profound inauthenticity when compared with the Grateful Dead. Acts of that kind were a last vestige of a passing era, one in which Warner/Reprise was losing interest. **Mo Ostin:** "To me, what I had learned from Norman Granz and Frank Sinatra—that the artist and the music should always come first at a record company, and everything else would take care of itself— became my mantra. I believed it, I told the people who worked for me to believe it, and I let the artists know it, too. Warner/Reprise now had a vision. My job was to make it as clear as day and build a record company from it."

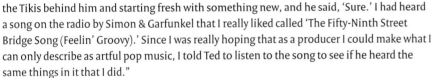

↑ The Mojo Men's only foray into the pop music charts was this version of Buffalo Springfield's "Sit Down, I Think I Love You" in 1967.
↑↑ The Tikis were Ted Templeman's band before he added Beau Brummels drummer John Petersen and renamed the group Harpers Bizarre.
↖ Harpers Bizarre in 1968: Eddie James, John Petersen, Ted Templeman, Dick Yount, Dick Scoppettone.

↑ Dean Martin, Mo Ostin, Frank Sinatra, and Sammy Davis, Jr., 1965.
↗ Frank, Tina, and Nancy Sinatra, 1968.
↗↘ Frank and Nancy Sinatra, 1967.
➜ Sinatra and his coterie of friends/admirers/business associates, 1962.
⊙ The Rat Pack gives its state of the union address, 1962.

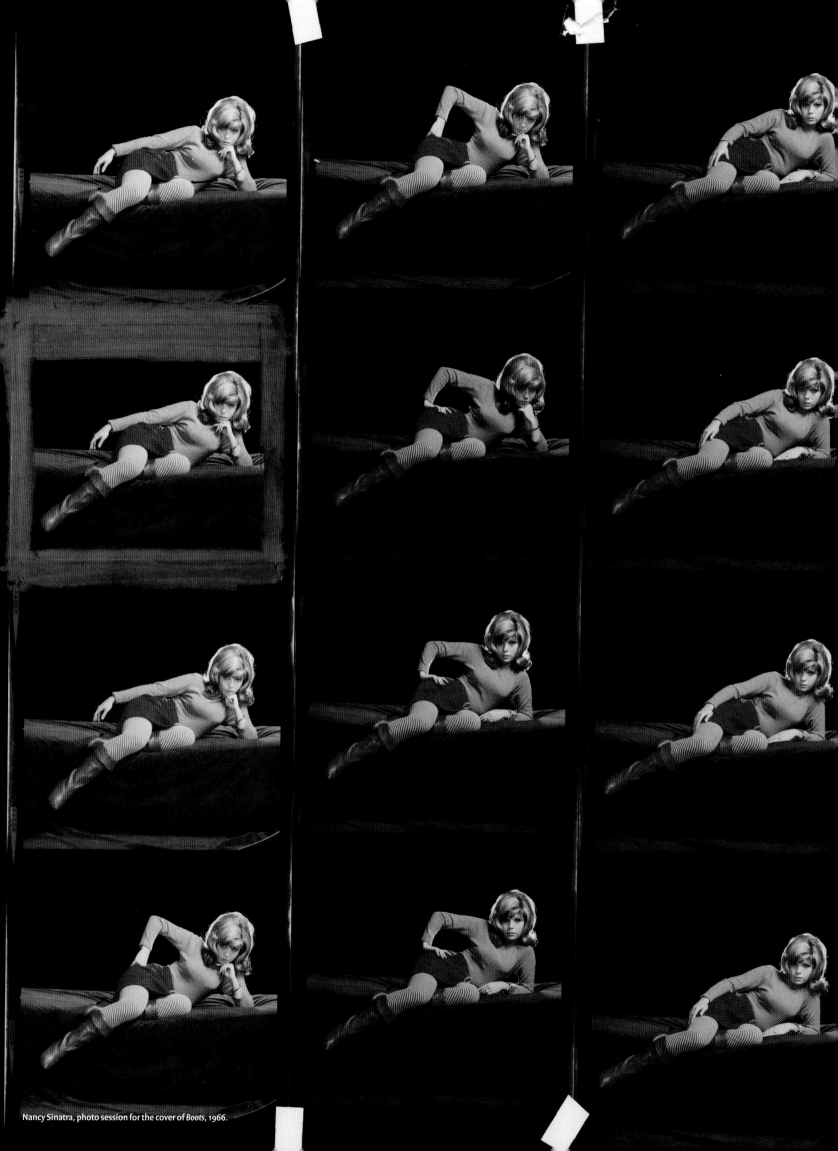

Nancy Sinatra, photo session for the cover of *Boots*, 1966.

A "STRANGERS IN THE NIGHT" TALE AS TOLD BY PRODUCER JIMMY BOWEN

A publisher from New York had given me the soundtrack for a movie starring James Garner. One of the pieces on the soundtrack was the melody for "Strangers in the Night." I heard it and said to myself, "My God, that's a song for Sinatra." I sent it to Frank, but he didn't like it. It just didn't knock him out. Two or three months went by. One night I get home from the recording studio about one o'clock in the morning and see that a package had been left for me. So I opened it up and there was a new version of "Strangers in the Night." I called up the publisher in New York—it was about four o'clock in the morning there—and said, "I'm taking 'Strangers in the Night' to Sinatra tomorrow afternoon and we're going to record it."

Sinatra finally agreed to do the song and we set a recording date for the next day. Well, I got to the studio early, got everything taken care of with the arrangement of the song, and then went over to a little place called Martoni's, which back then was a musicians' hangout. It's around 5:30 in the evening. The musicians are due at seven and Sinatra at eight. I walk into Martoni's and Jack Jones, the singer, is sitting there. I ask him how's he doing and he says, "Oh great, Jimmy.

I got this record that I know is going to be a hit coming out tomorrow. It's called 'Strangers in the Night.'" "Why that's nice, Jack," I said, "Good luck with it." Well, I got out of there and went right to the studio. I got on the phone and called all the Reprise promotion men around the country. I told them that I was cutting a Sinatra record that night and needed a big favor from them.

I just so happened to have in my pocket about $500 dollars or so in $20 bills that I had won in a golf game that weekend. Well, Sinatra cut "Strangers in the Night" and we were done by nine. I spent the next hour mixing it, and then went in the mastering room and started making acetates of the song. Then I had my assistant and other people at the studio take the acetates and the wad of $20s to the airport. Any flight that left that night that was going to a major city, they went up to a stewardess and said, "Here's $20. Take this here record with you and one of our promotion men will take it from you when you land." And that's what happened. Our promo men got acetates from the plane to friendly radio stations around the country and got "Strangers in the Night" on the air the next day. The record just took off from there, giving Frank a huge number one.

↑ Dean Martin at a 1964 recording session.
↗ Sammy Davis, Jr., mid-1960s.
→ Sammy Davis, Jr., late-1960s.
⊙ Neal Hefti with Dean Martin, mid-1960s.

▲ Sandie Shaw, 1964.
© Petula Clark, 1968.

BOB KRASNOW: FROM LOMA RECORDS TO FUNKADELIC AND BEYOND

Mike Maitland was running Warner Bros. Records at the time I came to start Loma Records. His idea of soul music was something along the lines of Ira Ironstrings. So he was looking around and called me, saying, "Look, we want to get into the black music business. I realize we don't have that much experience in it, but I know you worked with James Brown and Ike & Tina Turner." He asked me what I thought of starting something in that area for Warners. And, really, once I accepted the job and went to Warners, it was pretty good because no one—I mean, no one—knew what I was doing. They didn't have a clue. Their top guy at the time was Jimmy Bowen, and he was cutting songs like "Strangers in the Night."

So they gave me an office at the back of the bus. And I had a lot of fun there. I started Loma by reaching out to people I had met on the road with James Brown and other acts like Little Willie John. In those days, there were Cavalcade of Stars kinds of tours, with eight acts on the bill. In San Francisco everyone would stay at the Fillmore Hotel, right around the corner from the Fillmore Auditorium. And the Fillmore District, as it was called, was basically a black neighborhood. It was very lovely. I hate to say it was a miniature Harlem because I'm a New Yorker, and there is no such thing as a miniature Harlem, but it's as close as you were going to get to a self-contained black neighborhood. All the acts would stay there. And many of the people I met at that time and in that place were the ones I called when I started Loma Records for Warner Bros.

Warners saw what was happening with Atlantic, with some black artists crossing over. They were hoping I could do the same for them. But, unlike Atlantic, Warner Bros. was not steeped in ethnic or American music. The label was not set up to support black music. I'll give you an example: There was a California-based band, a black band, called the Olympics that I'd met on one of the package tours. When a friend of mine from New York called to say that he had a great song called "Good Lovin'," I suggested we cut it with the Olympics,

which we did. It went to number one in Los Angeles. Then Atlantic, our partner record company, cuts it with the Rascals and crushes us. Loma wasn't equipped—didn't know how—to cross a record over. And we had a six-month start on Atlantic! So, yes, it was lonely at Warner Bros. in the sense of getting support for something the label didn't understand. Not that they were bad, but Warners had just never been involved in anything like that. Same thing happened with an Ike & Tina Turner record, a cover of a Scepter recording called "Tell Her I'm Not Home." Again, it went to number one in Los Angeles. But the label couldn't cross it over.

Loma lasted for two years, then I was gone again. But I came back to Warner Bros. By the time of my return, however, my credibility was a lot higher. I wasn't a twenty-two-year-old kid. During that next period I had the George Benson record that sold eight million copies worldwide, for instance, and a Staples Singers song, "I'll Take You There," which was on a soundtrack and sold a couple million records. With those successes behind me, I was able to bring in Funkadelic.

George Clinton was someone I'd met at The Bottom Line. He had a band called Parliament, from which Funkadelic was a spin-off. Warner Bros. recognized that Parliament was a big band and this was a chance to capitalize on their success—it was an easy sell for me. And George, well, the more money he could make the happier he was. Like all of us. He was one of the funniest, most enlightened and talented guys I've ever worked with.

We had a big party for Funkadelic down in New Orleans. George was there with his new gadget called The Mothership. This was the first time he was going to use it—this thing that came down from the ceiling, made out of I don't know what . . . tinfoil, I guess. It was hysterical. But my team from Warners came down to see the show—and that's how we brought Bootsy [Collins] out of the band. Everybody saw Bootsy and thought he was great. I went back and told George that everyone really liked Bootsy. George said, "Yeah? Well we gotta make a record with Bootsy." And that was the next record. Then Roger [Troutman] and Zapp. The whole thing exploded. It was beautiful. When we'd go out on tour I'd say to my friends, "I'm not going out on the road, I'm going to a different country."

When I signed Devo, a very high IQ band, I saw that, like Funkadelic, they had a grasp of the visual and the musical. Bands with that kind of strength were bringing a lot to their situations. Really, what an A&R person does is to get out there in the culture and look for important messages. What a label is doing is reflecting everything that is going on around it at any given time. Whether with Devo or Funkadelic, here were bands making important cultural connections. The A&R person needs to stay open to see that happening—that's the job. If that is happening, it will be good.

PRODUCER/WRITER TONY HATCH ON PETULA CLARK'S "DOWNTOWN"

"Downtown" was a complete departure from anything I'd written, arranged, and produced before. It was like a stage musical in three minutes. I got the idea for the song on my first visit to New York. On my initial evening there, feeling somewhat jet-lagged, I walked from the Essex House Hotel on Central Park down Broadway to Times Square. Naively, I thought this was "Downtown." I found the atmosphere just incredibly exciting.

I spent several days visiting music publishers, trying to pick up new songs for my UK artists. When I returned to London, I remember sitting in the quiet and darkened Pye No. 1 Studio after a recording session, doodling on the piano while I waited for my engineer [Ray Prickett] to repatch the mixing desk for a mixdown of whatever I'd just recorded. I was thinking about "Downtown," and very quickly a tune and the general shape of the song emerged. The only line at that moment was, "When you're alone and life is making you lonely you can always go downtown." I thought it might be good for the Drifters, but I didn't necessarily write it with them in mind, though I really liked "Up on the Roof," and "On Broadway."

Shortly after this I visited Petula's home in Paris to select songs for her next recording session in the UK, where most of her records, in French and in English, were made. We probably "routine-ed" (a quaint verb used at that time to cover setting the routine of a song plus the key, etc.) some French songs, then turned our attention to the English titles. She told me that if we couldn't find the magic formula this time, she would only record something in English if it was really special. I played her three songs I had found on my New York trip, but could see she wasn't keen on any of them. When she asked me if I was working on anything new, I was reluctant to pitch more of my songs to her because she'd recorded several without ever having any success. I was disillusioned. Nevertheless, having nothing else to show her, I played her my "new idea," which had not advanced from my original doodles. Her reaction was instant. She said, "If the

lyrics will be anything like the tune, it will be a fantastic song. I want to record it!" It was her encouragement that inspired me. I couldn't have done it without her. I then thought about a stranger in New York and a lot of lines came pretty quickly.

I returned to London and immediately booked Pye No. 1 Studio, the orchestra, and a conductor/musical associate. I completed the lyrics and arranged the musical score, still finishing the lyrics half an hour before the session—in the gents toilet, to be precise. Then the orchestra, Petula, and the backing singers, the Breakaways, arrived. Everybody recorded together in those days. The session began, and while I rehearsed in the studio, my balance engineer, Ray, worked hard getting a basic mix together—it was great to work with someone regularly because they know intuitively what you want. When I thought we were ready, I went to the control room, said something crass like, "Let's wax a hottie" or "Tense up," and we started recording. I hate lots of "takes." They demoralize everyone. I like to rehearse a lot but have only two or three actual takes. The "Downtown" master was take two.

Even as early as the first rehearsal, I noticed the good reaction from the musicians and backing singers—my musical associate Johnny Harris said, "F. . . ing 'ell. That's sensational." Even Ray, my engineer, somewhat prone to understatement, said, "Very good, Tone!" I thought then we could be making history. The song sounded so fresh and different, and I hadn't—for a change!—copied anyone. After we had finished recording "Downtown," Petula said to me, "I don't care if it isn't a hit. I'll always be incredibly proud of this record and pleased we did it." When Joe Smith said it was great, I started to believe it!

My recollection of how the record came to Warner Bros. is this: Pye Records had a deal with the label to distribute WB product in the UK, and Joe Smith came over to the UK to meet with Pye execs and possibly secure Pye product for release in the States. I had recently finished the mix on "Downtown" and had already played it to the weekly A&R meeting. This meeting included Pye MD Louis Benjamin, all Pye A&R staff, plus heads of other departments. The meeting was designed to get feedback and plan future releases. As I remember it, the record got a mixed reception, but the decision was made that if Petula and Claude Woolf (her husband and manager) wanted it released, the date would be subject to Petula's UK schedule. One afternoon shortly after this meeting, Louis Benjamin called and asked me to come to his office—and bring the new Petula Clark record with me. On arrival, I was introduced to Joe Smith. He listened to the record and I'm sure this was the first time he'd heard it. His reaction was immediate. He wanted it for a US release. Petula's contractual arrangements with Pye were somewhat complicated at the time, with a Swiss company and French Disques Vogues also being involved. Nevertheless, a US deal was done. The "Joe Smith" factor, moreover, had an amazing effect on Pye—for suddenly "Downtown" became a major priority for the label.

I was delighted to have such success in America. You break America and the world is yours. (Well, sometimes, for some people.) And as far as Warner Bros. is concerned, you deal with people—not labels or companies—and the people I dealt with were great, especially Joe Smith. The real interaction came after "Downtown" started to climb the charts. When it went to number one, they were never off the phone, just making sure I was alive and well and thinking about a follow-up and an album. More music was made.

The song "My Love" was recorded in LA. Neither Petula nor Claude could make up their minds if they really wanted it released. Joe Smith had the final say. Another number one in the States. We recorded "Colour My World" in New York. I hired the city's only sitar player who could read music. He arrived with the rest of the orchestra, but we had to put his contribution on after the session—nobody told me he needed three hours just to meditate! With everything we did, it wasn't *my* sound or the *English* sound—it was Petula's sound.

PETULA CLARK

DOWN- TOWN

The Kinks in 1964, (back) Dave Davies, Mick Avory, (front) Peter Quaife, Ray Davies.

LENNY KAYE ON THE KINKS

When I formed my earliest band, the Vandals, and we were getting ready to play our first gig in November of 1964, our idea was to take a song that had just hit the radio and cover it. I was going to Rutgers at the time, and the Vandals wanted to be the first band on campus to feature a song no one else was playing . . . yet. When we heard "You Really Got Me," we immediately knew it was the one-up calling card we were looking for. Over the years I must've played it in dozens of settings, from formal gigs to everyone-knows-this-one jam sessions. A few years ago I had the privilege of backing Ray Davies at Carnegie Hall for a Tibet House benefit and got to take *that solo* and ride the key changes of the song. It was a remarkable moment for me, a self-circle completed, and one for which I am ever grateful.

The Kinks are intriguing because their early songs were very riff-based and somewhat disguised their inner complexities. Initially, they seemed closer to the Stones axis of the British Invasion than to that of the Beatles. They had a dissolute Edwardian image, brocade coats and ruffles and English teeth, with these heavy, rudimentary guitar parts driving their material. "You Really Got Me" is really a hook more than it is a composed, verse-chorus-bridge kind of song. Same thing with "All Day and All of the Night." Even "Tired of Waiting" is more about its sinuous guitar line. The simplicity, the immediacy of "You Really Got Me" is akin to "Louie, Louie." You could pick it up right away, play it within seconds of hearing it. The excitement and compulsion is there from the opening note. And like myself, as bands sprung up across the country in the wake of the British Invasion, many of them were covering the Kinks' first singles.

Yet the Kinks were not the semi-decadent Byronic characters of their self-presentation, and I think it puzzled audiences over here. Once you took the time to enter into Ray Davies' mindset, you saw that the Kinks were more than the sum of their riffs. Songs like "Dandy," "Afternoon Tea," even "Lola" had remarkable compassion and insight as regards English life, its eccentricities and misbegottens, its nostalgia for the trappings of empire and the vaudeville of the music hall and the hidebounds of the class system along with a bemused appreciation of human foible, all twinkled in Ray Davies' eye. If they weren't the group you thought they'd be, if all you knew was "You Really Got Me" as seen on *Hullabaloo*, likely you'd be surprised that a song like "Waterloo Sunset" could emanate from the same band.

In some ways they had a literary sensibility. The Kinks' character studies—even of themselves, since Ray is quite a character and the group history contains enough sibling drama to fill a *Masterpiece Theater*—remind one more of Evelyn Waugh or Anthony Powell than traditional pop music. Yet as their wonderful strangeness deepened, they became like those of whom they sang, both a part of the British Invasion and, so quickly, a remarkable anomaly amidst their peers.

↑ The Grateful Dead circa 1966.
➜ Joe Smith with the Grateful Dead.
⊙ The Grateful Dead in the studio, 1968.

BOB WEIR ON THE GRATEFUL DEAD

In San Francisco at the time of our signing, the musician community really thought it had a good thing going. There was a lot of interaction, a lot of musicians coming to the city and a lot of music coming out of the city. For a long time it was a hub. After the Jefferson Airplane got signed and had a hit right away, we weren't surprised to see more bands getting record deals. The record companies recognized that, obviously, this San Francisco music scene has got legs. They flocked to us.

We viewed working with record companies as a necessary evil. There was no alternative. So, if we were going to deal with a record company, we assumed they'd be who they were. They were going to wear their blue suits and see things the way they saw things. We weren't about to try to change them. Warner Bros. Records has to be credited with some degree of insight. They signed bands that may have tested them but ended up with quite a catalogue.

I vaguely recall a letter Joe Smith sent the band suggesting that we aim for a higher level of professionalism. We read it with some amount of derision. But we must have tried their patience enormously. If it's true [that Joe Smith described the Grateful Dead's *Anthem of the Sun* as "the most unreasonable project with which we have ever involved ourselves"], I'm quietly proud. We were anything but easy to work with. And that record didn't do very well—and they knew it wasn't going to do very well. We were headstrong. We were kids.

Back then the whole deal in the record industry was to get hit singles happening. Joe Smith liked my singing. He thought I had a hit singles voice or

something. We eventually got "Truckin'," we got "Sugar Magnolia," both of which sold some singles. He wanted us to work in that direction. But we were totally uncooperative. If anybody tried to tell us to do anything, most likely we'd head the other direction. We were fairly contrarian. We weren't about to be shaped or nurtured. That said, they put up with us and sold the records we gave them. And they did pretty well at that.

Record companies had to do some adapting around that time. Jimi Hendrix and Van Morrison wrote their own material. So did we. Frank Sinatra didn't do that. The folks in the A&R department had to sit on their hands—they didn't know what to do with these new kinds of groups. They'd make fledgling attempts to try to direct us in our writing, but they knew damn well that wasn't going to work.

I remember a few things in particular about working with Joe Smith. The Grateful Dead live record [*Live/Dead*, 1969] we wanted to call *Skullfuck*. Joe got on an airplane and came up to San Francisco to have a meeting with us about that. He managed to talk us out of it. He said, "You know, you can call it whatever you want. But if you call it *Skullfuck* no one will stock it in the stores." We acquiesced. There was another time when we were playing at the Universal Amphitheatre in LA and our crew—the band was complicit, but the crew saw this through—was hard at work trying to dose Joe, who had come out to see the band. They finally managed to do it. It might have been a beer, might have been a coke, but it had LSD in it. I didn't get a chance to hang with him after the show, but I'm guessing that he had a real interesting time that night.

LENNY WARONKER ON THE BEAU BRUMMELS

As a producer, I always tried to conceptualize an approach that would make a project unique. Usually it came from the artist. In the case of *Triangle*, I had what was pretty much a broken band. There were only a few members left, the most important ones. I became close with Ron Elliot. What I was attracted to first was what Ron was writing and, second, the acoustic quality of the work. Most everyone else recording at the time was working with an electric sound. So, combined with Sal Valentino's support—he was always very helpful, and a great singer—I thought we had a place to begin.

Ron's melodic sense and his abilities as a player led us. Then we started tracking, layering acoustic guitars. We brought in Jimmy Gordon on drums. It was like we had a little, tiny band that got bigger in the studio. *Triangle*, the title, had to do with the three band members. But, really, Ron was the force. He was introverted, very sweet, and wanted to do certain things. My role was to facilitate his vision.

Of course, the Beau Brummels had hits before coming to Warners. But I think Ron was realistic about what he was doing with *Triangle*, that it was far less commercial. He wanted to branch out, do it his way. I supported it, always hoping for a last laugh in some form, but we didn't get it.

For the next record, *Bradley's Barn*, we went to Nashville. I'd gone there when I was with my father's label, Liberty Records, and working for Snuff Garrett as a kind of gopher. He would take me to New York in the summers—I was in college and had the summers off—and I'd learn about what was going on in New York, the importance of publishers and songwriters in those days; then we'd go to Nashville, basically for the same reasons. That gave me a sense for what Nashville was like. And I had studied country music a bit and liked it.

But the idea of going to Nashville with Ron had to do with a couple artists coming out of Nashville who I thought were really good. The concept was to take this guitar player and songwriter from the West Coast and put him together with some of the young guys down there who could really play. That was the context for *Bradley's Barn*. And Ron wrote songs that fit into it. Ron and Sal loved players like Kenny Buttrey and Norbert Putnam. We got Jerry Reed, who was an unbelievable guitar player. Then we had Owen Bradley's brother, Harold, on guitar, also. It was a wonderful group of players—and they'd never heard anything quite like what Ron brought in. That record was like a little explosion. We did two or three songs a night for five nights.

When I go back to *Bradley's Barn* and listen to "Turn Around," the opening cut, I get so angry because there's a chorus there we could have used voices on. I was so overwhelmed by the guitars and the concept . . . I think I blew that one. You never know, but maybe if we had a harmony on the chorus and the drums were recorded differently . . . I don't know. I was really angry with myself. But I love it. I still do.

⬆ Lenny Waronker, head down at the board for a Beau Brummels recording session. This could be a producer focusing on a playback or a producer considering career alternatives.

↗ The Beau Brummels International Fan Club certificate circa 1966. They were as close as San Francisco would get to the Beatles—and then they became something else altogether with albums such as *Triangle* and *Bradley's Barn*.

The Beau Brummels in 1966. Ron Meagher, Don Irving, Ron Elliott, John Petersen, Sal Valentino

↑ The Jim Kweskin Jug Band, mid-1960s.
→→ Harpers Bizarre, 1967.
→ Napoleon XIV, 1966.
⊙ The Electric Prunes, 1967.

CHAPTER FOUR
GETTING EXPERIENCED

BY THE END OF THE LABEL'S FIRST DECADE, THE LAST VESTIGES OF ITS AWKWARD BEGINNINGS WERE ALL BUT GONE. YES, LIBERACE WAS ON THE ROSTER—BUT ALONGSIDE ZAPPA, THE FUGS AND TINY TIM, HIS PRESENCE MADE A NEW KIND OF SENSE. THE PARTY HAD BEGUN.

TURNING IT UP

Carl Scott: "In the late 1950s, early 1960s, I always considered Warner Bros. Records, in my small little mind back then, an accommodation to the film company. Soundtracks, 'Kookie, Kookie (Lend Me Your Comb)', Frank Sinatra, all of it an adjunct to Jack Warner. Then the music changed." That change was, of course, gradual and never all-determining. In 1966, for example, Warner Bros. Records released Johnny Sea's "Day for Decision," a pro-war anthem that went to thirty-five on the pop charts. **Stan Cornyn:** "Here we were: liberals, hip, wearing Nehru jackets, and Joe comes up with a single by a guy named Johnny Sea called 'Day for Decision.' I said, 'Joe?' To which he replied—and this was one of my better lessons in the record business—'Don't you believe in free speech?' And I think Joe was right."

In the same year that saw "Day for Decision" released, Jerry Samuels' profound oddity, recorded under the name Napoleon XIV, "They're Coming to Take Me Away, Ha-Haaa!", reached number three for the label. The valley between Johnny Sea and Jerry Samuels was, of course, wide and traversed only with care. If both Ostin and Smith would make benchmark signings in this time, these other, seemingly arbitrary additions to the roster suggest that creative freedom was operative in the burgeoning Warner Bros. culture. As tastemakers, Ostin and Smith would often head in different directions. But as architects of the A&R–driven culture that was coming into formation, they were often moving in the same general direction. If Smith had landed the Grateful Dead, Ostin would make an even greater impact in bringing Jimi Hendrix into the Warner/Reprise fold. The strength and character of the emerging culture would be determined by this and other key signings. **Ron Goldstein:** "When I got there we were still selling Don Ho, Trini Lopez, and Petula Clark records. It was an in-between era. I remember one of the first things I did was bring some dealers from San Francisco to see Petula Clark at Harrah's in Lake Tahoe. Two days later I'm back in LA at a Hendrix show."

JAMES MARSHALL HENDRIX

The Monterey International Pop Festival took place in mid-June, 1967, just down the coast from San Francisco. The bill included Janis Joplin, Simon & Garfunkel, the Mamas & the Papas, the Who, Otis Redding, the Grateful Dead, the Jefferson Airplane, the Byrds, and the Beach Boys. But for Warner Bros. this event would be remembered as the American coming out party of Jimi Hendrix.

Mo Ostin had become increasingly interested in British rock. Of course, Warner/Reprise had the Kinks, one of the most consistently inventive bands of the first British Invasion. But Ostin felt there was a lot more music to be mined across the Atlantic. He kept up with the slew of acts popping up in London, mostly by watching the British charts, reading the British music press, and listening to contacts who knew the city's music scene. **Mo Ostin:** "I became very interested in what was going on over there. It seemed like so much was happening musically that I figured I wouldn't be doing my job if I didn't pay attention to the scene."

The Jimi Hendrix Experience released its first British single, "Hey Joe," in December 1966 on Track Records, a small indie English label. By February "Hey Joe" had made it into the English Top Ten. Ostin had a copy of the single sent to him, and although he claimed not to fully understand where Hendrix was going, the music—and the band's look—caught his interest. In March, Hendrix's second single, "Purple Haze," came out just as he and the Experience

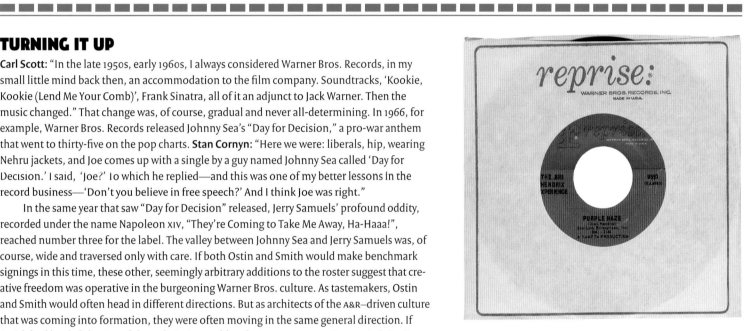

↑ "Purple Haze," the second Reprise single by the Jimi Hendrix Experience, was released in 1967 with "The Wind Cries Mary" on the b-side. You can't turn back from there.

← The many faces of Jimi Hendrix. Reprise gets its dose of psychedelia.

Opening spread: Jimi Hendrix, 1968.

were embarking on an English tour. Around the time Ostin heard "Purple Haze," he also heard that Atlantic Records had passed on signing the band.

Mo Ostin: "Atlantic had first option to all of the American rights of any of the companies that were under the British Decca label, which included Track. I couldn't believe they passed on Hendrix. Later, I had heard that Atlantic thought he sounded too much like B.B. King. But because Atlantic passed on Hendrix, he and his band were free to make another deal. I went after him very, very quickly. I called people in England whose opinion I trusted, and they told me what an astounding performer Hendrix was. And that look Hendrix had—it was phenomenal. I couldn't stop thinking about him. All of the elements were present in Hendrix to indicate that he might be something important, a major find."

With Atlantic out of the picture, Ostin signed the Jimi Hendrix Experience to a three-album deal. Out of the blue, Beatle Paul McCartney, who had seen the Experience perform in England, recommended to the Monterey Pop Festival organizers, Lou Adler and John Phillips, that the group be added to the bill. Neither Adler nor Phillips had heard the Jimi Hendrix Experience before, but they quickly took McCartney's advice and got the band on the event roster.

Despite unforgettable Monterey Pop sets by the Who, Otis Redding, and Janis Joplin, it was Hendrix who made rock history that mid-June weekend. In one short set, Hendrix launched a major career in the States. At the close of his set, Hendrix lit his guitar on fire. Ostin went to Monterey with other executives from Warner/Reprise. After the festival he was astonished at his good fortune in getting to Hendrix before Monterey. **Mo Ostin:** "I've always wondered if I would have been able to sign Hendrix after the festival. I mean, he was just so amazing there. Afterwards, I had A&R people from other labels coming up to me and asking me if I was interested in selling his contract."

Having Hendrix on Reprise had a transforming effect on Warner/Reprise as a whole. The artist's aura was conferred on the label. Ostin had taken a chance on a band that he had never seen perform and it worked. During his short time with Reprise, Hendrix released just three studio albums—but his presence on the label would be meaningful for years to come.

If this was a defining period for Warner Bros., due particularly to roster additions such as Hendrix, it was also a time in which the business as a whole was changing. The late 1960s saw the inventive spirit of the 1950s indie labels picked up by the majors and the larger indies. **Bob Krasnow:** "In England there was a revolution taking place, and the indies over here had little exposure as far as signing overseas acts. There were all of these English labels whose releases could be licensed. Hendrix was on Track. The smaller labels in the States didn't have access to that, and therefore the independent record distributors often missed out. It was the rise of the majors, in many respects." The first wave of innovation in the business of rock & roll would go to the indie labels, but as the 1960s came to a close it was as if the spirit of that first wave finally caught on at the larger labels.

THE EXTENDED FAMILY

Mike Maitland, Mo Ostin, and Joe Smith were watching a cultural changing of the guards. Jack Warner, "the Chief," sold out and retired. In walked Elliott Hyman and his company, Seven Arts, which purchased the Warner Bros. conglomerate for $184 million. While the film studio kept its name, the record label was now called Warner Bros. Records-Seven Arts. Hyman stayed away from the creative side of the record business. He got in it to make money, leaving the A&R work to others. As was soon evident, what Hyman really wanted was to make another deal, add a record company to the Warner Bros.-Seven Arts family. He found what he was looking for in Atlantic Records, a label owned and run by Ahmet Ertegun, Ahmet's brother Nesuhi, and Jerry Wexler.

Since its inception in the late 1940s, Atlantic Records was one of the great independent labels releasing black music, something with which Warner Bros. had little connection, save for the releases on Loma Records. Atlantic had released some of the most significant music in the post-War era. Everyone from Big Joe Turner and Ruth Brown, to LaVern Baker and Ray Charles, to the Coasters and the Drifters had made records for Atlantic. In the 1960s, the soul era, it was Aretha Franklin, Solomon Burke, Ben E. King, Wilson Pickett, Percy Sledge, and Joe Tex. With Atlantic's connection to Stax-Volt, Otis Redding, Eddie Floyd, Sam & Dave, and Booker T & the MG's came to the label.

After the Beatles broke, however, Atlantic also got interested in white rock, especially British rock. Ertegun signed Eric Clapton's Cream to Atlantic. Jerry Wexler signed Led Zeppelin. The other side of the Led Zeppelin story came from Reprise. **Mo Ostin:** "Led Zeppelin was the band that got away from us, and, much like what had happened with Buffalo Springfield, the culprit was Atlantic. A young A&R guy named Andy Wickham, who would become very important to Warner Bros. in the late 1960s and early 1970s, was a good friend of Jimmy Page. The Yardbirds had broken up, and Andy found out that Page was starting a new group. I flew Page and his manager, Peter Grant, to Los Angeles to start contract negotiations. We actually had a contract being drawn up when Jerry Wexler got wind of the impending deal. And Jerry did what he and the rest of the Atlantic team were very good at: swooping in and grabbing the act before pen went to paper. Just like that Led Zeppelin became an Atlantic act."

Elliott Hyman didn't much care about all this. All he knew was what Mike Maitland and his financial advisors told him: If you want to buy another record company, buy Atlantic. In October 1967, Atlantic Records became part of the growing Warner Bros. music family. Ahmet and Nesuhi Ertegun and Jerry Wexler stayed on to run the label. **Jerry Wexler:** "Looking back, it was the wrong decision. Ahmet didn't want to sell, but I did, and so did Nesuhi. I was a craven coward. I saw all these other small labels disappearing. And I didn't see any reason why Atlantic would endure. We made a big mistake. We undersold. I regret it, and always will."

If the decision to sell Atlantic was a bad one for the Erteguns and Wexler, it was just the opposite for Warner Bros.-Seven Arts. **Mo Ostin:** "Acquiring Atlantic was enormously important. Bringing them into the fold made Warner as a record group so much stronger. Now we had this powerful East Coast operation to go along with our powerful West Coast operation. Plus we got these incredible record men in Ahmet, Nesuhi, and Jerry Wexler. They were in an area of music that we were not strong in, so they complemented Warner Bros.-Seven Arts in a very big way. The whole thing was just an incredible coup for us."

ECLECTICISM FINDS ITS FORMAT

Warner Bros. and Reprise were signing new acts on a regular basis. In 1967, in addition to the Jimi Hendrix Experience, Ostin and Smith signed the enigmatic songwriter Van Dyke Parks, Arlo Guthrie, son of the legendary folkie, Woody Guthrie, the Fugs, a New York–based group that mixed politics, profanity, street theater, and folk-rock, and Kenny Rogers and the First Edition, among others. The following year the pace quickened: Joni Mitchell, Randy Newman, Neil Young, and Frank Zappa headed the signing list. In 1969, Jethro Tull came onboard, and new affiliate labels, such as Tetragammaton (Deep Purple), Bizarre (Frank Zappa), and Straight (Alice Cooper) contributed to the bounty. That same year Frank Sinatra scored with another big hit, "My Way," while comedian Bill Cosby, Peter, Paul & Mary, Sammy Davis, Jr., and Rod McKuen released equally significant records. A 1970 in-house roster list includes the Beach Boys, Lenny Bruce, Ella Fitzgerald, Liberace, Van Morrison, Tiny Tim, Jethro Tull, Dion, and more.

Lenny Waronker: "Everything was coming together. These things happen from time to time, when radio changes, artists' outlooks change, a youth culture of sorts comes around with a different sense of things. Record companies have to be quick on their feet." The growth of FM radio and the underground press supported the changing roster at the label, as if the one was tailored for the other. The same Tom Donahue who had sold Autumn Records would be the driving force behind the rise of FM. **Joe Smith:** "We couldn't get any AM radio play for the Grateful Dead. It was a controlled, Top Forty format. When Tom Donahue took over KSAN in San Francisco: That's when we got the Grateful Dead played." Donahue's vision spread

through the end of the 1960s into the early 1970s, FM free-form radio eventually becoming the home base of rock music. **Eddie Rosenblatt:** "FM radio was definitely a major part of the success of any of the companies that went after rock & roll. It was a fabulous time for getting airplay for acts that never got airplay before."

With the rise of FM not only did a range of performers now have a chance to be played on the radio, the eclecticism of the format propelled a further eclecticism on the label's part. **Lenny Waronker:** "I remember talking to Tom Donahue and praying that he would be able to get this format he was talking about off the ground. The first day the station in Pasadena went on the air, he called me and said, 'Turn on the radio.' I figured out how to do it, and there was Van Dyke Parks. It was an affirmation, for sure." With that affirmation a reversal of sorts took place: The growing underground displaced Sinatra and Dean Martin as the focus of the label's efforts. In the realm of A&R, a group of young producers would build something like a creative community in which the ideals of the era were manifested in the music making. The Burbank scene was compared to what one might find at other majors in an article from *Stereo Review*, 1970: "In a mammoth record company, artists can pass each other in the halls with barely a nod of recognition. In Burbank they are interested in each other's work and often get personally involved in it. The first album Gordon Lightfoot did for Reprise had John Sebastian playing bottleneck guitar on a couple of cuts, Van Dyke Parks playing harmonium, and Randy Newman doing some of the string arrangements. That album was co-produced by Lenny Waronker, and I mention that because Waronker also produces Parks and Newman—an indication of how interwoven and personal the working arrangements are at the company." Ry Cooder, Van Dyke Parks, Randy Newman, Lenny Waronker, Ted Templeman, Russ Titelman: These names would stick around Warner Bros. Records for decades, providing the human support for Mo Ostin's vision of an A&R-led music company.

Lou Dennis: "Mo always described the company in this way: The most important part of the company is A&R. The second most important part? Promotion. That means publicity, radio, and all that stuff. Third most important part? Mo always called it 'distribution.' Sales. If you don't have the music to start with, nothing else will follow. I used to tell people that if all it took was money, General Motors would be in the record business."

CREATIVE SERVICES

Eddie Rosenblatt: "In his world of creativity, Stan Cornyn knew no bounds. His was an integral part of the company." In establishing the character of Warner/Reprise, the work of the Creative Services department was a key factor. Almost like a marketing counterpart to the relatively unrestricted A&R department, Creative Services was given ample room to move. Through that department the consumer engaged with the company, the company as an idea and, in many respects, a personality. From the minds of such people as Stan Cornyn and Ed Thrasher came the words and images that established both a look and an identity for the company. The ad copy that Cornyn created defied convention, pissing off a few artists along the way. Projects such as the so-called *Loss Leaders* compilations set the tone. Subversive, ironic, self-reflexive: Cornyn's efforts undercut the traditional advertising model. **Stan Cornyn:** "My boss at the time, Joel Friedman, went on a sabbatical to study law. Mo came down to my office and asked if I could do ads while Joel was gone. 'Okay.' I looked in *Billboard* and turned the pages, seeing all of these nothings ads. 'Rocketing Up The Charts!' with a full-page picture of the performer. I said, 'We're wasting our money here. No one's looking at these things.' I figured we should do something that stops people, that gets their attention."

↑ Van Dyke Parks from the back cover of *Song Cycle*, 1968.

↗ The once and future building. An architect's rendering of the A. Quincy Jones-designed offices at 3300 Warner Boulevard. Jones worked with Warner Bros. art director Ed Thrasher on the plans. The building remains the company's headquarters.

→ Ed Thrasher, Joel Friedman, and Stan Cornyn, 1964. Their Nehru jackets would be shipped within three years.

"Once You Get Used To It, His Voice Is Really Something," declared the ad for a Randy Newman album. "Joni Mitchell is 90% Virgin." "(While Supplies Last) Free Dirt!" More than ready to make fun of the "fat, hard-of-hearing, paunchy executives at Warner Bros. Records," the ads dissolved the wall between consumer and company. **Mo Ostin:** "Stan Cornyn was breaking new ground in music marketing. He was doing things, writing things that no one in the business had ever done before. The ads he created were controversial and stopped you in your tracks. Stan's role in the success of Warners during the heyday can't be underestimated. He had a lot to do with creating the image of the company. All of the creative marketing areas fell under his responsibility, and they all turned out things that made us shake our heads, at other times laugh, and sometimes think we'd be sued. But the stuff worked."

Art director Ed Thrasher left his own lasting mark in that same period. As one of the figures associated with raising album packages to the level of art, Thrasher had an ability to match the visuals to the artist. Whether with the Jimi Hendrix Experience's *Are You Experienced?* or the Doobie Brothers' *Stampede* or Van Morrison's *Tupelo Honey*, he helped to establish Warner Bros. as a label that would consistently find creative ways to foster the dialogue between sound and image, between sleeve and content. Thrasher created artwork for the generation that grew up staring at record jackets while LPs played.

In 1973, when Frank Sinatra ended his early retirement, it was Thrasher who came up with the images and the tagline for the "Ol' Blue Eyes Is Back" campaign, with which Sinatra immediately fell in love. His art direction, which sometimes revolved around his own photographs, led to twelve Grammy nominations. Thrasher's design sense was so closely tied to that of Warner Bros. that he eventually extended his services to work with architect A. Quincy Jones on the building at 3300 Warner Boulevard. But Thrasher's most lasting gift lay in his capacity to leave any one project behind and adjust his sensibility to whatever might come next. Each album project he led was developed on its own terms, an approach that would carry over through the years in various Warner Bros. art departments. **Adam Somers:** "Ed had an extraordinary eye and was a brilliant photographer, which informed his point of view. Stan, who applied his considerable intellect to the issues of the record business and was a torrent of ideas, is a formidable writer, which informs *his* point of view. The tension between those two points of view, I believe, led to the trendsetting 'Warners look' as well as the 'Warners voice' in ads, posters, covers, sales presentations, etc."

CHANGING HANDS: A CORPORATE BEST-CASE SCENARIO

By the late 1960s Warner/Reprise had established itself as a tastemaker company and a profit machine. In that same period, Steve Ross, Ted Ashley, and Kinney National Services, a company the two men owned that had a part in everything from parking lots to one of the largest funeral casket businesses in America, approached Elliot Hyman about selling Warner Bros. to Kinney. Likely Elliott Hyman had never intended to hold onto Warner Bros. for very long. He was in the business to make money. In the case of the Warner Group, he served to make a remarkable profit. In the summer of 1969, Hyman received about four hundred million for Warner Bros.-Seven Arts, which included Atlantic and Warner Bros. Pictures. Frank Sinatra,

ED THRASHER
ART DIRECTOR

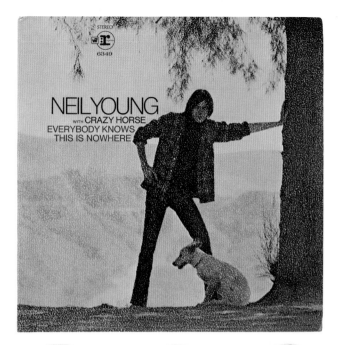

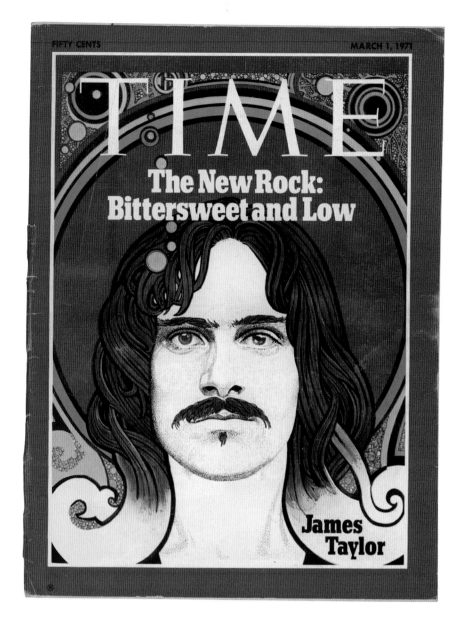

who owned a significant piece of Warner/Reprise, agreed to the deal. Both the Atlantic and Warner/Reprise record executives were told to carry on. All that was supposed to change were the owners of the company—and the name of it. Off came the hyphenated Seven Arts. Warner Bros. Records became just that again. If the scale of the exchange was staggering, the biggest surprise might have been Steve Ross himself. **Joe Smith:** "Steve Ross was the ideal boss. He'd say to you, 'This is your company. Don't bother me about anything. We'll talk financials at the end of the year, half-year. Go sign the artists'."

Mike Maitland was still head of the company, but the end of his tenure was coming. In some respects, Mo Ostin and Joe Smith had outgrown their boss. But that was not the problem that brought about Maitland's departure. Ahmet Ertegun was. To Ahmet, Maitland's efforts to be boss to Ostin, Smith, *and* the Atlantic team were misguided. **Stan Cornyn:** "I think Ahmet liked to be left alone." In order to keep Ahmet and the Atlantic team in place, Ross and Ashley quickly realized that they had to intervene. In January 1970, Mike Maitland stepped down as head of the company.

The Mike Maitland years at Warner/Reprise had allowed what was generally safe passage from the Conkling era. Maitland didn't stand in Ostin and Smith's way, even when he knew that the manner in which the presidents did business was different from that of the other major record companies. But, by this time, that was precisely the point. Warner/Reprise became commercially successful and artistically valid because it did things differently.

AN EMERGING AESTHETIC

Ron Goldstein: "When I got there Neil Young's *Everybody Knows This Is Nowhere* had just come out. I went crazy over it. So I took Neil—and this was when hardly anybody knew who he was—down to Pico Boulevard where there was a whole line of what were called 'one-stops.' They were like wholesale record warehouses. The young kids that were working there, the clerks, went out of their minds, and the owners didn't know who he was because they were still dealing with our Dean Martin and Frank Sinatra records at the time." Warner/Reprise helped to establish the rise of rock in the late 1960s. But as a counterbalance to the rise of rock,

a more acoustic-based, introspective sound, leaning heavily on the confessional mode of songwriting, came to the fore. By the early 1970s the golden era of the singer-songwriter had begun, with Warner/Reprise at the vanguard. **Mo Ostin:** "The singer-songwriter era came upon us without a whole lot of fanfare. We were fortunate because a lot of them lived in or around LA. Being in Burbank meant we were right there. We could go see them perform in clubs like the Whiskey. Plus, Lenny Waronker, who produced a number of singer-songwriters for us, had a great feel for the music."

In the year 1970 alone, Warner/Reprise released James Taylor's *Sweet Baby James*, Van Morrison's *Moondance*, and Gordon Lightfoot's *Sit Down Young Stranger*. Morrison's album, the follow-up to *Astral Weeks*, his first Warners release, would come to be seen as among the finest albums of the singer-songwriter era. But, simply put, Gordon Lightfoot and James Taylor sold lots of records. Their projects yielded Top Five songs for the label in "If You Could Read My Mind" and "Fire and Rain," respectively.

Lou Dennis: "I think James Taylor was one of the turning points. With his first Warners record he made the cover of *Time*." James Taylor's self-titled debut had come out a year earlier on the Beatles' Apple label. Despite the connection with the Beatles and strong material, the album stalled in America. *Sweet Baby James* made up for that. Produced by Peter Asher and including such players as Carole King and Russ Kunkel, the album made James Taylor a major star, and gave Warner Bros. still more critical acclaim for signing an artist with a poetic pop vision that spoke to the historical moment. For many, *Sweet Baby James* set the tone for the singer-songwriter era of the early 1970s. **Stan Cornyn:** "We just kept going on and having fun and having more fun until one day an event occurred that said to me, 'Oh, I guess it's over now.' It was the day that I got *Time* magazine and there on the cover was James Taylor. I said, 'That's not the *LA Free Press* anymore, is it?' By then, I had a custom Cadillac, a good income, and a showbiz wife. I should have seen it coming."

When "Fire and Rain" made it to the number three spot on the singles charts, the song's confessional quality sent fans digging for more details of Taylor's experiences, leading to apocryphal tales of the singer's personal life. But the mystery around the lyrical content fueled Taylor's career and signaled a shift in how the audience was approaching songs, now listening as though words were a keyhole into the artist's private life. The teenagers who had grown up on rock & roll certainly hadn't listened to the Coasters that way. But the audience had changed in tandem with the artists and the company that made their records.

Gordon Lightfoot's *Sit Down Young Stranger* produced a Top Five hit with "If You Could Read My Mind." Earlier, Lightfoot's material had been covered by Peter, Paul & Mary, among others, but this was the album that broke the artist in the States. Produced by Lenny Waronker and Joeseph Wissert, the album had enough mainstream appeal to solidify the label's position as a key player in the high-stakes game of sales and charts, but its sound was grounded in the work of a supporting cast that included Ry Cooder, Van Dyke Parks, and Randy Newman. Within that group lies the other story that was being told at Warner/Reprise in the singer-songwriter era.

↑ Gordon Lightfoot, *Sit Down Young Stranger*, 1970. Along with James Taylor, Joni Mitchell, Neil Young, and Van Morrison, Lightfoot helped to form the nucleus of an artistic community that put Warner Bros. in the lead position throughout the singer-songwriter era.

↑↑ James Taylor, *Sweet Baby James*—outtake, 1970. As with Tiny Tim—but in a different way—Taylor's looks were not lost on his audience.

GOD LOVES AN ECCENTRIC

It was in this period more than any other that Warner Bros. Records established its identity as an artist friendly label, as a place that allowed creative freedom. If that had been policy in-house, now the world seemed to be getting it: James Taylor helped Warners keep acts like Captain Beefheart around. It wasn't as if the label had a Gordon Lightfoot simply so that they could be sure another Van Dyke Parks record was on the way. It was a matter of spreading the wealth generated by one artist in order to maintain a creative culture for the many. Put another way, failure in the marketplace didn't mean you had to pack your bags. **Carl Scott:** "It was all about the artists. The artist and the music always came first, and the record company came in second. And that pissed people off. But it never pissed artists off."

For many of the performers who later signed to Warner Bros., they did so because of a certain sensibility at the label. Elvis Costello, R.E.M., The Flaming Lips, Tom Petty: All have cited a particular history at Warner/Reprise, a history that included the names Van Dyke Parks, Randy Newman, and Ry Cooder, as the reason they came to the label. The guys who played on Gordon Lightfoot's hit were magnets to the artist community, were artists who attracted artists. While a story that ran in a 1970 issue of *Vogue* associated Parks, Newman, and Cooder with "a commitment to understatement," there is plenty of good cause to challenge this reading. One of the reasons that these three, and others such as Captain Beefheart, Wild Man Fischer, and Frank Zappa, didn't fare well in the mainstream, where James Taylor lived quite peacefully and profitably, is that they *refused* understatement. No doubt the *Vogue* critic, when describing the music thus, was thinking of acoustic guitars and harmoniums. Randy Newman's *Good Old Boys* did not, after all, suffer from anything like an understatement.

Ry Cooder signed with Reprise in 1969 and, over the next several years, released a series of records that chronicled his musical travels. **Mo Ostin:** "Ry's work, I think, epitomized what Warner/Reprise was all about back then. He made these really great albums—his debut, *Into the Purple Valley* and *Paradise and Lunch*—and we really loved them at the label, though they weren't big sellers. It didn't matter. The music was great. It meant something to have Ry Cooder on our roster." Van Dyke Parks was often lumped into the singer-songwriter group simply because no one knew where else to put him. Another talent raised in Hollywood, Parks was the songwriter, producer, arranger, singer, musician, and friend who worked with Beach Boy Brian Wilson on the legendary *Smile* project. **Lenny Waronker:** "Van Dyke's musical genius just killed me. I didn't think people could be that smart when it came to music. He wanted success, just like any other recording artist, but he wanted it on his own terms. Even

† Captain Beefheart & His Magic Band's third LP, *Trout Mask Replica*, was released in June 1969 on Frank Zappa's Straight Records.

†† Van Dyke Parks, 1968. One of the architects of a particular Warner Bros. Records moment, Parks remains among the most distinctive and sought-after musician/arrangers of his time.

when it didn't seem like he was in control, which was for much of the making of *Song Cycle*, he very definitely was. At one point during the recording we went to a Russian restaurant in LA where this 80-year-old Russian musician played Russian music for the guests. Van Dyke was very impressed with him, so he hired him on the spot. The next day I went to pick him up to bring him to the studio. The poor guy had no idea what he was supposed to do. He had a very thick accent, so we could barely understand him, and he could barely understand us. The studio, the music, the people—nothing made sense to this old Russian musician, and yet who he was and what he played that day in the studio made total sense to Van Dyke."

Warner/Reprise had other artists who fell into the singer-songwriter category. Randy Newman was thrown in there—despite the fact that he didn't go near the confessional mode of address. Thinking more like a short-story writer, Newman wrote character-centered songs that, in many ways, couldn't have been further from Gordon Lightfoot and James Taylor. He was the living reminder of just how much could be done in the context of a pop song. If others avoided controversial themes, he went after them, finding in them a human story that didn't necessarily lend itself to slow dances but which elevated the three-minute song to a new level of art.

Other giants associated with the singer-songwriter movement would continue the label's string of breakthroughs, Neil Young and Joni Mitchell most profoundly. Both artists would defy the category in short order, but not before leaving major albums behind, albums that affected most every person writing songs at that time. You couldn't tell the story of that era without talking about the Warner/Reprise roster and the recordings produced under the label's banner.

↑ Early Randy Newman, circa 1968. Born into a family that included major Hollywood composers, Newman marked out a songwriting territory that set him apart from other singer-songwriters. In many respects, he inadvertently exposed the limitations of the "confessional" mode of songwriting and showed just what devices the songwriter could borrow from the world of the fiction writer.

↑↑ Ry Cooder, circa 1971. Like Bonnie Raitt and others, Cooder never sold a lot of records while at Warner Bros., but he was always a calling card for the label. A regular fixture as a session player, his exploration of American music's back alleys and open fields led to a series of celebrated recordings.

↑ Rod McKuen, late-1960s.
↗ Kenny Rogers and the First Edition, 1968.
↘↘ The Grateful Dead live in the Haight-Ashbury, late-1960s.
↘ The Association, late-1960s.
☉ Gordon Lightfoot, 1969.

ENGINEER EDDIE KRAMER ON ARE YOU EXPERIENCED?

I was at Pye Records in 1963 and 1964, working as an assistant engineer. I was involved with the Kinks and Petula Clark projects that would come out in the States on Warner/Reprise. But if I were to compare a Petula Clark session, for instance, with the Hendrix sessions, it would be like comparing chalk and cheese. There is no comparison. With Petula it was an orchestra, an arranger, everyone playing and singing at the same time, very structured, very disciplined. It would be three-hour sessions with tea breaks and so forth. In late 1966 and early 1967, the whole industry changed. I went to Olympic Studios, an independent—and that's where I would work with Hendrix. The studio manager came to me and said, "Hey, Eddie. There's this American chap with big hair—I think you should do him because you do all the weird acts anyway." That's how I got to record Jimi.

I had read about Jimi, heard about him, seen things in *New Musical Express* and *Melody Maker*. He'd already put out "Hey Joe" and "The Wind Cries Mary." But they were very unhappy with the way things were being recorded. That's why they came to Olympic. So I got to re-record some things, do overdubs on some, record new things, and mix it all, which was fabulous. It was an honor for me.

Prior to coming to Olympic, the band was not able to record at the volume they wanted to record, they were not able to record at the times they wanted to record, and they didn't like the sounds they were getting. Being independent, we could go all night, make as much noise as we wanted to, and I was able to translate what he was doing in the studio onto tape, so that when he came into the control room he said, "Wow! That's cool. I love that." Then it became a matter of us challenging one another, raising the bar. He loved how I interpreted his sound—that was the key.

I think I was too bloody nervous to pause long enough to get the depth of what we were doing. My head was down. My job was to get it on tape as effectively as I could. I wasn't really aware of the impact until after that first album was out. Jimi was always so funny in the studio, too, that you didn't necessarily think

about bigger picture issues in that fashion. The sessions were hilarious. He'd take the piss out of all of us, without losing his tremendous focus.

I remember being at the Saville Theater, a venue owned by the Beatles' manager Brian Epstein, to see Jimi play one time. I was up in the dressing room five minutes before they went on stage, and there's Jimi with a little record player, showing the guys in the band how to play "Sgt. Pepper's." They rehearsed it quickly, ran downstairs, and opened the show with that song—and in the audience were the Beatles, who freaked out. It was Paul who would recommend Jimi for the Monterey Pop Festival.

Now I wasn't at Monterey, but I had the pleasure of mixing the recordings. You definitely get the sense that this was Jimi's chance, coming back to the US with the potential to be a hero, to really make his mark. And he was prepared to do anything to ensure that the public knew he was back. I think it was like whatever was inside of him he was going to bring out. Of course, that determination was compounded by the confrontation with the Who regarding who would play first. Both bands wanted to be the first to blow the audience's minds with their performances. In the kind of rivalry that followed, Hendrix managed to come out on top. That image of him burning his guitar at Monterey lasted above everything. He made his mark. At Monterey Jimi Hendrix showed himself as the superstar he was going to become.

I had some wonderful moments with other artists. Certainly Zeppelin, the Rolling Stones, Traffic, and many others. But if I had to look at just one artist, really Jimi is the pinnacle. He's the one I'd refer back to. The three albums: *Are You Experienced?*, *Axis: Bold As Love*, and *Electric Ladyland* are monuments. It was a privilege to be there, making records that would have such an impact on the world. It's music that really does stand the test of time. Jimi Hendrix is the benchmark, the reference point.

The Jimi Hendrix Experience in 1968, Noel Redding, Jimi Hendrix, "Mitch" Mitchell.

DR. DEMENTO ON THE LOSS LEADERS

FROM A 1971 LOSS LEADERS SERIES SLEEVE:

These Warner/Reprise specials are full stereo, double albums in deluxe packaging. The double albums ($2 for two records) average about 28 selections, each of them is filled with the best of the artists' work, plus some extra collectors' items (like unreleased singles, even an Ice Capades commercial by our Van Dyke Parks).

You can't buy these albums in a store; they are available only by mail, for the ridiculously low price of $2 for the doubles, $1 for Zappéd, and $3 for the deluxe three-record set, Looney Tunes & Merrie Melodies.

We can get away with that low price because these celebrated artists and this benevolent record company have agreed not to make a profit on this venture. We (and they) feel it's more important that these samples of musical joy be heard.

If you're as suspicious of big record companies as we feel you have every right to be, we avert your qualms with the following High Truths:

This is new stuff, NOT old tracks dredged out of our Dead Dogs files. If our Accounting Department were running the company, they'd charge you $9.96 for each double album. But they're not. Yet.

We are not 100 per cent benevolent. It's our fervent hope that you, Dear Consumer, will be encouraged to pick up more of what you hear on these special albums at regular retail prices.

That you haven't heard much of this material we hold obvious. Over 8000 new albums glut the market (and airwaves) each year. Some of our Best Stuff has to get overlooked. Or underheard. Underbought. Thus, we're trying to get right to you Phonograph Lovers, bypassing the middle man.

Each album is divinely packaged, having been designed at no little expense by our latently talented Art Department.

DR. DEMENTO (LOSS LEADERS PRODUCER FROM 1971 THROUGH 1979)

The Loss Leaders series started a few years before I began working for Warners. It was Stan Cornyn's baby. When I worked at the label, I was writing for their freebie publications, first *Circular*, a weekly, then *Wax Paper*, a monthly. These would have some blurbs about the latest Warner product and some other stuff to keep people interested. I was involved in a lot of that "other stuff," which was generally record lore of some kind.

Then, starting in 1971 with the *Whole Burbank Catalog*, I was brought in to take over for Stan in the nuts-and-bolts assembly of these collections. Stan would still come up with the title and cover concept. He would come to me and say, "The next one is going to be called *Deep Ear*." Of course these collections weren't available in stores—you'd send $2 to the label and get a record in the mail.

The Loss Leaders records were samplers that served a basic commercial purpose. But they also seemed to have a life of their own, each having its own concept and character. What was happening on those records was not unlike what we were doing at underground FM radio, which was trying to play a wide variety of music but make it flow together and, under ideal circumstances, tell a story. I relished the opportunity. Really, I was doing radio shows without talking. So the art of the Loss Leaders series was the art of the sequence.

On Stan's very first record in the series you had Wild Man Fischer leading into Jethro Tull, the Jimi Hendrix Experience leading into Miriam Makeba. Later on, I would sometimes put little funny noises and soundbites between the tracks. For the collection *Burbank*, I found a comedy record from circa 1912 that featured a skit about Luther Burbank, the botanist, and isolated the word "Burbank," speeding it up and slowing it down for effect.

The purpose, as I understood it, was to expose lesser-known artists on the label. Someone might buy a sampler for James Taylor—but suddenly Captain Beefheart was in their house. There was a Trojan horse effect. Hirth Martinez, who the company believed in but who didn't break or get airplay, is suddenly being played.

I also think the series was an honest conversation with the customer. It was a conversation about music that might not have been heard, but it was also Warner Bros. showing that their interests often went beyond the bottom line, that the music came first.

Here's how I approached it: When records were nearly ready to come out, they would distribute test pressings to certain staffers. And I was on the list. So, usually a month or two before an album was released, I would get a test pressing. That early, I'd listen and make notes, marking tracks that seemed like they might be good for Loss Leaders.

Some artists, though very few, resisted the idea of being included on Loss Leaders collections. On the other hand, I once had an artist yell at me for *not* including them on a compilation. By that time the series had attracted its own fan base, had taken on a life of its own. Not surprisingly, we started to see other labels begin to try their hands at this.

STAN CORNYN

➡ Celebrating Stan's "Veeping" are Stan, Mo Ostin, Joe Smith, Lenny Waronker, and Ed West.

I was writing liner notes and other editorial jobs at Warner Bros. in the early 1960s when I was asked to write copy for some advertisements that the company needed for new releases. I hadn't done that before, but I looked at the ads in such trade magazines as *Billboard* and thought I could try my hand at it. From the start, I knew I didn't want to write the kind of ads that everyone else was writing in the record business. They were boring and bland and just plain bad. I took some of my sassiness and put it to good use writing ads. I got bolder when I saw that Mo [Ostin] and Joe [Smith] hadn't complained about what I was writing.

The idea was to get people's attention. All the ads coming out of the other record companies boasted about the music to the point where it just became a whole lot of hype and you didn't have to be too smart to figure it out. My way was to do something different: some white space, a catchy headline, a couple of paragraphs, a small photograph, some wit, all the while embracing the artist.

This was in parallel with what was happening with the A&R side of the company. The myth is that all Warner/Reprise signed during the late 1960s and early 1970s were weird, fringe acts that didn't sell a lot of records. That was only partially true. There were a number of very successful acts on the company's roster that weren't from the far end of the spectrum. But there were fringe acts that were often signed inexpensively and were increasingly worth embracing, whether they came from Laurel Canyon, San Francisco, or lower Manhattan. The ads I did weren't the kind to embrace Top Forty music. Instead it was "Bottom Forty" music. We were very successful in the underground rock press that was just beginning to surface in those days. The price of a full-page ad was something along the lines of a couple of hundred dollars, so it was cheap enough to experiment, which I did. The attitude of these ads was such that many people believed that Warner/Reprise was more interested in great music than great profits. Actually, we wanted both. But the ads accented the former and over time, the company's reputation with the hip music-buying crowd was very positive.

↖ Neil Young, early 1970s.
◎ The Beach Boys, 1970.
← Tim Buckley, early 1970s.
↙← Alice Cooper, 1971.

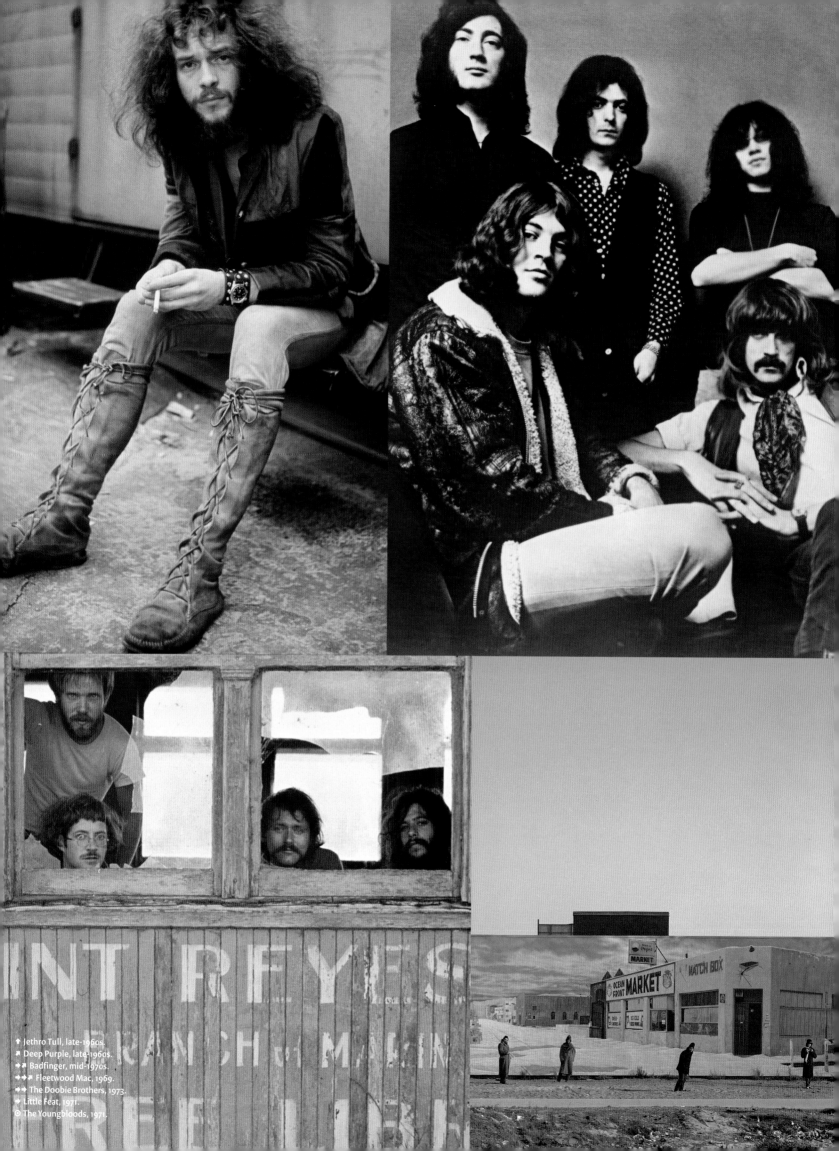

↑ Jethro Tull, late-1960s.
↗ Deep Purple, late-1960s.
→↗ Badfinger, mid-1970s.
→→ Fleetwood Mac, 1969.
→↘ The Doobie Brothers, 1973.
↓ Little Feat, 1971.
© The Youngbloods, 1971.

TONY IOMMI ON PARANOID

We made the first Black Sabbath record, both recording and mixing, in two days. Making *Paranoid*, however, was a thing of luxury—we had five. The band had been on tour in Europe, supporting the first album, and in the course of that often had the chance to jam songs. If we had a couple hours, we'd do that, which meant that a number of the song ideas were started before we went into rehearsals. Rehearsals themselves went for a few weeks. So by the time we got into the studio, we could essentially play the album. The recording was done live in the studio. Many of our ideas we came up with on the spot in rehearsals, sometimes later in the studio, which was often the case with *Paranoid*. In the instance of the song "Paranoid," we didn't have enough material, and that one just fell together once I came up with the primary riff.

My favorite tracks on *Paranoid* are "Iron Man," "War Pigs" . . . I still hear it on the radio and, like most artists confronting their own work, I'll hear things I might change today. The quality of the sound strikes me—you listen to the drums and it's like, "Oh, my God! That boxy sound!" But *Paranoid* was right for the time. And the technology was the *technology* of the time. We made those sounds. It wasn't a matter of buying a bloody keyboard with a gong, timpanis, and God knows what else on it, as you can now. You had to make whatever sounds you needed.

Paranoid was cut at Regent Sound, same as the first record. It's a very small studio in London. Recording is done very differently today. But when you went in and recorded live, there was a kind of magic to it. When you polish it up too much, you lose a certain sound. There's a rough sound to *Paranoid*, with all of us being in this little, tiny room, with just a slight partition between your amp and the next person. It worked.

The first Black Sabbath album was on the charts in America for a while. But when *Paranoid* came out it opened the door for big tours. That album took off pretty quick. Our first tours were as the opening act—we went out with Mountain, a couple with Rod Stewart . . . really peculiar bills some of them. But in those days such bills worked. Then before we knew it, we were headlining.

In England, of course, *Paranoid* went to number one. This certainly increased the pressure. It becomes a matter of, "Where do you go from here?" From there on out we needed to be as good as *Paranoid*. If we didn't get a number one, it wasn't going to be as successful. It forced us to put more thought into what we were going to do next. But, really, it remained a matter of first seeing if *we* liked what we were creating; if that was the case, then we proceeded. That's how we've always done it.

Given all that came after this album, I think it's hard for people to remember that we were a blues band. I don't think they even think of us as coming from blues roots. But I was very fond of John Mayall's Bluesbreakers, for instance. I also listened to quite a bit of jazz, the guitarist Joe Pass being among my favorites. For some among the Black Sabbath audience this might come as a surprise, simply because the band's history has been filed under Heavy Metal and, as a result, our origins are often obscured.

It certainly means a great deal to see young bands acknowledging our contribution. *Paranoid* pushed a lot of people out there. I'm so proud of that. To see bands like Metallica, Nirvana pay tribute, it's fantastic. When Metallica played our songs at the Rock & Roll Hall of Fame inductions, I wished I could have been up there with them, really. And Warner Bros. has been a part of that story.

Black Sabbath in 1971, "Ozzy" Osbourne, "Geezer" Butler, Tony Iommi, Bill Ward.

↑ The Pentangle, 1969.
↗ Richard Thompson, 1972.
↘ Norman Greenbaum, 1969.
↘↘ The Allman Brothers Band, early 1970s.
© Steeleye Span, 1972.

↑ Mason Williams, 1968.
↗ Arlo Guthrie, 1969.
→ Van Dyke Parks, 1968.
⊙ John Sebastian, 1970.

RY COODER

I was working with Jack Nitzsche, who was friends with the Stones, and he got the *Performance* soundtrack job. He went through an important door, which involved pop music in film, and was a really good arranger with interesting compositional abilities. In those days movie people looked askance at the idea of pop music in film, of drums and bass—it was all wrong as far as film theory was concerned. But Nitzsche got the job. The idea of world music had occurred to him. Milt Holland could play the tabla. Buffy Sainte-Marie came in with her mouth bow. He brought in Roy Hart. Some great people who could play some crazy things. Nitzsche had a really good idea there. They'd screen the film—projected in those days—and the director would wave his arms and talk in aphorisms, like English people do sometimes, trying to get you to know what he wanted you to feel and play. It worked pretty good.

We cut "Memo from Turner" to a recording of Jagger's voice and a click track. I used to go home from these sessions with a splitting headache, thinking, "What's the world coming to? This is about the nastiest looking thing I've ever seen, this film." It scared me. It made me ill. But the next thing I know everyone's running around like headless chickens raving about *Performance*. And that probably did have an impact on the Warners people. Likely they thought, "Hey, we can do this, too"—meaning make that English thing happen. Everyone was dying to do that, without even knowing what it was. But when *Performance* came out, people suddenly realized that this soundtrack came from Hollywood—"Hey,

that's Sunset and Gower!"—and figured they'd keep trying. And along the way I got a record deal. You should never assume that people knew what they were doing, not in a business as primitive as the record business.

When I got signed I was pretty young. I considered myself a folk musician in the general sense. But I think they thought . . . in fact I know they thought I was going to be one of these guitar hotshots who would do the rock guitar thing. That's what Jack Nitzsche had told Lenny I could do. But I didn't do that because I didn't even know what that was. They got the wrong guy. I always thought it was a mistake to sign me because I didn't do what they really needed. I wasn't a good team player—you've got to want it, got to get in there and say, "I want to do what the company wants me to do, and I'm going to do it as hard and as fast as I can." Somebody once told me, "Get a pair of leather pants and get hip to yourself." That was a piece of advice I got from someone at Warner Bros. I thought, "What the hell's he talking about?"

When I talk about folk music I don't mean the folkies from Washington Square. That's something else. I'm talking about people like Blind Alfred Reed who literally starved to death. Or Sleepy John Estes who went off a bridge blind in a car and drowned . . . but came back—that's a song! That fascinated me. I could see it. Within that folk music is some of the greatest philosophy and some of the greatest storytelling that ever was. I come from Santa Monica. There's no more prosaic place. It's a grid of streets, with sidewalks and lawns and duplex houses with linoleum floors. Let me just tell you, when Johnny Cash goes, "Hey Porter," I'm gone. Folk music told of other places. Other ways of life. It was fascinating. When I say "folk music," I mean the music of rural America. The music of failure is what it really is.

So what I wanted to do around the time I started with Warners was this: I'd listened to hillbilly—let's call it country and western—since I was a kid, and I thought, wouldn't it be good if you could take these old tunes that I liked and put them with a combo. I learned to like the sound of drums and bass from doing sessions with Terry Melcher. Once you hear a guy like Earl Palmer playing drums five feet away from you, you never go back. And I loved bluegrass, Jimmy Martin and all that, but they'd already done it, so why did I need to do it? If it was done to perfection, why the hell would you go and do it again?

American music is all about morphing things together. When the bluegrass guys kicked the tempo up from the old-time records, they were doing something pretty radical. To get from Charlie Poole to Flatt and Scruggs is to travel light years. And it was probably done in a heartbeat—because Earl Scruggs could do it. He saw that fast was good. Loud was good. It's much more interesting to hear a Mastertone banjo played with metal fingerpicks than it is a frailing banjo. I like frailing, too, but it just doesn't move you, doesn't kick at you like the bluegrass does. Or with their harmony, for instance; they took harmony from shape note singing and old church music, sacred harp, and they turned it into three or four part hillbilly bluegrass singing. Once you hear that live, you never forget it. It's imprinted. Or gospel music with electric guitar. Pop Staples thought it would be cool to have this vibrato guitar simply because he walked into a music store and they had it. He thought, "This'll be good." He added that guitar—and look at the result: First time I heard it I thought I was going to pass out. People take something and change it. The notion of purity in music is false. My idea, as I said, was to put the old-time tunes together with the combo sound. But I didn't sell records.

I do know that every time George Harrison came to the office, Mo would give him a copy of my new record. It's nothing I'm pissed off about—I realized that they had to play every angle. So I began to get it. I went, "I see. I don't make money and don't sell records, but there's a service I'm able to provide somehow." I like to make records, grew to love it after my initial fear, and figured if I'm being tolerated, because I serve this purpose, then I'll get to keep making these things. I was given the chance to keep trying, to improve. Nobody would do that now.

RANDY NEWMAN

ON LENNY WARONKER

Lenny's father was the violinist in the 20TH Century Fox Orchestra when my uncle was the head of the Fox music department and doing a lot of pictures. They became friends, and, ultimately, Lenny's dad became close with my father. I must have met Lenny when I was one year old. By the time I was four I remember going to Roxbury Park with him.

I was already playing piano and studying music when he suggested that I try to write some songs. We both listened to pop music and what was on the radio; and his father had started Liberty Records. So I followed Lenny's suggestion, and he showed some enthusiasm for what I'd done. He started me off, really, and was always the first person I played anything new for . . . for thirty or forty years now. You are, of course, in a fragile state when you write something. If you play it and someone reacts badly, and you don't have a great deal of confidence—and I didn't—it can squash you. But Lenny was always a supporter. He was my backbone.

We'd go see publishers and writers together, guys like Lou Adler or Lieber and Stoller in New York. Lenny had access to these people. Like Mickey Rooney and Judy Garland. We were young kids and we were going to put on a show [laughs]. But really, without Lenny . . . I suppose I would have done *something* in music, but I was kind of shy and insecure. And he wasn't. He was around people who knew what the good stuff was. And I could hear it, too—you know, that Carole King was really special, for instance. I signed to Metric Music, Liberty's publishing company, when I was sixteen or seventeen. I got a Fleetwoods record, which ended up on the backside of a hit. I earned about $800. I should have earned more, but that's what I got, I think.

When I started my career as an artist, I had two offers: one from A&M—they were going to pay me $10,000 to sign—and one from Warners, represented by Lenny, I guess. I was going to sign with A&M. They were going to pay me something, and it seemed like that meant they were into me a little more. Lenny was angry at that. I think he thought somehow . . . he often thought somehow that I didn't have to make a living. He never considered that side of things. The way I wrote, and have written all my life, it sounds like I haven't thought about it either. But I guess they matched the offer or something, and I signed with Warners. Luckily.

ON GOOD OLD BOYS

Good Old Boys was set in motion by one song. I'd written "Rednecks" and I felt that it needed explaining, that I had to further delineate the character. The singer, this Southern guy, needed more. So I wrote "Marie." Then I wrote a handful of other songs that might fit into a song cycle of some kind. "Birmingham" was appropriate to it. "Rollin'." "Back on My Feet Again." That focus, that exclusive focus, went away, but Lenny was always trying to get me—and maybe everyone else he dealt with—to do something bigger, like, "Oh, that song could be connected." He was encouraging me to do that. But I did reach a point at which it didn't necessarily work anymore as a really integrated collection of songs. There was a demo version, which has actually been released, with more Southern stuff. But I didn't like it. I didn't want to dig deeper into the clichés about the South. I don't know if Lenny regrets that, but I don't. When I heard it again, I went, "Oh, I know why I didn't do it."

There was a widespread belief that the North was morally superior to the South in its attitude towards African-Americans. That patently isn't true. Yes, the racism was written into the law in the South—I could see it in the signs when I was a little boy in New Orleans, "White" and "Colored"—but this city, Los Angeles, is a segregated city. There are very few cities that aren't segregated. In the South it was often different. So, that moment that I capture in "Rednecks," when Lester Maddox is on *The Dick Cavett Show* in New York City, ridiculed, *set up* really, encouraged me to look at the complexities of the situation, through the viewpoint of a Southerner who might already see New York City as a center of evil, a place where everyone sees all Southerners as stupid. The character felt to

me like an accurate portrayal of a guy from Georgia who might have seen Maddox on *The Dick Cavett Show* and how he might have felt watching that.

ON WARNER BROS. RECORDS

Whenever a mystique forms around a corporation, as it has with Apple or Microsoft, and as it did around Warner/Reprise, I always think it's excessive, because it's still a corporation. And when you dealt with Warners on business, you may as well have been dealing with a mortgage broker. They were tough. Mo, Joe Smith, whomever you dealt with. Though not on record budgets—I never heard that I couldn't use an orchestra, for instance. The main thing about the label, though, is that they gave you the chance to fail. They put up with you if what you were doing was good in, let's say, an aesthetic way. There was no A&R department that passed judgment. If it felt like somebody was doing something—they'd let you fail, and fail again, and fail again. And fail forever. Like me, and Cooder, and Bonnie, for a time. Now that's gone. You can't find it. And that's a very big thing.

⬆ Randy Newman, Lenny Waronker, Bob Regehr, Bob Merlis, mid-1970s.

I was living in Laurel Canyon in the late 1960s. One evening, Phil Ochs, the folk-singer, who was a good friend and former roommate of mine, came over to the house and brought with him another folksinger, Tom Rush. Phil and Tom were sitting around and playing songs. One of the songs that Rush sang was "Urge for Going." The song struck me at once. It was a great song. You could hear the artistry in it—the melody, the lyrics, the way it was put together. I asked Rush if the song was his. "Oh no," he said. "It was written by Joni Mitchell."

I didn't know who Joni was at the time, but I did remember that another song that I liked, "The Circle Game," was written by a "J. Mitchell." Rush told me that "The Circle Game" was also Joni's song and that J. Mitchell was indeed Joni Mitchell. He told me that she lived in Ann Arbor and had a lot more great songs. Rush happened to have Joni's address, so he gave it to me. I had just gotten a job with Warner Bros. Records as Director of Special Projects. I had been to the Monterey Pop Festival and had met Mo there. I loved what this label was starting to do with some really great acts, so I accepted his offer to join the company.

The first thing Mo said was, "So what do you want to do first?" My answer was, "Sign Joni Mitchell." I wrote to Joni; my letter was effusive and naive. I said "If you come to Los Angeles, I'll take you to Disneyland." What a thing to say! But it worked. Shortly thereafter I got a lovely note back from Joni on lavender paper saying that she'd take me up on my offer.

I never took Joni to Disneyland, but I did sign her to the label and we made an album that was produced by her boyfriend at the time, David Crosby. People think there is some kind of magic in all this talent-finding, but sometimes you have to do very little and suddenly some great artist surfaces and great music is made. Joni Mitchell became one of the great artists that Warner Bros. produced, but I couldn't claim credit for any of what she did except to bring her to the label. It was really that simple.

Her First
Album
On Reprise
Records

JONI
MITCHELL

STEREO RSLP 6293 *reprise* r

↟ Earth, Wind & Fire, 1971.
➜ Charles Wright and the Watts 103rd Street Rhythm Band, 1970.
ⓞ Herbie Hancock, early 1970s.

MARK ENGLISH

MO OSTIN ON NEIL YOUNG

As I've often said, Neil Young was a very important artist for us. Neil was always somebody who was respected by his peers. We had, of course, tried to sign him as part of the Buffalo Springfield. Brian Stone and Charlie Greene, two fellows with whom I'd had something of an incident, managed the Springfield. The incident was this: Some time earlier Jimmy Bowen had signed a group called Caesar & Cleo. I never saw them perform—Jimmy was the head A&R guy, and we made a standard deal with them. I trusted Jimmy's judgment. Soon after, Brian and Charlie came in and played me a master of the song "Baby, Don't Go" by Sonny & Cher. I was so excited by that song that I gave them a big royalty, an advance, bought the master and signed the artist—and then found out that Sonny & Cher were Caesar & Cleo, an act I already had! I was duped. I signed the same act twice. So, I found that unacceptable. I called Sonny into my office and told him I couldn't continue to work with Brian and Charlie. But Sonny said he would not change his management. I was so upset that I decided not to continue with Sonny & Cher—even though "Baby, Don't Go" was a local hit and they showed promise. Then what happened was that they ended up with Ahmet at Atlantic. The first record they made there was "I Got You, Babe."

Once Ahmet got his tentacles into Brian and Charlie, he owned them. And as it turned out, of course, they managed the Buffalo Springfield. But the Buffalo Springfield was so good that I was willing to work with Brian and Charlie just to get that band. And I went after them whole hog, had them over to my house for dinner and so forth. But Ahmet had it wrapped.

Now, Ahmet, for whatever reason, thought that Stephen [Stills] was the key guy in the Buffalo Springfield. And, in part because of that, Neil always felt like he was being treated as a second-class citizen. Jack Nitzsche let me know that Neil was very unhappy and suggested that I might be able to pry him loose from Atlantic. So I spoke to Ahmet, who said okay, as long as Neil was part of the family. Because we were under the same corporate umbrella, he would allow us to do it. That's how we ended up with Neil. The first record was *Neil Young*, which had "The Loner" and a bunch of great songs. The second album was *Everybody Knows This Is Nowhere*. And that was huge.

People began to recognize how important and special Neil was. He was a totally unique artist and a huge risk taker. When everybody else would go right, Neil would go left. He would always do the unexpected . . . with great, great results. He became so important to the label. In some ways, he was as big a signer as anyone in the A&R department, simply because he was a magnet for other artists. Even later on. R.E.M., Dinosaur Jr.: Acts like this would sign with Warners, telling us that Neil was a big reason. He was a beacon. It was devastating to me when David Geffen started Geffen Records and convinced Neil to go over to his label. But, ultimately, Neil came back to Warners. Neil was one of those artists with whom I became lifelong friends.

CHAPTER FIVE
FULL THROTTLE

IN THE 1970S, WARNER BROS. RECORDS ENTERED A PERIOD THAT WOULD BE REMEMBERED AS A GOLDEN AGE. ADDING AFFILIATE LABELS FOR STRENGTH AND ARTISTIC BREADTH, RESPONDING TO THE VERY LATEST IN MUSIC CULTURE, BREAKING NEW ACTS, PROPELLED BY WEA DISTRIBUTION: THE COMPANY HAD BECOME A FINE, WELL-BALANCED MACHINE.

WEA

Adam Somers: "When they put WEA into effect and fleshed out the whole system, sales just exploded." In 1970 Steve Ross ushered Jac Holzman's Elektra Records into the fold, bringing Elektra together with Warner/Reprise and Atlantic. Later, in 1973, David Geffen's Asylum Records would join that trinity. **Joe Smith:** "There was a great picture in *Fortune* magazine of Ahmet Ertegun, Nesuhi Ertegun, Jerry Wexler, David Geffen, Mo, and myself, all standing around the diving board at the Beverly Hills Hotel pool. The photographer was taking the picture, and I said to Steve Ross, 'If this diving board goes, you're out of the record business.' He yells, 'Get 'em down! Get 'em off that board! Take 'em on the ground!' He was a perfect boss." Even before Geffen's entrance on this scene, a branch distribution system, WEA (Warner-Elektra-Atlantic), was created to handle the extended team's releases. No more would the labels go through indie distribution. It was a change that would affect every one of the participating labels. **Russ Thyret:** "Obviously, the heads of the labels decided that we should be in charge of our own destiny as far as manufacturing and distribution goes. Joel Friedman was the first guy they hired to pull it all together." It was a business decision that would remove Warner Bros. from a world that went back decades. **Bob Krasnow:** "Doing business through WEA was much classier than doing business with those indie distributors in Chicago, where who knew if you were going to get paid or killed? Indie distributors were like punk rockers, didn't take shit from anybody. Real Damon Runyon characters. I loved it."

Branch distribution would have considerable benefits when figured in relation to the increasingly diverse roster at Warner Bros. **Eddie Rosenblatt:** "Indie distributors handled many, many lines, many different record companies. As such, when working with records they went on the strength of sales. Obviously. Artists like Ry Cooder, Randy Newman, and Captain Beefheart, wonderful artists, were very, very difficult to market. FM radio was still getting going. Mainstream radio didn't understand these acts. So, with the exception of a few retailers, it was tough getting these artists out through indie distribution. WEA changed that."

In business as in music, it was the end of an era. **Ron Goldstein:** "When they decided to start WEA, Joel Friedman called me and said, 'You're going on the road with me. We're going to pull the line.' *Pulling the line* meant we'd be ending our relationship with the indie distributors. So first we go to New York to see a Greek guy named Harry Apostolaros. We go into this bad neighborhood where his warehouse was, go in, and there's Harry. Joel says, 'Harry, how are you doing?' Harry doesn't say anything. He reaches over, and with his right hand pulls open the desk drawer. He takes out a lead pipe and slams the thing down on the desk. There's a dent about four inches deep. I jumped out of my chair. Joel, a really smart guy, says, 'Harry we're leaving right now. Meet us at 5:30 at . . .' Joel names some restaurant on Central Park South. I'm scared to death. Sure enough, Harry shows up at 5:30. First thing Joel does is order a bottle of Ouzo, this Greek after-dinner drink. Then they get shitfaced drunk. Just out of their minds. By they end of the evening they were hugging and kissing and all of that."

wea

⬆ Jerry Wexler, Mo Ostin, Nesuhi Ertegun, David Geffen, Ahmet Ertegun, and Joe Smith at the Beverly Hills Hotel, 1974. Six species of "record men."
⬅ Bootsy Collins, mid-1970s. Brought into the fold when Bob Krasnow signed Funkadelic, Bootsy honed his art in James Brown's band and became an ambassador of funk.
Opening spread: The inner gatefold spread from Alice Cooper's 1971 *Love It to Death*.

THE SHOW RETURNS

Bob Merlis: "I remember going to the Troubadour to see Dory Previn, and I thought I was going to slit my wrists. I sat through it and thought, 'This isn't really fun. This isn't the same as having Etta James do the dirty dog onstage at the Roxy'." The prominence of the singer-songwriter movement, which in many respects was the logical conclusion of changes kicked off in the Beatle era, had visible effects on artist performances. Singer-songwriters such as Gordon Lightfoot, Joni Mitchell, and James Taylor eschewed the baggage of show business. The theatrical elements of performance, costume, dance, and stage banter, disappeared—intimacy was, for better or worse, made the new priority. **Bob Krasnow:** "They were lily-white. Not to denigrate what was going on, because let's face it, Joni Mitchell's one of the greatest songwriters who ever lived. James Taylor is iconic. Neil Young is unbelievable. But, yes, it was lily-white. I had worked with James Brown. *That* was a show." But the early 1970s could never be reduced to what was happening with the singer-songwriters. As had been the case for some time, Warner/Reprise cultivated a diverse roster. **Lenny Waronker:** "There was the idea of building a roster that had a certain kind of balance to it." Through acts including Alice Cooper, T-Rex, Black Sabbath, and Kiss, varying degrees of theater would come back into play like the return of the repressed. In the face of the anti-spectacle that surrounded the singer-songwriter movement and the worlds of Ry Cooder, Van Dyke Parks, and Randy Newman, these other acts would banish subtlety to the back of the room.

In part through the influence of glam rock, overtly theatrical and always playing with sexual boundaries, there was a renewed connection in popular music to the Vaudevillian spirit. When Warner/Reprise brought T. Rex into the fold, they secured an artist who would become an icon, Marc Bolan. But the theatrical impulse would find a stronger advocate still in the person of Alice Cooper. Later enshrined as a father of heavy metal, Cooper's roots were both in the garage and in rock's more aggressively performative traditions. **Carl Scott:** "When you compare, say, Ry Cooder and Van Dyke Parks to Alice Cooper, you're talking about a salon mentality next to street rock. I was always more partial to the hammer-it-over-my-head stuff. I loved Kiss because of the theatrics, Jethro Tull because it was Jethro Tull. I would have preferred Deep Purple to the other side of things. But, pointedly, there was a place for both traditions. Onstage, Alice Cooper was behind a mask of makeup, in leopard leotards, had a live boa constrictor around his neck. *Song Cycle* this was not."

As would be the case from here on out in Warner Bros. Records' history, a lot of the balance came through the growing family of affiliate labels, including Chrysalis (Jethro Tull), Bearsville (Foghat), and Capricorn (The Allman Brothers). Alice Cooper and his band made their first recordings for Frank Zappa's Straight Records. Sensing that Cooper was maturing as a songwriter, Warner Bros. brought him onto the mother label, which released *Love It to Death* in 1971. What followed was a run of best-selling records that took Alice Cooper into the mainstream, both as a well-loved entertainer with a string of singles to his credit and an object of parental anxiety. "Eighteen," "School's Out," "Elected," "Hello, Hooray," and "No More Mr. Nice Guy" were all Top Forty hits, while *School's Out* (1972) and *Billion Dollar Babies* (1973) went to number two and number one, respectively, on the *Billboard* album charts. Artists like Cooper gave the label a chance to go off the deep end with promotion. **Joe Smith:** "Bob Regehr decided that we were going to have a coming-out party for this debutante, Alice Cooper, at the Ambassador Hotel, one of the most prestigious hotels on the West Coast. The Ambassador had done coming-out parties for Presidents' children and so forth. They had no idea. We brought our whole roster of artists from Straight and Bizarre Records, Wild Man Fischer, the Cockettes. It was a party with every deviant from Seattle to Acapulco showing up. The guys at the hotel could not believe what was happening to their place."

Guiding Cooper's career at the time was Shep Gordon, one of the many managers with whom Warner Bros. worked over the years but certainly among the best remembered. **Bob Krasnow:** "Don't start giving Warner Bros. credit for Alice Cooper. That was Shep Gordon, his manager. I remember the arguments he used to have with Mo about doing something like throwing fifty thousand pairs of girls' underwear out of a plane into the Hollywood Bowl." If managers were the link between the act and the label, not all of them knew how to make the most of the company. Gordon, however, was exceptional. **Russ Thyret:** "Shep Gordon was a very colorful, very creative guy. He made his presence known in the building, slowly wore a lot of people down."

With Black Sabbath's *Paranoid* also hitting in 1971, and Deep Purple's *Machine Head* following in the next year, Warners was laying the groundwork for an era of heavy metal that would surprise many in its staying power. But no one was ready to call it heavy metal just yet. For Tony Iommi of Black Sabbath, his peers included Led Zeppelin, and his roots went back to the blues. Only the convenience of history would subsume Cooper, Black Sabbath, and Deep Purple under a banner that was only just percolating as a banner in the early 1970s. Warners was in early, if only by instinct. **Joe Smith:** "I couldn't hear Black Sabbath, but I knew something was happening with them. When they'd come to the States they would want me to hear the new material, and I would say to them, 'The new material sounds like the old material'."

From another angle came progressive rock, which also engaged the deeper theatrical possibilities of the stage, if with less humor. Playing with costume, narrative, the instrumental vocabulary of rock, and, at times, the patience of those who wished rock would maintain its connections to rock & roll proper, progressive rock helped increase popular music's possibilities. At Warners, it was Jethro Tull who would represent prog rock with the most force. Releasing *Aqualung* in 1971, Jethro Tull joined Black Sabbath, T. Rex, and the Faces as a new generation of British bands on Warner/Reprise. As with every decade at the label, England was providing key elements that would bring scope and strength to a roster that had become known for its diverse character and, certainly, diverse characters.

But if *show* is the subject, Bob Krasnow, whose on and off tenure with Warners went back to the mid-1960s, must be credited with playing a major role in giving Warner Bros. a piece of that action. Krasnow had handled the short-lived Loma label, but he would also later be responsible for bringing Funkadelic to the label. With George Clinton, Bootsy Collins, Zapp and Roger and others coming into the fold through the Funkadelic connection, Krasnow ultimately provided Warner Bros. with some of the heavy R&B that they'd never had. Funk was a sound and a culture that was crucial to the 1970s and certainly a foundation stone upon which hip-hop later built. Having worked with James Brown earlier in his career, Krasnow forged a link between his own past and one of the most vibrant scenes in American music. What he helped to build would set the stage for a peak in the late 1980s and early 1990s, when Warner Bros. executive Benny Medina, Tommy Boy Records, Giant Records, Sire Records, and Quincy Jones' Qwest Records would all help to give Warner Bros. the deepest relationship to black music that the label would ever have.

FROM A&R TO ARTIST RELATIONS

In this period record companies were releasing albums at an unprecedented rate. In 1976 alone, Warner Bros. and its sister labels had released more than 300 albums; nearly a fourth of the total of all major labels. Over three hundred albums meant WEA was handling approximately six albums a week. If offering a contract to a new act was always a risk, in the mid-1970s that risk was more than tolerable as profits rolled in from established acts already on the label.

The Warner A&R team included Lenny Waronker, Ted Templeman, Russ Titelman, Tommy LiPuma, and at different times, John Cale, Richard Perry and Andy Wickham, among others. Producers dominated the A&R staff. Artists Waronker worked with in the studio in the 1970s included Maria Muldaur, Randy Newman, Ry Cooder, Gordon Lightfoot, and James Taylor. Templeman signed the Doobie Brothers in 1971 and made them into one of the top rock bands of the decade. He also worked with Van Morrison on *Tupelo Honey*, Nicolette Larson, Little Feat, and, later on, Van Halen. His production style shared some ground with Waronker's *and* with Titelman's, but in his telling, he let the artist determine the aesthetic, a viewpoint he shared with *Record World*. **Ted Templeman:** "If you listen to the Doobies or Little Feat, you can't really tell who produced them. I think that's the mark of a good producer. It's just an album, and you recognize the artist, you don't hear the producer—you don't say, 'That's a Ted Templeman sound' or something. I try to make sure my trip isn't on their record."

When Titelman joined Warners in 1971, bringing to the label Lowell George's Little Feat, he fit snugly in the company's A&R and production machine, working with Waronker on

↑ From the photo shoot for Deep Purple's classic, *Machine Head*, 1972. Warner Bros. Records launched several acts that would later be credited with *and* blamed for the rise of heavy metal.

↑↑ It seemed like everyone fell in love with Marc Bolan, the mind and body behind T. Rex—*Electric Warrior*, 1971.

Warners' Newest SuperGroup:

Waronker, Wickham, Templeman, Titelman & Cale

In this business, cities have sounds. New Orleans and Kansas City got known for Dixieland sounds. Memphis has its, and so does Detroit. Nashville, too.

And incredibly, there's

The Burbank Sound

It's the responsibility of Lenny Waronker.

He is leader of Warners' A&R staff, the company's latest supergroup.

The Burbank Sound may be his responsibility, but if you were to ask Mr. Waronker what the Burbank Sound is, he'd say he never heard of it.

Other people, of course, have: among them Captain Beefheart, John Cale, Ry Cooder, The Doobie Brothers, Arlo Guthrie, Gordon Lightfoot, Little Feat, Van Morrison, Randy Newman, Van Dyke Parks, Ed Sanders, for sure.

Each of these artists has recorded with a producer from the ranks of Warner's new supergroup—with Lenny Waronker, Andy Wickham, Ted Templeman, Russ Titelman or John Cale—the five pictured above.

Good Men.

(Ted Templeman, for instance, has most recently watched his latest Burbank Sound single—"Listen to the Music," by the Doobie Brothers—capture America.)

Sweated Subtleties

The Burbank Sound is, in essence, the result of a drive—often near interminable—toward perfection.

The drive to get a single or album recorded plumperfect. To redo and redo a record, even to the point where producer and artist spend hours sweating over subtleties that might well go unheard on the final record.

That sweating costs money and spirits, but it earns a Sound with capital S.

Earlier in '72, for example, Lenny's artist Arlo Guthrie had been long overdue for an album. The merchandising guys at the other end of the humble Warner/Reprise building were a-gnash. They bitched about "losing momentum" (as they put it) because "Arlo's been off the market so long."

And Lenny would listen and nod gravely, and he would say yes that certainly is so and what a shame but Arlo just hasn't felt like it 'til recently, fellas.

Mirable dictu, that settled the matter.

When Arlo did, however, feel like recording some more, the Burbank Sound and the Burbank Supergroup were available. Month after month, available, until Mr. Guthrie and Lenny knew it could be no better.

And at that time only did Lenny Waronker slip the album to Warners by-then rather randy sales boys.

Out of that album smashed Arlo's "City of New Orleans."

History should note: the City of New Orleans owes a lot to Burbank, and Burbank's Sound.

Thank you Arlo, but thank you Supergroup, too.

That Supergroup is why the Burbank Sound sounds better and better.

Even if it takes longer.

Even if it costs more.

Supergroups like Waronker, Wickham, Templeman, Titelman, and Cale happen neither cheap nor hasty.

But they happen in Burbank.

Where they belong.

⬆ Warner Bros. Records' talent wasn't limited solely to its artists. The A&R brain trust assembles for a little press.

⬈ The photo collage that appeared on the insert for *Rumours*. All that smiling was for the cameras.

⬆⬈ Fleetwood Mac's *Rumours* album cover.

⬈ Mo and Evelyn Ostin at the Fleetwood Mac party, 1976. Evelyn's intimate connection to Warner Bros. Records was a defining aspect of the label's culture.

albums by Ry Cooder (*Paradise and Lunch*) and James Taylor (*Gorilla* and *In the Pocket*). But, supporting Krasnow's efforts to get the label a presence in black music, Titelman also developed and produced the black funk group, Graham Central Station, fronted by former Sly & the Family Stone bass player Larry Graham, and soul-funk singer Chaka Khan. **Russ Titelman:** "Lenny and Mo had this philosophy of getting the best people to do the job of finding and producing artists. They were never threatened by any of the people they brought in. In fact, they embraced us, made us feel like we were part of the family. Over time, everyone fell into their own niches, one of mine being black music, since I had grown up loving doo-wop and R&B and had continued to keep connected to the music. I don't know if other labels enjoyed this same camaraderie, but at Warner Bros. we certainly did."

Tommy LiPuma came from Cleveland where he discovered R&B and jazz early on and worked as a promotion man. While working for Liberty Records he met Lenny Waronker. In 1966, LiPuma produced records for A&M Records before joining Bob Krasnow to form Blue Thumb Records. When Blue Thumb was sold to ABC-Paramount, LiPuma went to Warner Bros. Records, quickly setting out to give the label a presence in the jazz market. **Tommy LiPuma:** "Joining Warner Bros. in the early 1970s was like joining Murderer's Row. What talent the label had in the A&R department! There was also this elbowroom to do your own thing that was just amazing. Yet at the same time, you knew you were connected to something bigger." LiPuma brought a number of jazz artists to the label, including Michael Franks, Al Jarreau, and Randy Crawford, among others.

With A&R driving the company and bringing in acts of every kind, one obvious challenge became that of breaking the unknowns. A number of the artists who, in retrospect, are major acts were introduced to the market by a department that was a Warner Bros. creation dreamed up by Carl Scott and Bob Regehr: Artist relations. **Carl Scott:** "I had this idea that the record company was in the best possible situation to do what the movie studios did in their day. They had control of the artist roster and a solid responsibility to utilize that control in a positive way, in order to bring up the bands. I was a movie buff and really knew the studio system, as a fan. I thought to myself, 'The record company can do this.' So what happened was that I started out doing these tours, and I had no title. Tour department. At that point, Bob Regehr came to Warners. He was brilliant. He got it right away. Regehr became the champion of artist relations at Warner Bros. There was no such thing prior to that. We'd go out with the talent and make sure the promoter was tied into a radio station that was approved and working with our promotion department, get as much airplay as we could possibly get in that town, get posters up, get stuff in the newspapers, get people in to see these bands, and hopefully create an awareness in the marketplace around the country, city by city by city. None of it could have been done without Bob Regehr. He was fearless, courageous, smart, had creative vision. It was all about the music for Bob."

Artist relations began by supporting acts that were just developing, many of whom did not have managers with the sensibility or drive *or* wherewithal of, say, Alice Cooper manager Shep Gordon. **Ron Goldstein:** "Bob Regehr brought with him an entirely new concept. That department was essentially an in-house management company. Most managers were incompetent or didn't know what they were doing. Carl Scott and Bob Regehr really managed the acts. They really did. If an act had good management, then they complemented them. They were amazing. This was definitely an innovation, no doubt about it." The efforts of the artist relations department, while benefiting the artists themselves, also helped create the brand of the label. In one instance, Regehr and Scott, with the help of Georgia Bergman, put together a European Warner Bros. tour featuring various acts that introduced the label as much as it did the bands on it. **Lenny Waronker:** "Bob Regehr was coming at it from this high-powered publicity angle. Carl Scott was coming at it from the managerial side. There was this explosion when they came together. They were so smart. Every time they had an idea, it seemed to make sense—and it seemed to go hand-in-hand with the kind of roster that we had. For instance, they put together these tours, whether in Europe or at colleges over here, that maybe didn't make money but really got the company out there."

In time, Warner Bros.' artist relations department would be emulated at other major labels. Bands would come to expect the services that Regehr and Scott had invented. **Georgia Bergman:** "Artist relations had an enormous impact on the business. And Bob Regehr was critical to life at Warner Bros., a principal architect of the company's spirit. I was approached in 1973, not long after I'd finished working for the Rolling Stones. Carl Scott called, and I asked, 'What will I do?' He said, 'Oh, just come in.' Nobody really knew what artist relations was. It was like covert operations. One thing I did was to help put together a survival guide for performers that was called *The Book of the Road*. It included information on lighting gear and equipment, restaurants and hotels, record stores . . . everything, even fun stuff like VD clinics." Through A&R practices and artist relations' efforts, the "artists first" philosophy emerged as a practice. And Warner Bros. became known as the place where it could be seen in action.

A FEW SOLD AT THE END OF THE 1970S

In 1975 Joe Smith left Warner Bros. to lead Elektra/Asylum. **Joe Smith:** "David Geffen, who was running Elektra/Asylum, wanted to get into the movie business. He badgered Steve Ross and others until he got his way. The problem was who, then, would head up Elektra/Asylum? Since there was dual leadership at Warners [Smith and Ostin], one of us was needed to make the jump." By that time, Mo Ostin was already chairman of Warner Bros. With creative services conveying a sense of the label's character, artist relations getting the brand on the road, sales and marketing filling the stores and exploring new possibilities, Warner Bros. Records was defining just what a label could do to break an act without losing its connection to the art of it all. The marriage of the creative side and the business side was unique to the label. **Hale Milgram:** "We call that period at the label 'Camelot'." There were no guarantees that an unknown act would, if they could make a good record, break—but when everything lined up, Warner Bros. could now do more than it ever could to capitalize on early success. No example speaks to this quite like that of Fleetwood Mac.

Fleetwood Mac had been with Warner/Reprise since the late 1960s. A British blues rock band led by Peter Green, a guitar player routinely overshadowed by the likes of Eric Clapton, Jimmy Page, and Jeff Beck, Fleetwood Mac was floundering when Mo Ostin signed the group to Reprise. Citing spiritual reasons, Green quit the band in 1970. A series of largely overlooked albums followed, including *Future Games* and *Bare Trees*. In most any other era and with any other record company, Fleetwood Mac would probably have been dropped. As they had with Little Feat, Bonnie Raitt, Ry Cooder, and others, Warner Bros. established a commitment to the band. **Ron Goldstein:** "One of my favorite bands within the label was Little Feat. And for the first three records we hardly sold anything. But we kept at it. That was the atmosphere of the place. It was incredible." Mo Ostin kept Fleetwood Mac on the label, hoping that he'd see his belief paid off. That happened in 1975.

After further personnel changes and relocation to California, two new members were added to Fleetwood Mac: Stevie Nicks and Lindsey Buckingham. The two new members gave the band an infusion. The chemistry got everyone interested. What resulted was *Fleetwood Mac*, an album that wound up selling more than five million copies and earning a number one spot on the *Billboard* album charts. But it was the follow-up, *Rumours*, that made the company fat. *Rumours* delivered four Top Ten singles—"Go Your Own Way" (#10), "Dreams" (#1), "Don't Stop" (#3), and "You Make Loving Fun" (#9). It also went to the top of the album charts, staying there for thirty-one weeks, and won the coveted Grammy Award for Album of the Year. It broke the ten million mark and kept going. **Mo Ostin:** "It was an incredible record, and it had incredible success. It was hard to fathom. Here was a band that seemed like it was all but over, and then out of nowhere they record this magnificent album. I don't know why it happened then, and with Fleetwood Mac of all bands. But suddenly we had one of the biggest acts in the world on our roster."

↑ Dueling belt buckles, Fleetwood Mac vs. the Ramones.

AFFILIATES: A LITTLE BALANCE COMES INTO THE PICTURE

Warner Bros. made remarkable use of its affiliate labels. In Mo Ostin's view, he could extend his A&R base by bringing on labels that had areas of specialization. In doing so, the company stayed abreast of the latest developments in popular music without having to contort to chase the trends. Affiliates functioned as outposts of sorts. **Bob Merlis:** "Early on you had Capricorn, Bearsville, Chrysalis. It may have been a world domination rationale, but when you think about this as a strategy, it's very effective. How could a national label have an A&R department in Macon, Georgia? Through Capricorn we could have a presence there." But the reach was both geographic and stylistic. Affiliate labels gave Warner Bros. a broad identity. It would be crucial at the end of the 1970s.

All things in the music business being cyclical, the prodigious success of that period would inspire a backlash in certain pockets of the audience. With acts like Fleetwood Mac selling millions and the divide between audience and performer growing as rock got bloated in the 1970s, that cyclical thing was due to kick in. Punk came about as a musical, cultural, and social reaction. It rejected the artistic pretensions of progressive rock, the self-investigations of the singer-songwriters, the safety of mainstream pop, and most everything else that had defined the late-1960s and 1970s. Punk was, in some respects, a cleansing agent. Not everyone saw it that way—but the sophistication of Warner Bros. was such that they could be on both sides of the conversation, making it all work. In this context, Seymour Stein's Sire Records would play a crucial role, bringing the Ramones, the Talking Heads, Richard Hell & the Voidoids, the Undertones, and more into the offices that were handling Fleetwood Mac. **Liz Rosenberg:** "Seymour Stein is a genius. A great person with a remarkable eye for talent." Sire got Warners into the right part of New York City at the right time—and after that he'd take them everywhere he went, an obsessive talent scout. **Russ Thyret:** "It seemed to me that Seymour liked everything that he signed until it had a degree of success. As soon as it had a degree of success, he didn't care about it anymore. That may be the opposite of how he really was, but, I swear to you, that was the impression I got from working with him for twenty years. As soon as any of his acts got a little taste of success, it was like, 'I don't want to talk about that, I want to talk about this new signing.' In a lot of ways, it was an admirable thing. And he had a remarkable ability to get out and recognize acts."

Like Bob Krasnow, Stein had worked for King Records and was a listener of the most passionate kind, known for storing the history of popular music in the back of his mind, even as he remained on top of the very latest underground movements. With Sire and Seymour Stein showing the way, Warners found itself at the forefront of a burgeoning New York scene. In came the Ramones, the group that was perhaps the most responsible for breaking punk Stateside in the 1970s. **Seymour Stein:** "I really loved the Ramones. And I told everyone I could at Warner Bros. why they should love them, too. I went office to office." His next signing was the Talking Heads. **Seymour Stein:** "Look, all I did was hear good music and get it signed to Sire. I was out in the clubs all the time. I knew what kids were listening to and what meant something to them. Punk just pulled in all different directions at once. You couldn't believe the energy that was coming from the stage. I had no idea how big punk would get. When I was hanging around CBGB's it was still an underground thing." The connection to CBGB's was only the beginning of the A&R work he would do while connected with Warner Bros. But what that connection meant for the identity of the Burbank company cannot be overstated. **Steven Baker:** "There were times when Seymour was absolutely crucial to Warner Bros. Records. We were

such a big company that we didn't always move as quickly as we needed to. But Seymour—and sometimes members of his team, certainly Joe McEwen—was always out there, looking for the next moment of vitality."

Lou Dennis: "I once went to his apartment on Central Park West. We were going to have a progressive dinner. In his apartment he probably had the largest 45 collection I've ever seen. He loved to talk 45s with me, because I was in radio in the 1950s and remember a lot of them. So we went out for this progressive dinner, where we went to one place for this, another for that—this was an Italian night, my background is Italian, my parents were born in Italy. We were all dressed up in those days, always a suit and tie for me when I was on the road. After dessert he said, 'You want to go to CBGB's?' I said, 'Yeah.' We were the only guys there in suit and ties, and all these people were with pins sticking out of their cheeks, and I didn't know what the hell they were talking about . . . . Richard Hell and the Voidoids? Why not? Let's go."

PISTOLS GOING OFF

To this day the debate over punk's origins continues. New York and London vie for the credit. But without a doubt, punk was an intercontinental phenomenon. Over in England, punk's most celebrated and vilified representatives, the Sex Pistols, provided the media with the sound bites and news shots that pushed the band into the front of the picture. The Pistols had originally signed with EMI Records in England, but were dropped from the label for, among other things, insulting the Queen. In the States, A&M had the band, but when that deal, too, went up in flames—as did most things the band touched—Warner Bros. got interested.

Mo Ostin sent Bob Krasnow and artist relations man Bob Regehr to England to meet with the Pistols. **Bob Krasnow:** "Mo calls me—I'm in New York—and he says, 'Look, there's a band in London I want you to go over and look at. Bob Regehr is gonna meet you there.' So we get to London, and the name of the band is the Sex Pistols. We go to meet this guy, their manager, Malcolm McLaren, who I really liked. A brilliant guy, another in the visionary category. So he says, 'I'm going to take you to where they're rehearsing.' We go down, not *up* into a building, down four flights of stairs. We went to hell. Here are these scroungy, horrible guys that were just gross. It was like stepping in shit. And they can't play their instruments. The whole thing was a disaster for me. We get back, and I leave a message for Mo saying, 'Mo, that's the worst shit I ever saw in my life.' Bob, on the other hand, calls him, and says, 'Mo, we've got to sign them. They're going to be huge.' Mo calls me back and says, 'Did you guys go together?'"

Lenny Waronker and Ted Templeman hated what Ostin had played them. **Mo Ostin:** "They thought it wasn't music. They didn't get it, and they had no interest in bringing the band into the company." Ostin flew to England to do the deal. **Mo Ostin:** "I got to London and looked all over the city for Malcolm McLaren. I finally found him and we agreed to meet, but every time we set a date, he'd break it. It was incredibly frustrating. Finally, we sat down and I offered him a deal. Malcolm said yes, but only if Warner Bros. agreed to finance a film [*The Great Rock 'n' Roll Swindle*] he wanted to do. What attracted me to the Sex Pistols, given their history? I don't really know. Perhaps it was a perverse side of my personality that led me to them. I wasn't afraid to take a chance with them. And it paid off. The Pistols made only one album—*Never Mind the Bollocks, Here's the Sex Pistols*—but what an album. I still think it's the seminal album in punk.'"

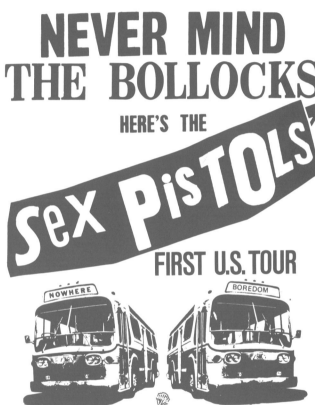

↑ An ad for The Sex Pistols' first (and only) US tour, 1978.

↑↑ The Flamin Groovies. By the time the band signed with Seymour Stein, they had already released recordings on several other labels. But, teamed with producer Dave Edmunds, they would do their finest work for Sire.

◄↑ The Dead Boys. Formed in the mid-1970s, they came from Ohio, the state that deserved punk rock more than any other. Another Sire iron in the fire of punk.

◄◄◄ Roxy Music, 1972.
◄◄ The Meters, 1972.
◎ Little Richard, 1971.
◄ Alice Cooper, 1971.

In the early 1970s I was a reporter for *Record World*, a trade magazine that covered the music business, when I got the job to become a publicist for Warner Bros. in New York, where I lived at the time. The company had its main publicity department in Burbank but used outside publicity firms in New York to deal with the media until I was hired, along with another publicist. I wrote press releases, artist biographies, and tried to get attention for our artists and records. I didn't know much about publicity back then, but I did know that Warner Bros. was the hippest label around because it had my two favorite bands, the Kinks and the Beach Boys, and it had those incredible ads, the Stan Cornyn ads. I figured I'd learn on the job, which is what I did.

Back then being a publicist at Warner Bros. meant you got to do some funny things. Alice Cooper was about to release his *School's Out* album, and I was assigned to do publicity for it. The interesting thing about *School's Out* was that when you opened up the album, you found that it was wrapped in disposable mesh panties. Well, before we got the opportunity to put them onto the

records, the US Customs Department had seized the panties. They confiscated them when they were en route to the pressing plant where they were to be inserted in the album. The reason they gave: The panties did not meet federal flammability standards.

We couldn't believe it. I called the Customs Department and talked to someone there who told me that the panties were made of the same material that surgical masks were made of back then. "You mean the kind of masks that doctors wear?" "Yes," he said. So I asked him that if you wore the panties on your face, you'd not be in violation of any code, but if you wore them under your clothes then that would be a problem. Amazingly, he said yes. I couldn't believe that I got someone in the government to say something really stupid. I turned the whole thing into a press release, which the *Washington Post* picked up and turned into a story called "Alice Cooper: (Under) Pants on Fire." The record got tons of publicity because of my little stunt. I'm sure the feds weren't amused, but I was, and, I think, so was Alice Cooper.

School's Out on press, being die-cut and being dressed.

Something/Anything?

← Todd Rundgren, 1972.
↑ Sparks, 1971.
© Captain Beefheart, early 1970s.
← Flo & Eddie, 1973.

↑ Gram Parsons, early 1970s.
→↗ Maria Muldaur, 1973.
→→→ Nicolette Larson, late-1970s.
→ Bonnie Raitt, mid-1970s.
→ Bob Seger, early 1970s.
⊙ Emmylou Harris, 1976.

↑ Marc Bolan of T. Rex, 1971.
→ The Faces, early 1970s.
⊙ Fleetwood Mac, 1976.

LINDSEY BUCKINGHAM ON FLEETWOOD MAC

If you look at the first Fleetwood Mac record that Stevie and I did, you have to consider it in terms of the Fleetwood Mac situation. The band had been languishing on the label. It's to Mo Ostin's credit that he allowed the various incarnations of Fleetwood Mac to exist on Warner Bros. Really, there was a series of albums that were non sequiturs in terms of style and band lineup. Mo had the intuition to say, "Well, they're not really making any money here, but let's wait and see what happens." That kind of mentality does not exist today. The willingness to take risks is at a historical low, and, by extension, so is a label's capacity to nurture acts.

So when Stevie and I came in, we joined a band that was not selling a lot of records and needed to make a new recording pretty quick. What we did was sit down in the basement, choose songs, and rehearse in such a way that we were completely ready to record. We needed to be ready so that we could enjoy a process that was as efficient as possible. Couple that context with the presence of Keith Olsen, who was the engineer and co-producer, and you can begin to understand how we approached that first record.

Keith had worked with Stevie and myself, and he was able to move things along quickly. The sense was this: Let's get it done and get it right, full-speed ahead. Keith's style was a lot softer, more refined perhaps. When compared with the lineup that made *Rumours*, you could say that Keith knew what he was doing to a greater degree. He was also constricted by what he thought was correct and what he thought wasn't. The end result of that album is a very competent, state-of-the-art kind of recording. It's a wonderful collection of tunes, and it does show this chemistry that we had as a fivesome, which was something intangible—you can't put your finger on why things worked as well as they did, they just did. There was a sense that this incarnation of Fleetwood Mac was onto something. That's pretty much the way I perceive that first album. And, of course, it was quite successful.

When you move on to *Rumours*, I think because there were certain . . . how can I say . . . boundaries that Keith Olsen was fond of putting around things to keep results in the realm of what he thought was good, at that point we wanted to move outside of those boundaries, to give ourselves more freedom, to make the process, if you will, less efficient. But it was also more eclectic. And by then, you also have to consider what was going on within the band.

It may be true that Stevie and I were poised for a breakup by the time we joined Fleetwood Mac. And certainly John and Christine McVie were poised. But we were still two couples intact and remained so for the making of that first album. I think success was the catalyst for the breakup of those two couples. It happened at the beginning of the making of *Rumours* and unfolded throughout the process. You had this whole backdrop of angst and, really, pain, if you want to call it what it was. And it was driving that machine. I like to think I did a lion's share of the producing on that first record—credited or not—but by *Rumours* I was really in the trenches doing much of it. So, I was having to live in denial, to compartmentalize my emotions, sealing off the things that were unhappy and getting on with those that needed doing because, obviously, we had this destiny we were trying to follow.

Rumours was more of a wild animal in terms of the people involved, their sensibilities, the emotional world in which we were embroiled. And all of that came out in the music. That was one of the things that made *Rumours* attractive to people—it brought out the voyeur in everyone. People knew what was going on with the band and could hear it being addressed in a very authentic way in the songs. But it really was not a very fun time, I have to say.

While there is, as I said, an eclecticism to *Rumours*, it doesn't necessarily wear that on its sleeve. In many ways, if you're doing the work properly, people aren't hearing the elements of a production, the parts. If you take those parts away, however, the songs aren't records anymore, records in the sense of something that is produced that transcends the song itself. A song like "Go Your Own Way," for instance, uses the drums a little differently than one might expect. I remember a reaction from this guy B. Mitchell Reed, a Los Angeles deejay. I was

in my car and the song had just been released as a single. He plays it and says, "That's the new Fleetwood Mac, and . . . I don't know about that one." I got to where I was going and—in those days I was feisty enough and, in that moment, curious enough to do something like this—called the station, and got him on the phone to ask what he was talking about. He said, "I can't find the beat." And he was right in many respects. We were offsetting the norm, disorienting people for a bit until they got it, particularly in that first verse. That was something Mick and I worked on for about a day.

In considering the whole of the album, having a side one and a side two was freeing. Side one was obviously the more aggressive, with more songs in major keys. Side two became interesting by virtue of putting almost too much of the same thing together—it's broken up by one song in a major key in the middle, but basically you have a whole side in the minor key. It's a dark thread running through. The forward motion of side one becomes a feeling of disintegration—and that's exactly what was happening within the band.

When it was first released, I don't think anyone could have foreseen this ridiculous situation, this moment of Michael Jackson–land sales. We weren't thinking that way. We knew we were a good band, that we had good songs, and that we had an appropriate follow-up. But at some point the success of *Rumours* detached itself from the music, the phenomenon becoming about the phenomenon itself. It was a moment in time that you couldn't repeat—why try?

There's this thing in the business: "If it works, run it into the ground." That loomed large in my world—and not just from the record company but within the band as well. And I was not comfortable with that. I think you should just go with what's engaging you. As a musician, as a writer, as a producer, the idea that there might have been pressure to make *Rumours II* put me on the precipice of having to do something for the wrong reasons. There's a danger, if you repeat yourself, of losing yourself in the process. So *Tusk* was a left turn. It's also my favorite Fleetwood Mac album and mix.

Somehow the Beach Boys loomed large in this moment. Brian Wilson has always meant a lot to me. You don't try to reach his level, but you can take lessons from the choices he made. I can't think of a better 45 rpm than "I Get Around" b/w "Don't Worry Baby." It's ridiculous, really, just in the construction alone. But Brian's struggle to grow, certainly more difficult and more tragic than my own, is something I also related to. His move away from making hits, in order to grow as an artist, meant a lot to me. He had very little support as he attempted that move. Yes, there was *Pet Sounds*, but it got hairier after that. He wanted to go places no one had gone, and he had this group, which was basically his family, around him, none of whom really supported what he was doing.

Brian's example helped me to see that if I wanted to explore some new turf, it wasn't going to be that easy. By the end of it I think everyone in the band embraced what we had made, until—and here's the thing—until it didn't sell sixteen million albums. Then we had this meeting where I was basically told, "Well, Lindsey, you can't do that anymore. We're going back to the old formula." That was the beginning of the end for me in terms of Fleetwood Mac. That was the tragedy of Fleetwood Mac: We didn't all want the same things for the same reasons. Had we all wanted the same things, we could have done any number of amazing pieces of work.

To have a sense of humor about it, I would have liked to have been a fly on the wall when they took *Tusk*, a double album, and put it on at the Warner Bros. Thursday meeting in the boardroom. They probably sat around the big, long table, all listened to it, and, then, silence. But that's part of it. As a band, we took the chance we were allowed to take.

RUSS TITELMAN: CROSS-POLLINATION

The popular music on the radio in my youth was stuff like "Mockingbird Hill," "Tennessee Waltz," Jo Stafford, Les Paul & Mary Ford. But there was also the doo-wop revolution, music that grew out of the Ink Spots and black vocal groups. Needless to say, there was a lot of cross-pollination—and not just between white and black traditions. So many of the great writers were first- and second-generation Jewish immigrants. The music was always about cultural mixing. That's what gave it its life.

My musical education went to the next level when I was in junior high and met Phil Spector, who came into my world because my older sister's boyfriend, Marshall Leib, was Phil's best friend. Both of those guys were in the Teddy Bears. Their big song was, of course, "To Know Him Is to Love Him." The Teddy Bears practiced in our living room. When that song went to number one and the band was on *American Bandstand*, this certainly made an impression on me. I idolized Phil, even taking lessons from his guitar teacher. I got good enough to play on some of his sessions, like the Paris Sisters.

At that time, the radio was important to all of us. And it was pop radio *and* R&B radio, great black artists. I remember going for drives with Phil Spector, listening to Hunter Hancock on KGFJ, a white deejay on an R&B station. It was Jackie Wilson, Sam Cooke, and all that. Phil would tear apart the records. I remember—vividly—driving with Phil and "Willie and the Hand Jive" came on. I said, "Listen to that guitar!" And Phil explained, "Look, that's not one guitar. One guitar player is doing this and the other guy is doing this." He'd dissect the record, how it was made. Really, this was when a big door opened. I started listening, and thinking, more like a producer.

The music community in Los Angeles at the time—the record companies, publishers, and studios—was a place of open doors. You could really hang out. It could be with Lou Adler at Screen Gems, Don Kirshner . . . and I would hang with Lenny Waronker, who at the time was at Metric Music, the publishing division of Liberty Records. Lenny would be in a white dress shirt, collar open with a tie hanging down—like a newspaper man—smoking like crazy. We'd listen to music, whether the new Burt Bacharach or what have you. We were all just looking to see what might be the next thing, listening, always listening.

Eventually Lenny moved over to Warner Bros., and through him I met Mo Ostin. Their offices looked like a barracks. But I'd go over and hang out at the offices. I remember Mo taking me out to lunch at Chow's Kosherama, which was a Chinese restaurant and a Jewish deli, and asking me if I might be interested in working with the label. I was probably twenty-three or twenty-four years old. For a few years I passed on the offer simply because I didn't want a job. I would go to the Warner offices every day. I was a part of the family. But I didn't want a job—I was a hippie. I remember [Ry] Cooder was there. Teddy Templeman. I think Richard Perry was there for a short time. Andy Wickham. John Cale came over there for a short while—we shared an office. When I finally signed on, it was a relationship that would last for almost twenty-five years.

One of the first acts I brought to Lenny was Little Feat. I brought Lowell George and Bill Payne into Lenny's office, they played "Willin'," "Truck Stop Girl," and some others. The music stopped and Lenny said, "That's really great. Go upstairs and make a deal with Mo." That's Lenny. Unpretentious, appreciative of great talent. There's no fanfare, no silliness, no posturing. But Lowell was a major talent, and Lenny saw it right away.

Working at Warner Bros. meant working with a number of guys who were raised, musically speaking, on black music, just as I was. Ry Cooder, Lowell, Randy Newman. For a song like "You Can Leave Your Hat On" from Randy's *Sail Away*, we were really trying for a Southern sound, for a Muscle Shoals feel. We even added horns, hoping to get the Memphis Horns thing going. By the time I'm working with artists like Larry Graham, from Sly & the Family Stone, or, later, Chaka Khan, I'm not really thinking of that as a departure. It was all on the same musical continuum. The cross-pollination was just a part of the story of this music. So when I went to cut "Ain't Nobody" with Rufus, with Chaka Khan singing, I didn't see it as a shift necessarily.

What was different on "Ain't Nobody" from my earlier productions had more to do with what was in the air at the time: drum machines, the beginning of sequencing. What led the way for the record, really, was Hawk Wolinski, who wrote the song and made the demo that we worked from. Contrary to what people think, only the very beginning of the song is programmed. It sounds like it's programmed, like it's drum machines and sequencers, but it's not. That's Hawk and, on drums, John Robinson. These guys are amazing players, and they captured the feel of the demo—which did have programmed drums—to such a degree that, ironically, they made it sound like machines.

We also built "Ain't Nobody" part by part. Different from, say, Ry Cooder's *Paradise and Lunch*, this doesn't sound like people playing in a room . . . because it isn't. There's no bleed through because even the drums were recorded piece by piece; the hi-hat first, then the kick and snare, and later the toms. Even the cymbal crashes were overdubs. But even as early as the first time I heard that song, I knew Hawk had brought in something really strong, something we had to do. You heard that thing and knew that, if you made a good record, it was going to be a hit.

And then there was Chaka. Talking about Chaka Khan is like talking about Aretha Franklin. She's one of the greatest singers in the genre. Recording with her was often really easy. When later I found myself working with Steve Winwood on "Higher Love," it felt natural to ask Chaka to come in. In fact, Steve Winwood's managers at the time had brought me into the *Back in the High Life* project *because* of "Ain't Nobody." So, when Chaka came in to sing, it was exciting for me and for Steve. She worked fast. And, again, the track was lifted to the next level. Steve was just beside himself. We knew something was working. And, really, the last thing you're thinking about in such a moment, with this music coming at you, is what part of this is a white tradition and what part is a black tradition. There's a lot in there, no doubt, but like the best music it's all running together. That's what happened for me time and time again at Warners, musical traditions flowed together, becoming something new in the process. There was a lot of that around at Warner Bros., for a long, long time.

↑ Little Feat, 1979.
☺ Steve Winwood, mid-1980s.
← Rufus and Chaka Khan, early 1970s.

ONE NATION UNDER A GROOVE

⊙ A Funkadelic ad, 1978.
⬈ George Clinton, late-1970s.
➔ Bootsy Collins, mid-1970s.

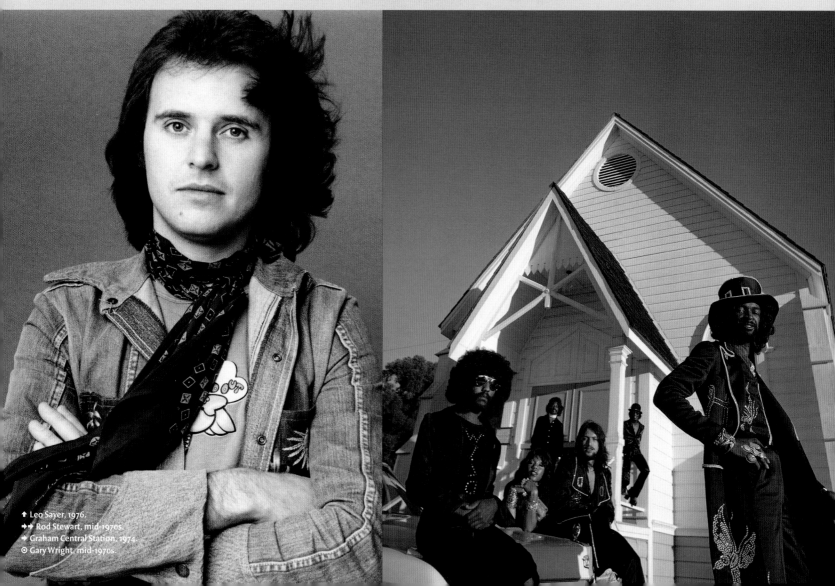

↑ Leo Sayer, 1976.
↦ Rod Stewart, mid-1970s.
↪ Graham Central Station, 1974.
☉ Gary Wright, mid-1970s.

TOMMY LIPUMA ON GEORGE BENSON AND *BREEZIN'*

I was always into jazz and R&B. I loved the emotional qualities that you'd find in those two types of music. I was a big fan of Wes Montgomery, one of the great guitarists in jazz. I didn't know that anyone could play with his finesse and fluid style until I met George Benson. It was in 1971 in San Francisco at a club called the Keystone Korner. My friend Bob Krasnow and I were just knocked out by his playing, but we couldn't touch him because he was already making records for Columbia.

One day Krasnow called me and said, "I got a marriage made in heaven." I didn't know what he was talking about. "I got a chance to sign George Benson," he said, "and I want you to produce him." I couldn't believe it. To me, George Benson was a dream gig for me. So I told Bob to sign him and I'd be his man in the studio.

As much as George Benson was a jazz artist, and a great one at that, he also had a strong pop sense. And even though he was the closest thing to Wes Montgomery that I ever heard, he could also sing. I heard him once at the Keystone and he did "Summertime." He just blew me away. I never forgot it. When we started working together, we'd drive to a restaurant and in the car he'd be singing

Nat King Cole one minute and Sam Cooke the next. So I asked him if he would sing on the album we were making. At first he was reluctant because the jazz purists didn't want their best guitarist making pop records, especially vocal pop records. But then he decided to give it a try, and it was then that we were on our way to making a great record.

I introduced him to a song by Leon Russell called "This Masquerade" that he loved. He jumped into it and very quickly made the song his own. With musicians like percussionist Ralph McDonald and bass player/rhythm guitarist Phil Upchurch backing him up, that song and the title song helped make *Breezin'* a phenomenal album. And we had it both ways: George sang and played guitar, and nobody could deny the combination turned out great.

Later, after *Breezin'* was a big hit for George and Warner Bros., George pulled me aside one day and said, "Tommy, remember when we first met and you asked me about my singing and how you wanted me to sing on the album?" "Sure," I said. "Well, that was when I knew you were the producer for me. That's what I wanted and needed to do, and you weren't afraid to go after it with me. So thank you." It made me feel like a million dollars.

Rickie Lee Jones, 1979.

DAVID BYRNE ON TALKING HEADS: 77

Seymour Stein is a notorious piece of work. But Seymour does hear songs, in any genre or style, which was more than you could say about a lot of folks in the music business. In the case of the Ramones, he saw past the image and the press and heard that they had some classic—if hilarious—pop songs. I suspect he heard something similar with the Talking Heads, as he could warble some of our own material back to us over drinks and Chinese food. He wasn't making huge promises like some of the major labels were. He genuinely seemed to like some of the songs.

The first record was traumatic. Like so many bands, we were completely uncomfortable in the recording studio. I'm glad others don't have to go through that now, simply because they can record at home or at a friend's place. That first record doesn't sound the way I'd hoped or imagined it would, but it also wasn't as compromised as it could have been. I think we made it in about three weeks, and if we'd have had more time, we might not have known what to do with it. We imagined ourselves as a pop band—albeit a pop band in a new mold that wasn't too designed or slick or glamorous.

We imagined, naively, that the realness of our music and that of others like us would topple the rock dinosaurs from their comfortable thrones. While the band and others around us loved pop music, we also saw it becoming corporate, distant, cynically manufactured . . . but, of course, I think the Eagles' last CD was the biggest-selling recording in 2007. So that revolution didn't quite happen.

Talking Heads: 77 wasn't a huge success—lots of media attention but modest sales and radio—so we weren't catapulted into another universe immediately. We couldn't really get a decent gig in New Jersey until our third record, if that gives you an idea. We did in-stores and, at least at first, toured in a station wagon, as we were wisely advised never to get ourselves in debt.

One of the smart things Brian Eno did on our second record was make us more comfortable in the studio. We all tracked the songs playing together in a large room with minimal isolation. We were a tight live band, so that was a feasible way to go. On our third record we went even further, bringing a live recording truck to park outside our rehearsal loft. Those decisions, while one might not think that they were very musical, had a huge effect on our comfort level and therefore how well we played together.

By that third record, as is common, we'd exhausted our live repertoire, so I wrote more songs before we went in, and a few new songs emerged out of instrumental jams, which meant that the tracks at least were "written" by the whole band. I would later write a tune and words to go on top. This approach was of course championed by Brian—and, again, was not producing in the accepted sense but had a huge effect on our output. This improvised approach, while risky at first, proved to be easier and more revelatory than expected.

↑ The Ramones, 1977.
⊕ The Sex Pistols, 1978.

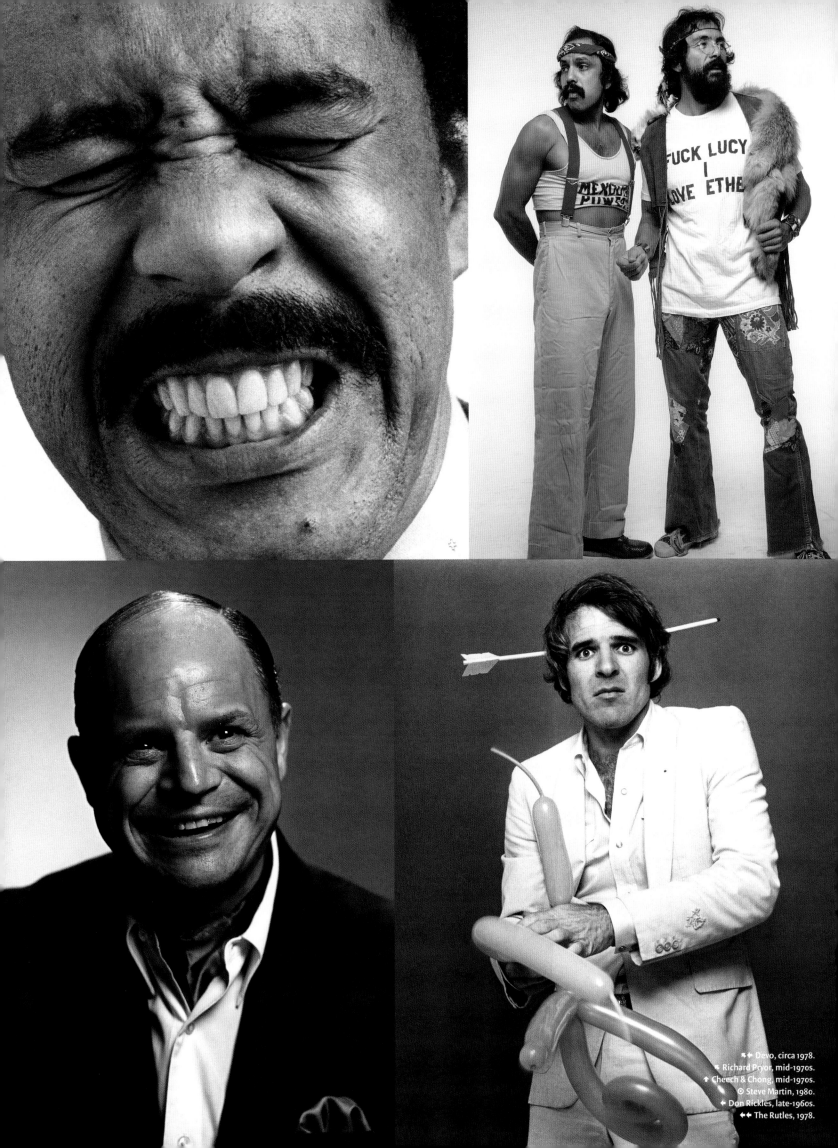

◀◀ Devo, circa 1978.
◀ Richard Pryor, mid-1970s.
↑ Cheech & Chong, mid-1970s.
⊙ Steve Martin, 1980.
◀ Don Rickles, late-1960s.
◀◀ The Rutles, 1978.

CHRISSIE HYNDE ON THE PRETENDERS

Seymour Stein had a place near Baker Street. And the Pretenders had signed with Sire Records. At the time I was in a very biker-cum-punk frame of mind and not feeling like I wanted to conform to a record company's idea for me. Nonetheless, I was given Seymour's address and walked over there, knocked on the door, thinking, "Well, if you own me, I may as well get to know you."

Seymour answered, asking me if I wanted to go out to a nearby antique market. *Okay.* So we walked over to a flea market and just rooted around. He ended up getting me this really nice little pin of a horse with a jockey on it. I love horses—and I still have that little pin.

Seymour and I bonded on what I love doing, and obviously what he loves doing. He loves going out to markets, and I love walking and hanging out. It was good. There was nothing about records or business, which worked well because *no one* can talk business with me; it's just not my subject. I suppose he instinctively knew that. We goofed off—and that's what I'm good at.

By the time we were getting ready to make that first album, we'd already played all those songs gigging—we had a good relationship with them. In fact, I heard a cassette of us playing at the Marquee Club just prior to the first recording, and practically the whole album is on that. The sound of the Pretenders was already in place. And what made that sound come together, really, was the chemistry with Jimmy [James Honeyman-Scott].

As soon as I heard the first demos we made with Jimmy Scott, I knew we were onto something. He and I didn't hit it off so well. I was defiant, a hardass girl-on-the-streets type. And Jimmy didn't have any time for that punk thing. If it had no melody, he wasn't interested, and he didn't care about the words. So there wasn't much of a rapport when we first met. It was only when I listed to those demos that I went, "Fucking hell! This is the guy." And he had exactly the same experience. At that point he was willing to leave Hereford, his girlfriend and job, and move to London to join us. He became my right arm. He made me much more melodic. He brought that out in me. Jimmy listened to Rockpile, Abba, the Beach Boys. I was in denial regarding my melodic inclinations.

As far as actually making the first record, understand that we never had A&R, to this day. The producer, Chris Thomas, came into the picture simply because I'd met him doing vocals on a Chris Spedding record. He was the only producer I knew other than Nick Lowe, who passed on the first album after doing our first single. I called Chris, asked him if he wanted to hear our stuff, and he agreed to make the record with us. That's how I've always worked. On occasion I was resistant to some of Chris's ideas—he was horrified because the song he thought was the single, "Brass in Pocket," wasn't my favorite song, my exact words being something like, "That will go out over my dead body"—but we thought of Chris as the fifth Pretender.

With that first record and the follow-up, we toured our asses off and had tremendous success. And then Jimmy and Pete were gone. Understand, there was no me without the band. I had no personal vision. I never in any way saw myself as a solo artist. I only existed with the band around me. It wasn't a lack of confidence—I don't think in those terms. All I ever wanted to be was to be in a band, so when I got them around me and it started feeling right, that was it. I brought my humble little songs in that I played badly on my guitar—and those guys transformed them into this sound that was the Pretenders.

After the two records and that success, to lose half the band . . . I could only say I was in shock. I was going through a lot of personal stuff. *And* I was pregnant, not knowing anything about children or babies. That was a much more feminine role than anything I'd anticipated. I was reeling in all of those changes. But earlier Jimmy had mentioned some young guitar player he wanted to augment the band's live sound, and that was Robbie McIntosh. I'm sure the audition process was strange for Robbie, and it was certainly strange for us. It was kind of like if your husband had died and your boyfriend walked in, having rooted through the closet, and he's wearing your husband's clothes. Like, "What the fuck are you doing?"

But it had taken a while to get a band—and then lose a band—so I wasn't thinking about going back, about getting a job modeling in an art college or as a cocktail waitress. I couldn't go backward. It had taken so long. And I'd put everything into it. It never occurred to me to walk away from it. And by that point I had other considerations. Hence the name *Learning to Crawl*. I was watching a baby learning to crawl, and I was watching my whole band start over again.

The Pretenders: Pete Farndon, Martin ... Hynde, James

CHAPTER SIX
LIKE NO PLACE ELSE

IF THE WORLD KNEW WARNER BROS. RECORDS FOR ITS ROSTER, WITHIN THE INDUSTRY IT WAS KNOWN FOR ITS CULTURE, IN THE BROAD, ANTHROPOLOGICAL SENSE OF THE WORD. FROM THE PLACE TO THE PEOPLE AND THEIR PRACTICES: WARNER BROS. WAS THE EXCEPTION.

BUILDING AMID CHANGES

Lou Dennis: "We had so little political bullshit going on at Warner Bros. that we were able to do our jobs. And have parties. Whenever we had a number one record, we had a party. We were always celebrating something. 'Oh, you've become a vice president? Let's have a party.' 'Someone new to the team? Let's have a party.' When I moved to California in 1972, Russ Thyret came out to the airport to pick me up—and he picked me up in a garbage truck. He rented a garbage truck just to get me. They steam cleaned it beforehand, of course. I put my luggage in, got into that garbage truck, and we drove to the office. When we pulled up there was a big sign that said, 'Welcome home, Lou.' And we had a party. It was that kind of a place."

David Berman: "When I left Warner Bros. and went to Capitol, Capitol was a blue collar, beer-drinking company, totally sales-driven, sales-oriented, not artist-oriented, not A&R-oriented. There's a difference. Warner Bros. was artist-oriented. When I got to Capitol I wanted, as much as I could, to duplicate the Warner philosophy. I made Tom Whalley, who had been at Warners, head of A&R. But Tom and I were the only two people in the company who understood what I was trying to do. I utterly failed. I did not change the attitude of that company. They just couldn't understand where I was coming from. I was coming from Warners."

In 1983 Mo Ostin celebrated his twentieth anniversary with the company. Two years earlier he named Lenny Waronker president of Warner Bros. Records. Depending on who you ask, that position had either been open for six years or, to make room for Lenny, Mo had split his own title in two, becoming chairman rather than chairman and president. Take the perception of **Stan Cornyn:** "I don't think there was a sense of waiting around to fill the presidency." Or that of **Ron Goldstein:** "There was this interesting period of time after Joe Smith left. His departure created a void. And Mo did not replace him for a long time. There was a rivalry, not actually out in the open, but everybody knew it, between Eddie Rosenblatt, Bob Regehr, and Stan Cornyn. Those were the three guys that were the candidates to take it." Or **Eddie Rosenblatt:** "I'll tell you my story. It's January 1980. We'd just come back from Christmas vacation. Mo comes in, says David Geffen has made a deal with Steve Ross, and we're going to distribute Geffen's new label. So I called David, because I had been with Warner Bros. at this point almost nine years. I wanted to do something else, be the president, I didn't know what. So I called David and I said I wanted to do this new label with him. David got very nervous, because he didn't want Mo to think he was poaching. He says, 'You have to clear this with Mo.' So I went to see Mo, and I said to Mo, 'Either I want to go to work with David or make me the president, either way.' And Mo said, 'Give me a day.' He came back a day later and he said, 'You can go with David if you can make your deal,' which I did. Many of us, I thought, were capable of running record companies." Or **Joe Smith:** "It could have been Rosenblatt. It could have been any of those people, and I wouldn't have been surprised. We were a very close group, and we'd all been involved in a lot of things in the company. But Mo leaned towards a creative man for that job rather than sales or marketing or anything like that. In the end, it was no surprise that Lenny was made president."

In many respects, with Lenny Waronker in that office, an old idea was merely manifest in a new way, writ large across the Burbank skies. The company had always been led by A&R. That was no secret. Every aspect of the Warner Bros. Records culture was touched by the A&R emphasis. Employees felt that if they wanted to champion an act, no matter the department

✦ Mo Ostin and Lenny Waronker. With Waronker named president of Warner Bros. Records, the company formalized the centrality of A&R in its philosophy and practice.

✦ The building at 3300 Warner Boulevard: Headquarters to Warner Bros. Records.

Opening spread: The B-52s gather around the hearth of sixties kitsch, 1980.

in which they worked, they could do so, feeding into the A&R process, helping to guide careers. Under Waronker this culture of empowerment reached its apex. **Lenny Waronker:** "I always felt if there was somebody who was adamant about an artist's worth, I'd better pay attention. It was fun to have people walk in your office and say, 'This artist has got the greatest record.' I might not have listened to it in that way. Bob Regehr and Carl Scott were really good at that. I think Eddie Rosenblatt and Russ Thyret were like that, too. When they heard something that was really great, even something that might have come to them from somebody on staff, they would bring the staff member along with them and say, 'You guys have got to pay attention to this.' It was an unbelievably open group of people. When somebody was hot on something, you paid attention. We used to get ripped for it, 'So many rabbis,' they used to say. That's what made it great."

EXPANSION IN EVERY DIRECTION

Russ Thyret: "I went home one day, and when I came back, the reception area in the old office was gone. Somebody had put two-by-fours on the floor and nailed up eight-inch phony wood fronts . . . that was my office. There was no table, no chairs, the coffee machine was still there . . . so for the first six months, people would just keep coming into my office making coffee and asking me how I was doing. Eventually they brought trailers in that were put in the parking lot, and people had to work out of a trailer. I'm not kidding. The new building was heaven-sent. Detractors described it as a ski lodge—fuck it, it was a ski lodge. It was great. It was beautiful architecture, laid out well. The building took a year or two years longer to build than was proposed because it was on the corner of a movie lot, and right next to it was the set for *The Waltons*, a huge hit. As hard as this is to believe, when they shot *The Waltons* during the day, the construction had to shut down. Because of that it went two years longer." In the new building, the company continued to grow. Seymour Stein's Sire Records accounted for some of that growth. Bob Biggs' Slash Records accounted for some. Tom Silverman's Tommy Boy Records for some. And there were others. Mo Ostin's strategy, to use affiliates to expand the A&R base continued to prove savvy.

When Seymour Stein's Sire Records came into the Warner Bros. family, Stein's territory was New York City. Soon enough, his activities branched out, particularly to England, where Sire had been active prior to joining Warner Bros. **Steven Baker:** "It would be hard to overestimate what Seymour brought to Warners. He really broadened our base. Yes, there was Madonna, the Talking Heads, the Ramones—all those important signings—but he then went to England

and got the Pretenders, the Smiths, Soft Cell, Depeche Mode, Erasure, and so many more, continuing to work the States and Canada all the while, bringing in the Replacements, Uncle Tupelo and Wilco, k.d. lang . . . it's just a tremendous history of signings, all of which meant so much to Warner Bros." In the first phase of the deal with Sire, Warner Bros. owned fifty percent of Sire. Within in a few years, they would own Sire outright, keeping Stein on as the label's visionary. He would sell outright, however, before Madonna hit. **Seymour Stein:** "I don't want to think about that."

Slash Records was based in Los Angeles but associated with a very different scene than that of Burbank. Punk bands Fear, the Germs, and X were among the acts that would make a name for Slash. **Bob Biggs:** "The Slash idea was to start with punk and then spread out in terms of styles but not attitude." When Slash signed the Blasters, Warner Bros. A&R got a sense for what Biggs was trying to do. The Blasters, led by Phil and Dave Alvin, had been mentored by Big Joe Turner and dedicated themselves to playing American roots without embellishment. The band hooked into the punk scene on just the basis that Biggs felt they should, on that of attitude. **Bob Biggs:** "Lenny Waronker and some of the others at Warner Bros.—Tom Whalley played a role in this—seemed to get it. And Lenny struck me as a really unusual cat in this whole music business menagerie." The in-house approach to Slash A&R became one of building acts on a regional basis. The Violent Femmes, out of Milwaukee, were handled in just this way, building slowly and becoming a force in the Slash catalogue. **Bob Biggs:** "It was like the independent labels in the 1950s, like Sam Phillips at Sun or the Chess brothers. We didn't try to conquer America out of the box. We built out, from regions where records started selling. But the connection with Warner Bros. meant that we could get behind something with new strength once Slash had a toehold. The *La Bamba* soundtrack that Los Lobos did is the best example of something taking off, with all of the elements behind it."

Tommy Boy Records gave Warner Bros. a place in the emerging hip-hop scene, bringing the Force MD's, De La Soul, Information Society, Naughty By Nature, Digital Underground, and others to the label. Affiliates Def Jam and Cold Chillin' would build that base and expand the urban department over the next few years, with Quincy Jones' Qwest Records bringing additional support. Historically weak in black music, with a few exceptions including Krasnow's and Titelman's important signings, it would prove a critical moment for Warner Bros. **Ron Goldstein:** "One of the last entrepreneurial young guys that came into the business and started a new trend was Tom Silverman. I'm not sure who has come along since him that's had a tremendous impact, other than Russell Simmons, Jay-Z and a few others." Silverman, accustomed to running his own show, felt that the connection to a major might get him where he couldn't otherwise go—that, and he needed the money. **Tom Silverman:** "Warner Bros. was the only major label that didn't feel like a business, that felt like a family. And I was concerned because I wasn't able to get pop radio for my releases because the indies and radio promoters had a lock on it. The only ones who could really get on the radio were the majors. But I was also in a downturn phase. I was between hits and a little bit in the hole. I needed to dig out, needed cash flow. I wanted to see if I could get the help by doing a deal where I gave them half of the company, and they would work my records."

⬆ Quincy Jones' Qwest Records was another Warner Bros. affiliate that would prove very meaningful to the company, bringing about a deeper connection to black music at a time when the company needed it more than ever.

⬆⬆ The Blasters, pictured here in the early 1980s, were among the first bands that attracted Warner Bros. Records to LA-based Slash Records. Featuring Dave and Phil Alvin, the band was known for Dave's songwriting, an explosive live show, and a sometimes bizarre sibling dynamic.

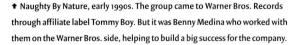

Naughty By Nature, early 1990s. The group came to Warner Bros. Records through affiliate label Tommy Boy. But it was Benny Medina who worked with them on the Warner Bros. side, helping to build a big success for the company.

De La Soul, seen here in 1989, were one of the first acts to break big for Tommy Boy after the label hooked up with Warner Bros. Records. But Tommy Boy's Tom Silverman would do it without WEA distribution.

Impossible to deny: Madonna, 1983.

Silverman's initial theory, that a major could do things for Tommy Boy that Tommy Boy couldn't on its own, did not, in Silverman's view, pan out. Though still at Warner Bros., he returned to his earlier model of operation. **Tom Silverman:** "I went back and renegotiated, said, 'Listen, we need to put the records out ourselves.' Mo said okay. So we put De La Soul out ourselves, through our distribution, and sold close to a million. And then we had a whole chain of million sellers that didn't go through Warner Bros., that they didn't promote. We did the promotion—they just got quarterly checks from their share of the profits." It was, in many respects, one of the strangest arrangements among all of the arrangements with affiliate labels. **David Berman:** "Tommy was unique in a lot of ways. First of all, he was unique in that he was the only person that I have ever seen with a struggling indie, makes a deal with a major label, and runs his operation exactly the same as if he's still a struggling indie. He still flies coach and all that stuff. Doesn't really utilize the perks and benefits you get from your major label affiliation. He ran Tommy Boy Records like he had before Warners invested the money. It was probably the best deal I ever made in my life."

With affiliates strong, Geffen Records (headed by Eddie Rosenblatt) in the fold, it was a period in which Mo Ostin continued to build. **Mo Ostin:** "I was really interested in broadening the company in terms of its artistic base. You always try to build and get bigger. That's what business is all about. You try to maximize your ability to make great music and reap better profits. Bringing in new labels was very important because you couldn't be every place at once. Pop music had grown so much; there were now so many different kinds of music that some labels were becoming specialists of sorts. These were the labels we wanted to work with."

POP STARS ARE SEEN NOT (JUST) HEARD

Mo Ostin: "Because Warner Communications was involved in creating the business plan for MTV, Steve Ross came to all the record companies and asked us what we thought about the potential of MTV; and we supported it very, very strongly." MTV's success, however, was not immediate. While companies had been making promotional films of artists, it was not yet standard practice. **Georgia Bergman:** "There was some concern that record companies might not be willing to make these 'films,' at least not in the abundance that a music video channel would need. But when people saw that a video like the Buggles' 'Video Killed the Radio Star'

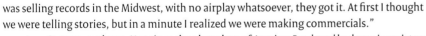

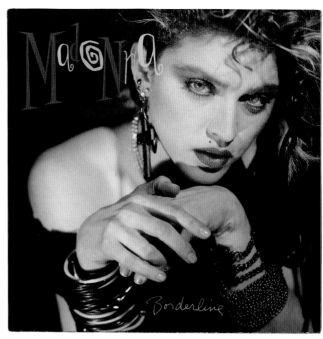

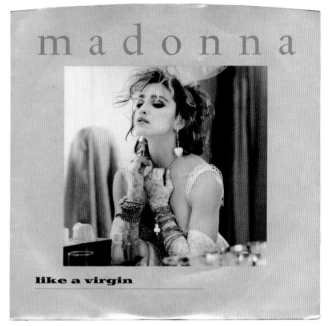

was selling records in the Midwest, with no airplay whatsoever, they got it. At first I thought we were telling stories, but in a minute I realized we were making commercials."

In 1982 MTV was born. Not since the glory days of *American Bandstand* had music registered this kind of effect on a TV audience. MTV didn't simply introduce new artists and emphasize singles the way radio did, it also, obviously, elevated the "look" of an act. Warner Bros. would use this moment both to launch and to reinvent careers. A different kind of superstar emerged, and several were associated with the label. After Bergman helped to create the video department within the offices of artist relations, the video staff grew. Among those handling video in the 1980s was Jeff Ayeroff, an executive who came over from A&M and left his mark not just on Warner Bros. but on the music business as a whole. **Diarmuid Quinn:** "Of all the people in the music business, Jeff Ayeroff is, to this day, the best at melding art and commerce." Ayeroff and Bergman brought in directors from a range of creative areas, using video to create stars not just among the performers but among the directors themselves, many of whom had not directed music videos before Ayeroff appealed to them. **Mo Ostin:** "Jeff is an amazing marketing executive. One of the greatest executives I've had the good fortune of working with. But he's also a good recruiter. If acts know Jeff is marketing their records, and he believes in them, they can be sure they'll get a first-class effort."

Among the many Warner Bros. artists in that era, Sire Records' act Madonna was the one who overwhelmed the company with a charismatic appeal that fit perfectly into the video age.

She quickly transcended category, becoming something like her own species. When introduced to Madonna by Sire A&R man Michael Rosenblatt, who had himself been tipped off by Danceateria deejay Mark Kamins, Seymour Stein grasped the situation. **Seymour Stein:** "She had a style all her own. She matched things like laced stockings and religious symbols and generally made you look at her. She wasn't afraid to separate herself from everybody else. She knew that by doing that, she'd get noticed. And it worked."

Because Madonna's initial deal was only for two singles, Sire released two dance tracks before putting out Madonna's debut. *Madonna* featured the hits "Borderline," "Holiday," and "Lucky Star," the last of which was co-written by Madonna, and all of which had an immediacy that made sense in clubs and at radio. But it was Madonna's second album, *Like A Virgin*, which made her a major star. The album generated multiple singles, including "Material Girl," and went to number one on the charts. Through video first, her visual presentation got her everywhere. **Seymour Stein:** "She dominated pop culture, just dominated it. There was no stopping her. Everything she did attracted media attention. She was controversial. She was beyond sexy. She had an understanding of style that few artists have. I would never have dreamed of signing anyone like Madonna if I wasn't with Warner Bros. I looked at Warner Bros. as the perfect place for her. Of course video was very important. But what Madonna also grew on was press. Liz Rosenberg did an incredible job."

Of the others among the label's video-age stars, Prince registered at a similar level. **Bob Krasnow:** "Russ Thyret plays the main role in getting Prince. It really is a great moment. There's a show, man. You've got everything. I remember when they played the demos for me. It blew my mind. Here's this eighteen-year-old kid, and I'm hearing Russ tell me that he played every instrument on the demo. I thought, 'Oh, my God'." Negotiating a deal wherein the label committed to three albums with no option to drop the artist before the completion of those three recordings, Warner Bros. beat out the competition to get Prince on the roster. **David Berman:** "One of the things Lenny and I always agreed on was that the signing of Prince was the perfect coordination of A&R and legal/business affairs. Without both those departments, it wouldn't have happened. I'm sitting through these meetings, Russ, Lenny, and these guys are raving about this artist's talent—not necessarily that he's going to come in fast with a hit single, but how enormously talented this kid is. I think he was eighteen at the time. And I said, 'If he's that talented, if you believe in him that much'—and everybody wanted him, A&M wanted him, Columbia wanted him—'Why don't we make him a three-album firm deal?' At the time that was unheard of. Lenny said, 'That's great.' And that's the reason we wound up with Prince." By the time of *Purple Rain*, Prince was a video-age superstar. The coordination of elements in the Warner Bros. office all worked, the force of Prince's talent dictating the terms while the executives responded appropriately.

↑ Looking not a little like Little Richard, Prince faces his listeners on a 1982 picture disc.

↑↑ ZZ Top, MTV superstars, pose with the car that became a video icon, 1983.

Russ Thyret: "When we made the deal, one of the things that concerned us the most—at least, at that time—was that Prince wanted to produce himself. Mo and Lenny were trying to make producer suggestions. But he insisted. Lenny said, 'Okay, I'll book a studio for a couple of days and get him in there and see what happens.' I remember, after that, Lenny coming in to see me and saying, 'He can do it all, he can do it, absolutely.' It turned out to be, obviously, a fortuitous day in my life. I can't tell you how happy I was for that."

ZZ Top and Van Halen, groups that broke before the video age, used video to take their careers to a new level. They found ways to expand their images, show themselves to be in possession of humor and artistic dynamism at one and the same time. This wasn't for the "Fire and Rain" crowd. If more unlikely as video stars, Dire Straits showed that the right match of song and image, what Ayeroff put in the category of "visual A&R," could transform an act without changing them musically. The force of the right visual, that alone could recast an artist's identity. And it was Warners' creative team that saw this as their role. "Money For Nothing" was the 1986 MTV video of the year, no dance moves or bikini briefs involved.

If video was demonstrating the ways in which artists could be invented and reinvented, Warner Bros. was showing how careers could be long and even longer. In this period, several breakthrough records were released by artists for whom the distinction "breakthrough" might seem odd, simply because they'd gotten there much earlier in the story. But such was the case. And it was a remarkable list: Paul Simon, Steve Winwood, George Harrison, Peter Gabriel, Don Henley, Eric Clapton. Every one of them came out with records that redefined who they were and what they did—and video played a role in every case. **Georgia Bergman:** "MTV gave more eccentric artists a chance to penetrate the mainstream without radio play being a limiting factor. Madonna and Prince were great examples. But then you had the other side in which established artists could be recreated through this 'new' medium."

Henley's "Boys of Summer" video, directed by Jean-Baptiste Mondino, was named MTV's video of the year in 1985. Peter Gabriel's "Sledgehammer" video, directed by Stephen R. Johnson, was MTV's video of the year in 1987. Steve Winwood's *Back in the Highlife* album, produced by Russ Titelman, saw the video for "Higher Love," directed by Paula Greif and Peter Kagan, *and* the song go to number one. Paul Simon's *Graceland* would rise to number three on the US charts in 1986, number one in the UK, and get the Grammy for album of the year and song of the year. The following year, as if emerging from hibernation with an appetite, George Harrison released *Cloud Nine*—and then he went even further, putting together the Traveling Wilburys with Bob Dylan, Tom Petty, Roy Orbison, and Jeff Lynne. The Wilburys would bring Warners one of the most beloved albums to come from a Beatle. Second acts were happening across the roster.

↑ Paul Simon, live in Central Park, 1991.

↑↑ The Traveling Wilburys gather around the mic, 1988. After the success of George Harrison's *Cloud Nine*, Warner Bros. Records' long-standing relationship with George Harrison would result in the company releasing *The Traveling Wilburys: Volume One.*

OUT IN THE COUNTRY

The mid-1980s did not mark Warner Bros.' first foray into country music. Artists such as Gram Parsons, John Anderson, and Emmylou Harris had all released important records with Warners well before that time. A&R man Andy Wickham, who had helped to sign Joni Mitchell and tried to help sign Led Zeppelin, even moved from Burbank to Nashville to give Warners a presence in the Music City. **Michael Ostin:** "Andy had a very, very distinctive and strong point of view and a love of country music. An Englishman in Nashville, wore a suit and tie to the office everyday. It was Andy who signed Emmylou Harris and Rodney Crowell." Further back still, country had come in and out of the roster with acts like the Oak Ridge Boys and Bob Luman. What *did* happen in the wider culture of country music in the 1980s, however, was that a renewal of meaning took place. **Bob Merlis:** "They invented this thing called the 'new tradition' around that time, meaning country music that actually sounds like country music." Very slowly, one started to hear a more stripped back sound that exposed the roots of the music. Steve Earle called it "the great credibility scare" in country music. Warners played a key role in delivering two artists in particular who went into the heart of that situation: Dwight Yoakam and Randy Travis.

In Nashville, Jim Ed Norman built the strength of Warner Bros.' operation even before the Travis and Yoakam signings. With a background as an arranger and producer, Jim Ed Norman took his first record company job when called by Jimmy Bowen to join Bowen in Nashville. **Jim Ed Norman:** "The idea was that I would come work for Jimmy. He had this vision of a succession plan. Next thing I knew, Jimmy left for MCA. That was seven months after I'd arrived! Mo Ostin came down to assess the situation, and a week later I was in the position of running the national division." Around that time, a "trade" with Elektra brought Hank Williams, Jr., Conway Twitty, Crystal Gayle, and Eddie Rabbitt to Warner Bros. **Jim Ed Norman:** "That became the nucleus of the label."

Only a few years later Yoakam and Travis would be signed to Warner Bros. Both artists embraced traditional country, each in his own way. **Jim Ed Norman:** "Harlan Howard's famous comment that 'country music is three chords and the truth' is one of those wonderful observations. But in country music there are times when we end up with about six chords and beating around the bush. Before long we've got eight chords and nothing to do with the truth at all. Yoakam and Travis brought it all back home." Yoakam was explicit regarding his debt to Buck Owens. *Guitars, Cadillacs, Etc., Etc.* was the kind of title that doubled as the start of a manifesto. Travis, launching his album *Storms of Life* with the song "On The Other Hand," had crisp, organic production courtesy of Kyle Lehning, songs from writers such as Paul Overstreet, and a vocal presence that recalled George Jones at his best. *Storms of Life* was one of those perfect albums. **Lenny Waronker:** "His was a big time voice. I just thought, 'Oh my god, this guy's unbelievable'."

Establishing Warner Bros. as a strong presence in Nashville, Jim Ed Norman would go on to sign Travis Tritt and Faith Hill, whose crossover success would require coordination between Nashville and Burbank. **Jim Ed Norman:** "At the end of the day, when it came to signing a great artist, I didn't get overly concerned with what they were doing. I signed Take 6, Béla Fleck and the Flecktones, Jeff Foxworthy, started a Hispanic label and a Christian division. The Nashville office didn't necessarily mean the country office. That was important to me."

ALTERNATIVE

Steven Baker: "A lot of record executives, even some at Warner Bros., were still in love with the Doobie Brothers and Fleetwood Mac in the early 1980s. Fair enough. But the trick for Warners would be to see that, at the same time, this alternative rock thing was about ready to explode. A lot of the bands that I really loved were not yet getting the most out of the artist-friendly culture. In the wider business, there were record company executives who had enjoyed great success in the 1970s but didn't grow into the next musical generation. They were suspicious of alternative rock because it was an alternative to what they were all about."

Baker, Roberta Peterson and others gave the company's A&R department new blood and a new outlook. The results were quick in coming: Hüsker Dü, Gang of Four, Jane's Addiction, and R.E.M. got deals, giving Warner Bros. a needed presence in a burgeoning scene. Waronker and Ostin made room for it, understanding that rock was in the process of reinventing itself. Lenny Waronker stayed open to new music. **Steven Baker:** "Lenny was interested in hearing new bands, which made him a main safety valve at Warners. Instead of pining for the old days, Lenny would listen to new things. The same was true of Seymour Stein. The two of them always had their ears open and really need to be credited with keeping Warners on the frontline." What was being built in alternative would in due course provide a basis for the new musical mainstream.

⬥ Hüsker Dü, *Candy Apple Grey*, 1986. A trio out of Minneapolis, the group's signing was an important gesture on Warner Bros. Records' part, particularly as "alternative" was bubbling under.

⬥⬥ Dwight Yoakam, 1989. Yoakam's conscious and reverential exposure of hillbilly roots struck audiences well beyond the confines of country music culture.

➥ Gang of Four, 1980. Associated with "post-punk," the band was revered in critical circles and a touchstone for musicians. Radio? That would be another story.

↟ Dire Straits, "Money for Nothing," 1985.
↗ a-ha, "Take on Me," 1985.
↟ ZZ Top, "Legs," 1983.
⊙ Peter Gabriel, "Sledgehammer," 1986.

I was a creative director when, because of MTV, video came into the picture. It wasn't necessarily something brand-new. We'd always done short films with artists, called "international films." But suddenly video became a matter of much greater importance. What happened structurally at record companies was that this expanding area, video, was subsumed under the creative departments. It was a good fit for me because when I listen to songs, I see visuals. My dad had a TV store when I grew up—what can I say? I grew up watching images.

When I got to Warners, Georgia Bergman was in charge of video and she was great at what she did. I was in charge of "creative marketing"—album covers, advertising, videos, posters, merchandise. Theoretically and in today's terms, creative marketing was where the bands were "branded." And just what we did with a band or a performer was contingent on the artists themselves; some people would walk in and know exactly who they were, some needed a little help, and some artists taught *you* stuff. The differentiation being that there were groups like Van Halen and the Talking Heads, from opposite sides of the rock & roll spectrum, both of whom knew exactly who they were, and bands like ZZ Top, who knew who they were visually but hadn't yet translated that into film. In the latter case, Georgia paired ZZ Top with Tim Newman, who did the famous ZZ Top videos, the man who basically styled those first videos, creating the keys and so forth. Billy Gibbons was already collecting cars, so there was a collaborative process between label, director, and band through which all the important pieces came together.

As the ZZ Top example suggests, what we did was something like visual A&R, putting directors and photographers together with performers, who often brought a lot of creative fire to the scene. From there, a collaboration between all parties would unfold, differently every time. We put Paula Greif and Peter Kagan together with Stevie Winwood for the "Higher Love" video, Don Henley together with Jean-Baptiste Mondino for the "Boys of Summer" project. In these two cases I brought in directors through other worlds of design. Paula was a New York–based friend and an art director at *Mademoiselle* with whom I'd worked on a number of projects, Mondino a Paris-based friend and a French avant-garde still photographer. You need to remember that video was so new as a mass phenomenon that there were no video directors proper—various visual thinkers, photographers, designers, film students, were coming from a range of backgrounds, picking up on video as just another medium of expression among those they already worked in—and because it was rock & roll it was more free and more fun and more creative.

It was a new moment in the music business and it required that we "discover" directors. There was a creativity in the air that inspired us all. There was an excitement. It was all moving very quickly. Suddenly artists were breaking or, as with Don Henley, redefining who they were through this new visual format. Look at "Boys of Summer"—Mondino gave it a European sensibility and an ennui, which you'd never expect from the quintessential American artist . . . an Eagle.

Because things were moving at such a pace, it was often a matter of staying open to the human and artistic connections that could be made. The photographer Steven Meisel, for instance, was "discovered" by Paula Greif, after which Steven became very important to Madonna's career—Madonna becoming something like his muse. Steve Barron, who I met because he had made Human League's "Don't You Want Me" when I was at A&M, wound up doing such work as Dire Straits' "Money for Nothing" and a-ha's "Take on Me." And the first of those two was a Video of the Year. I remember going to Don Henley's house for a meeting with Jean-Baptiste Mondino, a meeting which made little sense because Jean-Baptiste didn't speak English very well. Just imagine a guy who doesn't speak English very well trying to describe the "Boys of Summer" video to us. To Don's great credit—because he's so smart and intuitive—he said, "Let's take a go at this." It became another Video of the Year.

There was so much going on at Warner Bros., so much brilliant music coming from Mo and Lenny and so many brilliant visual thinkers coming through the building. During that period, when we really concentrated on what was in front of us—and there was time to concentrate back then—things happened. I remember a young band signing with Warners and coming to me, saying, "Hey, we met this guy at UCLA and want him to direct our video." I'm thinking, "Oh, I need this like a hole in the head." I ask to see this kid's reel. They send it to me and, shit, this kid's great, with a technique I've never seen. Fast forward to a moment when the Talking Heads are looking for a follow-up to "Burning Down the House." I turn David Byrne onto this same young director, Stephen Johnson, who ends up collaborating with David on "Road to Nowhere." I love what he does with that video, and introduce him to Peter Gabriel, and they go on to collaborate on another Video of the Year, "Sledgehammer." Then the Talking Heads' manager, Gary Kurfirst, turns me onto Mary Lambert, with whom the band went to the Rhode Island School of Design, who then makes the first three Madonna videos. And after Mary, I introduced Madonna to Mondino, and their twenty-year relationship gets its visual start with "Open Your Heart." Really, it was such a big grid of artistic interaction—visual and musical—and went so far beyond the music community. In the three-and-a-half years I was at Warners—for the *first* time—it was remarkable what magic happened with the visual intersection of film and music . . . and I've left off so much, important things like the discovery of David Fincher, the visuals of Prince. It was a special time.

SEYMOUR STEIN ON SIGNING MADONNA

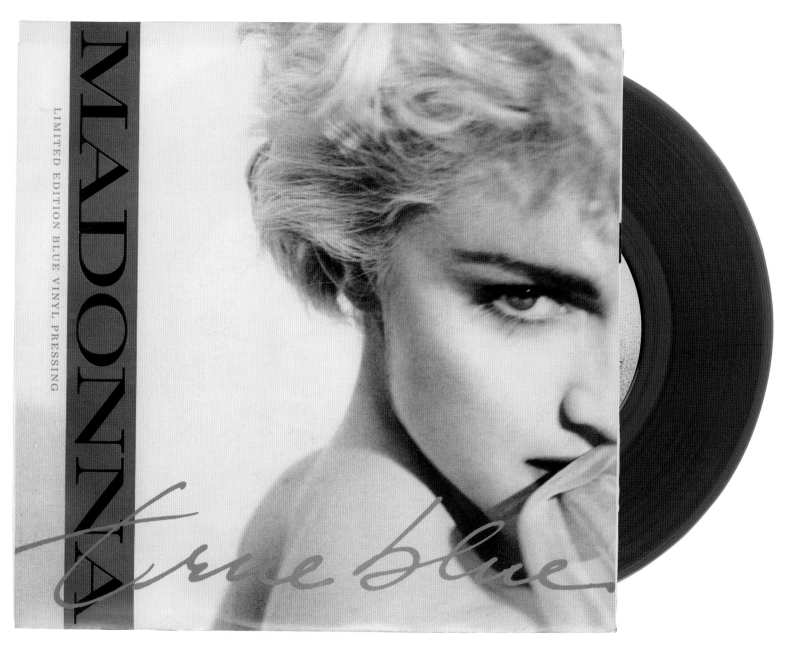

In 1982 I was in the hospital because I was born with a hole in my heart and bacteria had formed around that hole. The only treatment for it back then was a month's worth of rest in the hospital on a pencillin drip. Maybe it was because I wasn't behaving as good as I should have, healthwise—I don't know, but there I was stuck in this room, wearing a hospital gown and going out of my mind.

I had known about Madonna because a friend of mine, Mark Kamins, had told me about her. While I was in the hospital, I had read that he might be going to work for Island Records. That made me a little paranoid because I was really interested in learning more about Madonna. So, I called him up and told him that I wanted to meet her and that he should bring her to the hospital, never expecting that it would be that day. It was like two o'clock in the afternoon.

Mark called me an hour later. "Madonna wants to come tonight. We'll be at the hospital at eight o'clock." I was there in this hospital gown with a split down the back so that you could see my ass. I hadn't shaved or bathed. I looked like shit. All I was doing was listening to demos all day. Anyway, I called my secretary and she got me a pair of pajamas and a bathrobe. I showered and begged my barber to come to the hospital to cut my hair and shave me, which he did. I figured that I had to look healthy; it was the beginning of the AIDS epidemic and I didn't want Madonna to think that she was signing with someone who wasn't going to be around much longer.

Madonna came at eight that night. I could have been lying in a coffin; it didn't matter to her. All she wanted was a deal. We reached an agreement right there in the hospital. I told her to see a lawyer before she signed the deal. She wanted to sign right there and then. I said no, see a lawyer first, and I gave her a few names to check out. I was amazed at how focused she was, how sure she was that she wanted to sign with Sire and that she was going to have this great career.

Mark Kamins had arrived shortly after Madonna left the hospital. He was all excited and wanted to know what I thought of her. I said, "Are you kidding? Look, if today was Halloween and it was midnight and the shortest way to wherever she was heading happened to be through the creepiest graveyard in town, she'd pass through it without even thinking twice." He laughed, but it was true. Madonna was in a hurry. She knew what she wanted. She was so together. I told Mark, "You know, I love her music. But what I love even more is her determination. There's no way she's not going to make it."

Did I know that Madonna was going to become this big superstar? Absolutely not. But I believed in her from the get-go. She had a sense about her that was undeniable. Nothing was going to stop her.

LENNY WARONKER ON PURPLE RAIN

Russ Thyret, who was the head of promotion at that time, got a call from Owen Husney, Prince's first manager. Russ called me, said, "I have this meeting about a kid who sounds pretty interesting." I couldn't make it, but told Russ to let me know if it sounds good and, if so, that I'd listen the next day. Russ calls later and says, "You've got to hear this."

Next day in comes Prince. They played the stuff. I was amazed by how Prince, a teenager at the time, did those demos, just struck by his ability to play all of the instruments—this was before drum machines were commonplace. The only other person who could really do that was Stevie Wonder. I said, "Okay, let me live with this."

I played it for a few people in the A&R department, Steve Barri and Gary Katz, and they were very much taken by the material, which hadn't been my focus. I'd been looking more at the whole thing, this individual, what he could do in the studio, the entirety of it. When they singled out the songs, that put up a red flag for me. They thought there were a couple of hits on there. That really got me to pay attention.

So Russ and I took Prince in the studio soon after that. He put acoustic guitar down, then recorded drums, bass guitar . . . finally I just said, "Enough." No more evidence was needed. That kind of angered him because he was so immersed in finishing the track. But the thing that was most telling of all that day was not that he could *do* it but what he said. Prince was very quiet, hardly said anything. But when we were there in the studio, setting up something, a guitar or drums, in that tight space of the control room, just as I was moving past him to get something, he said, "Don't make me black." I thought, "Wow, what a thing to say." But he went on, letting me know that his idols, the people he was competing with, were Eric Clapton, the Beatles, Jimi Hendrix. It was an amazing moment—you know, when you're with an artist so special, so gifted and smart, and you're hearing something that is so important . . . but I couldn't quite get my hands on it then. All I knew was that we had to get this kid, that he was charting his own course. In retrospect, I think he made that comment to me in the studio when he had made up his mind that he wanted to come to Warner Bros.

The Prince negotiation got really hairy because Prince didn't want a producer and wanted a three-firm deal, which in those days was a big deal. David Berman, a legal affairs guy, who knew there was a buzz on this kid, came down and told me that if we could give Prince three-firm we could get him. So, I started thinking out loud, like, "Okay, this kid is eighteen. His first record will be a learning record. The second record—because he's so on top of it, will come fairly soon after. And we'll start to get a sense for who he is. And, after that, I know we'll be sitting in an A&R meeting wanting to make another record with him. So, yeah, we can probably get away with doing it because he's so young and talented." There was just no way we would have dropped him after two records.

Prince knew what he wanted. He really invented his own thing. At a certain point you stop trying to figure it out. We only had brief conversations early on. But it came on strong during *Purple Rain*. I remember when he had just finished "When Doves Cry." He was freaked out. His process was that he manufactures these records, building track by track. He'll record one thing, then do another, building it until it's done, pretty much on his own, though at that time he had some other people like Wendy & Lisa working with him. But he came to me, concerned because on "When Doves Cry" there was no bass. When he finished that record, he realized that and that frightened him.

So I got a call from his manager, asking if I would meet with Prince. I said sure, of course. He came in with his entourage, said, "Look, I just finished this thing, but there's no bass on it—I just want to see what you think." So I listened. And this record was just explosive, absolutely unique. The way it had been recorded, it had plenty of bottom end. I was like, what am I going to tell him? So I said, "Just out of curiosity, why didn't you put a bass on there?" Then he explains his process, how he starts then adds part by part until he's finished. Without thinking about it, he hadn't recorded a bass part. So I said, "You're finished, right?" He nods. I said, "Well let's put it out." That was the last track to go on *Purple Rain*.

TED TEMPLEMAN ON VAN HALEN

When Van Halen opened for Boston—and this was before anyone knew who Van Halen was—they had this thing where they stayed in a truck in the middle of the stadium, about a hundred and thirty degrees in there with only a coffee can to pee in, waiting as the stadium filled up with people. This took a long time. Then, just before the show, four guys in parachutes jump from a plane above the stadium, come out of the sky and land, one with a long blond wig to look like David. Then, when these professional parachute guys are on the ground, they get into the same truck, which then drives up to the stage. Then the band, wearing the same clothes as the parachuters, gets out of the truck, running on stage and breaking into "Runnin' with the Devil." There they are, looking like they just parachuted in. It was Dave's idea. They were great with that kind of thing. They had that mindset. Dave wasn't a great singer. He croaked away, and I worked with him, but he was brilliant with this stuff.

When I first saw Van Halen play, at the Starwood, there was nobody there in the audience. No one dancing, just a couple people watching. And the band played like they were in front of thousands of fans. They were sliding across the floor, doing their moves like they were playing for fifty thousand people. Ed was still playing those hammer-ons while he was jumping in the air. They knew who they were. Ed had Jimmy Page's moves down; he could play with a cigarette in his mouth. I signed them because of Ed, because he was such a great player. I figured, there's Art Tatum, Ornette Coleman, and this kid. So I got Mo Ostin down there, and we cut the deal. Bang! Like that.

People often ask what I did as far as recording them. With Eddie Van Halen what you do is put a mic in front of his amp. No mystery. Ed played his solos live on that first album. Donn Landee was a great engineer, and we did some stuff miking the room and so forth, but, in a lot of ways, they could have done that first album by themselves. They were driving the car. But we had a lot of laughs, a lot of fun. They were having a little more fun than I was—they would go into the other room, and I wasn't quite sure what they were up to. They had their own word for it: Krell. Ed would say to the roadie, "Call Krellman." I didn't figure it out for a while.

By the time of 1984, they moved up to Ed's house to make the record. Dave and I would get frustrated sometimes, because Ed would get up late and . . . it was hard to corral them. They were like the Marx Brothers, but it turned out to be one hell of a record. My role was diminished. When they did "Hot for Teacher"

they set up little chairs, like it was a schoolroom. I swear to God! They were a lot of fun like that. At that point they were so involved, I mostly just let them go. I think the Van Halen brothers wanted to take things to the next level. If you're a good producer and something's perfect, you just don't say a word. The highlight of that experience was "Jump," a track that Ed and the engineer actually cut the night before I came in—and it was perfect. We just recut a couple of things for sonic reasons. Then Dave wrote the words in about ten minutes sitting in the back of his Mercury convertible.

We had more fun than you can imagine. They were like that—they brought a tank into a show and ran over a Volkswagen. Really. But at the end of the day, it was simple: If you've got great artists, things are easy. Little Feat? Lowell George was a genius. Captain Beefheart was a genius. And Dave and Ed are geniuses. All I had to do was get a performance and make it sound good. I'm like a lighting man, that's all. I just got lucky with a bunch of those guys.

If it hadn't been for Lenny . . . I got a degree in history . . . I'd probably be working in a bookstore right now. If Mo hadn't given Lenny the freedom—and if Steve Ross hadn't given them the freedom—the Warners story would have been different. We had more producers on an A&R staff than any other label. Everybody was a producer, with hit records, all at once.

The story is really something when you think back to the beginning, when we were all working together: Randy Newman, Van Dyke Parks, me, Lenny Waronker, Ry Cooder. For instance, Ry Cooder and I did an arrangement for a Nancy Sinatra song called "Hook and Ladder" that Lenny produced. But it was Lenny who was the creative guy who put everyone together. He's a genius. He won't take credit for it, but he is. He was like Irving Thalberg in that he knew how all these artists could interact. And Mo—he could always hear a hit. I mean, he worked with Frank Sinatra. There was also Joe Smith, who introduced me to Van Morrison and allowed me to sign the Doobie Brothers. He doesn't always get the credit he deserves. And then there were creative managers like Elliot Roberts and David Geffen.

It gives me a smile. I wasn't in as good a mood as I am now. Just talking about it . . . all these memories came flooding back. But, basically, I think it's all about Lenny Waronker. He knew. He always knew. It was a musical company. And it was a special time.

BILLY GIBBONS ON ELIMINATOR

Why did we record *Eliminator* in Memphis? Well, Memphis was loaded with pretty girls . . . and at the time we were all single. There's *one* explanation. But add to this the fact they don't close the bars in Memphis. There are places down there that run 24/7. It's a lively environment. Of course, the bars don't close in part because they have so many musicians who are willing to work around the clock. I remember one particular nightclub called the North End, sister club of the South End. I wrote a song about it: "There's a little night spot about a block off Main / Ain't got no number, ain't got no name / You can walk right in, 'cause there ain't no door / Just a hole in the wall—and there ain't no floor."

But ZZ Top was also drawn—for many years—to that interesting shop in Memphis called Ardent Recording. Ardent was a good household. A number of interesting characters came into the band's life through that establishment. And they helped us to explore the possibilities. *Eliminator* was, in some respects, part of a progression that led from *Deguello* and *El Loco*. Each phase was more refined than the previous outing. What set *Eliminator* apart, however, came through our experimentation with some new gadgets.

At the time of that recording most of the major players in the manufacturing of musical gear dabbling in this brave new world of electronica started showing up. And they had some things which caught the band's experimental, inquisitive side. We chased a few crazy contraptions down. And we were so enthralled with some of this unusual new gear that we kept poking at it until we found something that worked. Now keep in mind that we don't profess to be technological geniuses or engineers of any sort—in fact, I daresay we never read page one of any manual. We just started poking at buttons. But if you're resourceful in designing soundscapes, you can follow the truth of one of the oldest sayings in the world: Learn to play what you want to hear.

In working with this new gear, sequencers and so forth, we brought great attention to tempo—and *that* was a major cornerstone in creating this benchmark piece of work. There's great value in establishing a groove that's unfailing.

Now, that said, it's often been suspected that *Eliminator* was machine-made, synthesized. But the truth is quite the opposite. What worked was the *combination*, using these new, untried contraptions . . . but blended in with the real guys—*that* was what created something new. For that time it was rock solid. And it came at a moment when we weren't necessarily the only ones trying this—we just happened to get there first.

You know, when ZZ Top was first gelling as an aggregation—three guys trying to get their feet on the ground, trying to figure out what they were—it would be fair to say our most influential resources came from blues players. It was the kind of music that we liked to listen to, and we all struggled to interpret this great art form. At the same time there were guys like Bob Dylan, very introspective. Nonetheless, early on we realized we were more like Howlin' Wolf than Bob Dylan—but that doesn't mean we weren't influenced by many of the tendencies that were alive around us. That thinking, that awareness of other traditions, later allowed us to embrace some technology that, ultimately, led to something new for ZZ Top.

When *Eliminator* was brought to Warner Bros. for a first listen, I was in Monte Carlo hanging out with some pals, whooping it up over there. The presentation took place in my absence, even if I was still quite enthusiastic about bringing this recording forward. It was different enough that it was either going to be embraced or repelled. But at Warners you didn't just have great executives who knew the business, you had people who knew how to listen for interesting and valuable material. That was the bonus. They got it.

There's a lingering attractiveness to that red-and-white Warner Bros. shield. To this day it spells out fame and fortune. I don't think there's an hour of programming in radio, TV, or film that goes by without the Warner Bros. shield popping up. The team of players . . . Mo Ostin, the head man, Lenny Waronker, who was an ally of so many bands, Bob Merlis, the head of publicity, and on and on and on, those personalities made for a real attractive camp.

ELVIS COSTELLO ON SPIKE

I was quite proud to be signed to Warner Bros. In my time as a record buyer and music fan, Warner Bros., more conspicuously than any other label, was a supporter of artists who elsewhere wouldn't have gotten anything like a shot, let alone the budgets they had to make records—people like Randy Newman, Ry Cooder, and Van Dyke Parks, especially, who, to say the least, would be regarded as uncommercial by some other record labels. Clearly, Warner Bros. had a strategy for doing that, which is that they made money doing other kinds of music and could therefore bankroll such artists.

When I came along, I may have caught the very tail end of that philosophy. I think, with R.E.M., I may have been among the last such acts. Even Prince,

when he has spoken openly about Warners and not necessarily about the conflicts that came later, acknowledged that they gave him a huge amount of latitude and support early on, to develop in a way that acts just don't get to now. Performers today get dropped if they don't sell five hundred thousand copies of their second record. It's ludicrous. Some people aren't even getting started for a couple of records—they need to find their voice, and the only real way to do it is in public.

I had a meeting with Lenny and Steven Baker at the time of signing. I described five albums that I had in my head. I didn't have all the songs written, but I could describe the five albums that I imagined making from that point

188

on. Since I'd been through some frustrating times with Columbia, always feeling that no matter what I did or how good I felt it was or how much I put into it, it never seemed to be the record they wanted, I kind of threw it open to Lenny and Steven to select one of these five records I had in mind as the record I would make next, my first for Warner Bros. So, I described them, and Lenny said, "Make them all." So I did. The only problem was, I made them simultaneously. The result was called *Spike*.

If you listen to those tracks you'll hear that I was given license to go mad, in a way that I hadn't been encouraged to before that. The only time previously I'd given myself a bigger piece of paper to do the picture on and a little more time for myself in the studio was during the six weeks in which I created *Imperial Bedroom*. But Columbia had nothing to do with that album; they didn't know what it was or how to handle it. We made that in isolation, whereas Warners did kind of know what I was doing. I think it's absolutely impossible to imagine—whether or not you like *Spike*, or even whether I like it—anybody bankrolling a record with that kind of mad ambition. To record in five cities, juxtaposing all these elements, with me learning arrangements on the fly and using the tape to organize these different choirs of instruments, from New Orleans brass bands to Irish musicians . . . if I look at some of these songs and strip them to their essentials, I recognize with the benefit of hindsight that some of them are better served by simpler means. But I wouldn't have it any other way than that I had the opportunity to make a movie like that—because that's what it felt like, like making a big film. I mean, the budget was by far the biggest budget I'd had to work with. But *Spike* was also, coincidentally, the biggest record of my career. Numerically some of my early records outsold it over the course of thirty years, but *Spike* was the biggest selling in its own time. "Veronica" was the force behind that. But remember, I did have a secret weapon—I had a Beatle on bass. He walked in carrying his own guitar case, plugged in, and did it.

The recordings began in Dublin, with the Irish ensemble, which contained Derek Bell of the Chieftains, the great Christy Moore, Dónal Lunny, who assembled this disparate crew, and Davy Spillane. In New Orleans Allen Toussaint came in to play this extraordinary piano part which more or less arranged "Deep Dark Truthful Mirror" from the keyboard out. On that song we added the Dirty Dozen Brass Band, some percussion, and that was it. That particular track was very sparse, but rich. We cut "Chewing Gum" with the Neville's drummer Willie Green,

and with Kirk Joseph playing an outstanding bass line on the sousaphone. A kind of a funk record, just not using the typical sounds of a funk record. And then we went to Los Angeles and recorded a considerable amount of music there, involving all sorts of people—Jerry Scheff and Jim Keltner, both of whom had played on *King of America*; Roger McGuinn came in and played some twelve-string guitar; Marc Ribot, who I think really shaped a couple of the songs like "Let Him Dangle" and "Pads, Paws, and Claws"; Mitchell Froom, Michael Blair. Many more. Really, just an enormous cast. After that we went back to London, which was the only time it got a little out of control. We cut Paul McCartney and Chrissie Hynde to great effect, but when we tried to mix there we found that we had to return to Los Angeles, at even more expense.

With the artwork I always had this idea that I wanted to portray the last entertainer in the world, who had been shot and hung on the wall in the Warner Bros. offices—you know, having escaped Columbia. There was a satirical element. I was wearing this kind of weird clown makeup, half white, half black, satirizing those elements of show business. And this was not done with the computer. I was very carefully made up and, with great care, had to insert my head into that shield. Then I was photographed in numerous expressions, from repose to the smiling one that made the cover to hideous grimaces. From these we made enormous backdrops for the subsequent tour—they were horrifying if you looked around when you were playing and saw these grimacing faces. There's actually some film of me with my head kind of stuck in this thing like some nightmarish David Lynch scene, where I'm kind of growling and howling. But I guess someone looked at this shape—and you would think it wouldn't be possible to copyright a shape, just as you can't copyright a circle or a triangle—but that particular shield design is apparently too close to the Warner Bros. logo. Then, when the label's own publicity department made these buttons that had my initials on them where the "WB" of Warner Bros. would be, that's when the legal department had issues. But even the sleeve was a problem there for a bit. And I suppose what is really odd is that this was the first time I did album art entirely in-house in the whole of my career—up until the *River in Reverse*. I worked with their art director, Jeri McManus [later Heiden]—no relation!—whose name is on a lot of great sleeves. And there I was, in trouble with the in-house legal department.

↑ Chris Isaak, late-1980s.
➜ Brian Ferry of Roxy Music, early 1980s.
◉ a-ha, mid-1980s.

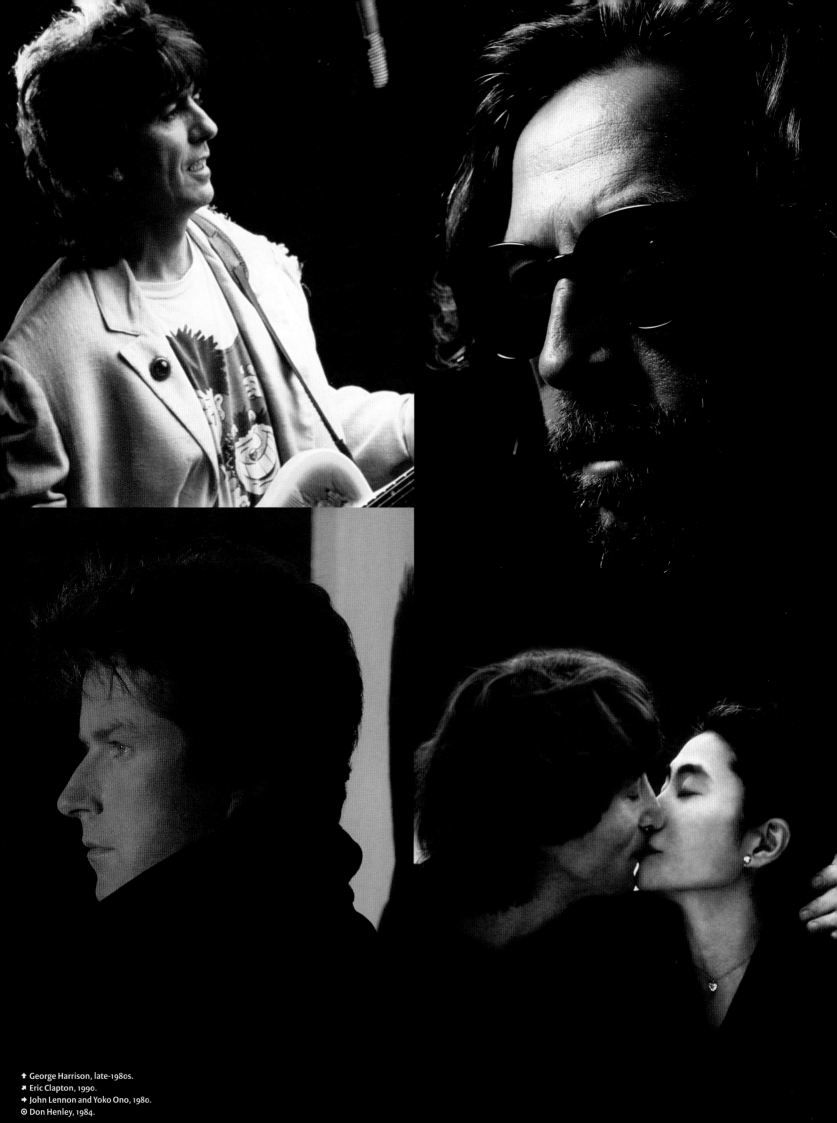

↑ George Harrison, late-1980s.
↖ Eric Clapton, 1990.
→ John Lennon and Yoko Ono, 1980.
⊙ Don Henley, 1984.

PAUL SIMON ON GRACELAND

A significant part of *Graceland* was conceptualized before the actual recording began. The first song that I heard that prompted this new direction was the "Gumboots" track. When I found out that it came from South Africa, I asked Mo if we had anybody in South Africa who could help me find the group that had recorded that particular track, the Boyoyo Boys. Mo put me in touch with Hilton Rosenthal, a record producer in South Africa who had worked with a group called Juluka.

Hilton Rosenthal sent me maybe ten albums of different styles of South African music. That's how I began to familiarize myself with not only the Zulu township jive style but also sutu music, shanga music. After the musicians voted on whether they wanted me to come, I went to South Africa and played with two or three different bands that came into the recording studio. From those bands I chose a few players to come and record in New York. That's how the tracks "Diamonds on the Soles of Her Shoes," "You Can Call Me Al," and maybe another one were recorded. The other tracks were recorded in South Africa—"Gumboots," "The Boy in the Bubble," "Graceland." Along the way I met Ray Phiri, Joseph Shabalala from Ladysmith Black Mambazo, and several others.

This wasn't the first time I had done something like I'd done on *Graceland*, meaning that aspect of bringing different cultural traditions together. "Mother and Child Reunion" was recorded in Jamaica with Jamaican musicians. Probably the first time I did it was with "El Condor Pasa," with Peruvian musicians. But there was an enormous learning process that went on with the South African

music that was different from my experience with the Jamaican and the Peruvian music. It had to do with the amount of material, in this case most of an album in South African idioms as opposed to individual songs.

Graceland involved an immersion in the music. I really had to analyze the music in order to write. I learned a lot about rhythm, about how they treated symmetry in guitar parts. It was unlike American music, though my first inclination was to relate to it—because it was three-chord music in 4/4 time. There was a feel in it that reminded me of 1950s music. And Ladysmith Black Mambazo sounded something like doo-wop, if distantly related. So the music wasn't altogether strange to me. That's why I went into the project with a kind of openness and a confidence. And, on the other hand, I didn't know it was going to lead where it did lead. I just began, thinking, "We'll see where this goes."

It was very stimulating. And I took the time that was needed. With the song "Graceland," it was a slow process; I kept singing that refrain, "I'm going to Graceland, Graceland." I was thinking, "I'm not going to keep this." I knew that it wasn't a song about Elvis Presley, I'd never been to Graceland, and I was working with South African musicians. But I couldn't shake the phrase from my consciousness. I finally said, "I'd better go to Graceland." And so I did.

I went there from Crowley, Louisiana, where I'd cut the Zydeco track—something I'd done because the accordion felt like my best link between the American and the South African music. I drove up Highway 61, I think, to Memphis, where "the Mississippi Delta was shining like a National guitar." That's where that line came from. The visit to Graceland then put the story in a certain context. If I hadn't made that trip, I wouldn't have been able to surround the story with that scenery and the circumstances. It gave me my emotional context for the song.

The thing that was different about *Graceland* in relation to South African music was that if, for instance, somebody played with a sutu band, they just played sutu music. And if they played in a shanga band—the song "I Know What I Know" is shanga music—they just played shanga music. Mixing the different musical styles would be akin to mixing R&B and bluegrass, making those styles coherent. At the time, this was an interesting leap in thinking for popular music. Now you see it all the time. People mix all kinds of eras and genres and sounds and cultures. At the time of *Graceland* it wasn't often attempted.

While I was making it, even when the excitement was building, I didn't share this with Warner Bros. My previous album, *Hearts and Bones*, wasn't a big hit. There were a lot of people saying, "Well, he's finished." So I felt when I went to work on the South African record that nobody was really paying attention—and that was a good thing. There wasn't the usual anticipation of me following up a hit, hearing, "What are you going to do now?" I was coming off a project that was not a big hit. Nobody was looking over my shoulder. It was a good time to be peacefully exploring, without anybody asking for songs, wondering what was going on.

Graceland had good luck attached to it all the time. It was a very positive thing. Even the political controversy and the questions that were asked of *Graceland* regarding multiculturalism and the use of one culture's treasures in another cultural context—all of those questions, which were fiercely debated at the time—really resolved themselves in a very positive way. People have been doing this constantly since then. I don't think *Graceland* was the first example, but it was the first really successful example of that thinking, reaching a mass audience. Ray Charles had done something along these lines when he recorded his country albums—but that was with American forms, so nobody said, "Where does Ray Charles come off singing country songs?" They said, "What a great insight." With *Graceland*, the matter was debated for many months. But the matter resolved itself with a sense that this is one world. It was a liberating conclusion, after the discussion took place.

RANDY TRAVIS ON STORMS OF LIFE

We went through the years of being turned down by all the labels, Warner Bros. being one of them. Record companies didn't think the traditional-sounding stuff would sell records. That's what we'd always hear when they passed. The *Urban Cowboy* era worked well for the industry, but in the end there wasn't enough good music to sustain and build the interest of the new audience that had emerged. The industry lost momentum. Everyone was trying to do the more pop-oriented sound in those years. When I knocked on doors with a traditional, country sound, I was having no luck. Years later, Grandpa Jones—and we were actually standing in the cornfield on the *Hee Haw* set at the time—told me, "I like what you do, son. I like that country stuff. If any of them people at that record label want you to cut that more pop-oriented material, you just tell them to kiss the part that shows the most when you pull the turnips."

Things turned around when Martha Sharp came into the picture. Martha was Warners A&R back in the 1980s and came out to the Nashville Palace, where I was singing and washing dishes. She listened to us play a set. I met her, talked to her for a bit. Then she left, and I figured she wasn't very impressed. I thought we'd be hearing another "no" soon enough. But within a month I was signed to the label, and we'd begun work on *Storms of Life*.

My contract with Warner Bros. actually started as a three-singles deal, meaning we'd release three singles and if nothing worked at radio I'd be dropped. Among the first few songs we found and recorded were "On the Other Hand" and "1982." "On the Other Hand" went out and got to, I think, number sixty-seven. Most radio folks wouldn't play the first single of someone they'd never heard of. Then we released "1982." And for whatever reason, that one worked. But, to tell you the truth, we were nowhere close to having an album ready at that point in time. So we released "On the Other Hand" again. Then we had a number one record and Song of the Year. That's when Kyle [Lehning, producer] and Martha and I got very busy finding songs and getting on with it.

Paul Overstreet's songs were a big part of *Storms of Life*. I heard a story about Paul calling his publisher—this was before we had a number one record,

obviously—and asking why they were pitching his songs to an artist he'd never heard of, because he felt they were some of the best songs he'd ever written. Then there was Kyle Lehning, who got involved when he called Martha Sharp, letting her know he'd like to try his hand producing me. I remember Kyle coming in for a meeting and asking what music I liked. I called off Hank [Williams], Merle [Haggard], obviously George Jones, and Lefty. He asked me, "Lefty who?" I remember thinking, "Good gosh! You want to produce a country record and you've never heard of Left Frizzell?" But as a producer, he was a huge part of making those albums, from picking songs to cutting the tracks to mixing. Seldom did Kyle, Martha, and I disagree on material.

When it came to making *Storms of Life* as a real country record, there wasn't much need to consider other directions. Heck, listen to my voice—what else could I do? But after those years of being turned down by labels for being too country, I believe there was a shift in the industry. There were always people doing traditional music, whether Ricky Skaggs, George Strait, Hank Jr., even Waylon & Willie, but now the industry began to see it. Really, I got signed for the same reason I'd been turned down.

The first artist who really showed us a kind of approval, like what we were doing was worthwhile, was Conway Twitty. We played at Twitty City, and he came out and watched probably four shows before I even had my first three singles out. Conway studied the business like no one I've ever seen. And he was the first one to really . . . well . . . be so complimentary. Later on George Jones actually came to me and sang "If I Didn't Have You." I grew up singing George's songs, so this meant a lot to me.

I came up through the clubs. I was singing in them by fourteen, full time by sixteen. *Storms of Life* was quite an experience for me. I remember Kyle coming to me, saying he wanted to make the best record we could make but that it was going to be me walking up on stage singing that material. "If you don't love it, don't do it," that was his message. I feel fortunate to say that's just what I've been able to do over the years.

↖ John Anderson, 1982.
↑ Dwight Yoakam, 1987.
⊙ k.d. lang, 1988.
← Hank Williams, Jr., 1982.

CHAPTER SEVEN
MUSIC IN THE FACE OF CHANGE

THE RISE OF WARNER BROS. RECORDS REMAINS ONE OF THE GREAT STORIES IN THE HISTORY OF THE AMERICAN ARTS. BUT THE COMPANY'S STRENGTH, AFTER YEARS OF STEADY GROWTH, WOULD BE TESTED IN THE MID-1990S.

LOCATING THE END

One critic, attempting a portrait of the music business, put forward this description: "A business filled with cynicism; a business that sees the frustrated, idealistic . . . young buyer simply as 'the youth market,' and the music they produce as 'product'." We hear a lot of such reports these days, no doubt. This critic, however, was writing in 1970. The point is that it's always been easy to condemn the music industry and sound the cry of loss. The end of Warner Bros. Records has in fact been declared many times. It all depends on where you're standing, who you are, and where you made your investments. The very notion of a golden age is, of course, as subjective a notion as one will ever find. But that's no reason to dismiss the idea out of hand.

In selecting *his* end of Warner Bros. Records, Nick Tosches looks to the moment in which Ice-T and Body Count took the song "Cop Killer" off their album due to public outcry: "Warner Bros. had lost its soul, and nothing without a soul can survive." In Robert Lloyd's "One Brief Shining Moment," written in 1988, Lloyd goes back much further to find the label's demise: "But finally, they were too big, too successful. In the 1970s, the record business went through the roof. Warner Bros. Records, by now part of the giant Kinney National Services (the parking lot people), took up residence in a new, sprawling building and began to diversify, to expand— and to lose its identity." If Lloyd sees the entrance of Steve Ross's company, Kinney National Services, as the end, it's worth noting that many more people count Ross's death, after so many productive years working with Mo Ostin's team, as the end of Warner Bros. Records. Jack Warner himself saw the end in 1958, at least until Bob Newhart charted a number one record. But it's 2008, Tom Petty and Neil Young both released albums this year. Clearly there's more to the story.

Rather than posit a golden age and indulge too much in the romance of loss, it's worth exploring the manner in which the Warner Bros. story includes both dramatic change and a significant measure of continuity. There is no escaping the fact that the music industry did undergo massive changes, and these changes affected Warner Bros. Records. The point is not to gloss over that upheaval, to wrongly suggest that all is as it was. Rather, the aim is to explore the manner in which the persistence of an idea, of a very good idea, based on putting the music first, carried on despite the weather.

THE CULTURE OF WARNER BROS.

If the story being told here is the story of that "very good idea," it's equally about the culture that grew up around it, a culture that emerged sometime in the mid-1960s. The most obvious way to arrive at a sense for that culture is, obviously, through its artists. **Joe Smith:** "Wild Man Fischer would hang around our lobby and expose himself. We had this girl who was our receptionist, a great looking redhead, a big girl, and she threatened to throw him out on the street. Fischer would be downstairs, and when the coffee truck came by he'd go out and say, 'I'll write a song for you. Gimme coffee and a sandwich and I'll write a song for you'." But one can also look to the cast of executives in order to understand, to *try* to understand the culture of Warner Bros. Records. **Hale Milgram:** "Bob Krasnow is a true record pioneer. Very, very savvy. And a nutcase. Mo Ostin brought in real personalities. He allowed all of these very different people to . . . think of Bob Krasnow and think of Lenny Waronker. Let's talk about two different worlds, two totally different worlds, productively coexisting." But, at the same time, the culture of Warner Bros. Records was born not just in its roster and in the upper reaches of management. Two individuals, whose names came up again and again in conversations with Warner Bros. employees and artists, offer as much human evidence of the label's day-to-day charac-

↑ Howard Washington tends to his garden, 1994. The man who kept peace in the Warner Bros. Records parking lot, Washington was for many years the icon of the Burbank building.

← "Cop Killer," 1992. This release by Ice-T's group Body Count would result in tremendous controversy for Warner Bros. Records, some of it unequivocably negative.

Opening spread: A detail from *Nothing's Shocking*, Jane's Addiction's 1988 release. The imagery was adapted from a dream recalled by frontman Perry Farrell.

ter as anyone: Evelyn Ostin, Mo's wife, and Howard Washington, the man who ran the Warner Bros. Records parking lot.

On Howard Washington. **Russ Thyret:** "Howard eventually rebuilt this thing we called 'the shed'—we never knew what else to call it—with air conditioning, cable television. It was great. He had his own garden there. This guy was a fatherly figure in ways I can't even describe to you. And there are famous stories of him not letting people park, not letting people on the lot, no matter who you were —the heads of other music companies, big-time attorneys, artists. If you didn't have a spot, you didn't get in, that was it. He was a gentleman. He was in a movie that I have a copy of, *Strangers on a Train*. In 1951, he played a porter in that movie." **Lou Dennis:** "Howard was the first person you saw when you came to Warner Bros. Records. If you were to come to Warner Bros. in those days you'd have to get past him. Howard was the guard up the street when we were in the old building. But when we moved to our new building, he said, 'I want to be with the record people. I like them.' He had a little—I call it a house—but it was a guard post with a television and air conditioning, a little garden outside that he could tend to. If you came in and said, 'I'm here to see Mo Ostin,' you had to get by Howard. He was the general. A wonderful, wonderful man. I think one year he played Santa Claus at the Christmas party." **Ron Goldstein:** "He ruled that parking lot like he was Mo Ostin."

Or Evelyn Ostin. **Tom Silverman:** "Evelyn was the spiritual consciousness of Warner Bros., from behind the curtain." **David Berman:** "I think she did, in part, set a tone for Warners. At her service, one of the things Jerry Moss said was that Evelyn was Mo's not-so-secret weapon, that every time he and Mo were going after the same artist, that if Evelyn got in the picture, he knew he was going to lose." **Russ Thyret:** "I'll tell you how she was with me. She would get you aside at various functions and say things like, 'Mo has his eye on you, he looks out for you, he respects your opinion.' But hearing it firsthand like that just made you feel like . . . unstoppable. I started in the company when I was in my very early twenties, and from early on, she always had a good word, was always there saying that Mo was in my corner. I can't tell you how much it meant to me. And I know I wasn't the only person she was encouraging. But I'll tell you this, if you had somebody that you revered as I revered Mo, and his partner would be saying things like that to you, you'd walk out of the room like, 'I can do this. I can fly! Watch!'"

The culture of Warner Bros. Records, something that was unplanned and grew organically, was finally the company's chief asset. The Warners story remains one of the great case studies of American business, as much as it belongs to the history of popular music culture. But, as early as the late-1980s, the strength of what Warner Bros. built would be tested in many ways. The twists and turns of the past twenty years are too many to be inventoried in these pages, but the great fact of the music industry and the changes it faced are the undeniable backdrop of the Warner Bros. narrative as it entered the 1990s.

A&R ONCE AGAIN

The celebrated A&R team at Warner Bros., the team that had created a roster of remarkable scope in the late 1960s and 1970s, was by the 1980s complemented by new members. Among them was Michael Ostin, Mo's son. **Michael Ostin:** "I started early, as a high-school student working summers in the A&R department. That was with Lenny Waronker, Ted Templeman, Russ Titleman. It was a great education. Ted had such broad tastes. In the same year, he could do a Van Halen record and a Nicolette Larson record. Russ was also very eclectic in the types of artists that he worked with. He and Lenny worked together a lot in the beginning, but then he started to venture off on his own, made a great Rufus record, a great Chaka Khan solo record, then went off and did Clapton, George Harrison. They all had focus but also tremendous respect for the rest of the building. They listened to others."

Ostin's first signing threw him into the deep end of the A&R pool. It was a heady start. **Michael Ostin:** "With Russ Titleman's support, I signed Christopher Cross. We made a record, turned it in, and though the company rallied around it, for some reason everyone felt the timing wasn't right. We decided to wait, putting the record out at the beginning of the next year. Then it just exploded. There were something like five hit singles, it won four or five Grammys, got Album of the Year and Single of the Year and Best New Artist. That was the first thing, for whatever reason, that I put the flag in the ground and said, 'This is something we should sign'."

Other signings, true to previous decades, remained diverse. If in 1967 Mo Ostin wrote a letter to Frank Sinatra, recommending that he check out the new recording by the Fugs, it was a gesture that revealed Mo Ostin's scope, from the Fugs to Frank. That breadth of taste would continue to inform the label's A&R practices. If "alternative" was a new category on the landscape, it was also a word to which the label had always been attuned and with which it had been identified. **Tom Biery:** "The first Rickie Lee Jones record, 'Chuck E.'s In Love,' that didn't really sound like what was going on at the time, not at all, you know what I mean? I always appreciated that about the label, that willingness to go where the music was leading." Dave

Stein, hired as a regional promoter in 1978 by Russ Thyret and brought to Burbank in 1994, viewed that sensibility as being the heart of the matter. **Dave Stein:** "I'll never, ever forget this big Top Forty station in Kansas City, which had fourteen of our records on their chart at the time, and Rod Stewart was doing a show out there, and I think the label was renegotiating their deal with Rod. So Mo came into the market, and I introduced him to the programmer and general manager of this Top Forty radio station. And Mo spent the whole time talking with these Top Forty guys about Laurie Anderson! That blew me away. It showed me that when I'm talking about music I should never be constrained by the person I'm talking to."

After R.E.M. and Jane's Addiction signed in 1987, there would be more important additions to the Warner Bros. roster over the course of the next several years. The aura established as early as the late-1960s still surrounded the label—and it was an aura that attracted artists. Elvis Costello released his first Warner Bros. project, *Spike*, in 1989. The Red Hot Chili Peppers had joined up one year earlier. Tom Petty signed with the label, in a clandestine operation spearheaded by Mo and Lenny, even before his MCA contract had run out, and started recording *Wildflowers* in 1992. In every case, the artists who came onboard cited the history of the label and its artist policies as the reason they did so. And, indeed, much of what made Warners an artist's label remained enshrined in the practices of the organization. **Michael Ostin:** "In A&R Roberta Peterson was the den mother. She was great. She had real strong opinions, great taste, cutting edge. She fought for stuff. We bounced off each other a lot, but Roberta was sort of a focal point. Her signings were super-eclectic, from Jane's Addiction to The Flaming Lips." The department left room for its staff to cross the terrain between the alternative and mainstream worlds with relative comfort. Michael Ostin proved a key player as Madonna's career continued to grow, eventually leading the A&R department. **Michael Ostin:** "I had the good fortune of finding material that Madonna really responded to. 'Love Don't Live Here Anymore,' for instance, which was the old Rose Royce record. I was driving into work one day and heard it on the radio, I called Nile [Rodgers] and Madonna, they were in the studio. I said, 'I have an idea, you know the old Rose Royce record, 'Love Don't Live Here Anymore'? Why don't you guys try it?' They cut it that day and put it on the record. There was a little bit of old school A&R-ing that went on there. But, really, Madonna was off and running. She was a holistic artist, she could do it all."

With affiliates continuing to play an enormous role in deepening the roster, giving Warners a presence in urban music *and* providing singles, the years between 1987 and 1994 were musically rich. But, as many recognized, a false sense of security had come over the music industry when CDs replaced vinyl. Had CDs not been a part of the picture, the dialogue

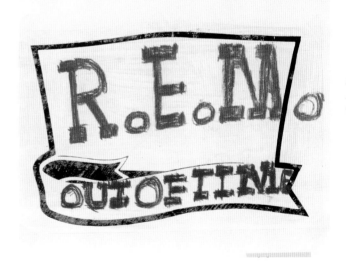

↑ Inner sleeve artwork from R.E.M.'s 1991 *Out of Time*, the recording that would take the band to the next level.
↑↑ Tom Petty during the making of *Wildflowers*. Made with Rick Rubin, *Wildflowers* was among Petty's most intimate recordings and the artist's personal favorite.

↑ Signed to Sire Records after breaking in England, Seal would go on to massive success with the song "Kiss from a Rose."

↗ Depeche Mode, early 1990s. Signed to Sire, Depeche Mode was late-breaking in the States but would ultimately be a defining band for both Sire and Warner Bros. Records. It was another case of Sire giving the label an invaluable presence in English music.

→↑ Green Day, *Dookie*, 1994.

→↗ The Prodigy, *The Fat of the Land*, 1997.

→→ *Under Cover, The Songs of Lou Reed*, 1996.

202

regarding "the end of the industry" would have been kicked off much earlier. **Lou Dennis:** "Then along came CDs. We were selling the same stuff all over again in a different configuration to people that owned the stuff before, and to new people. It was the golden age. When we released *James Taylor's Greatest Hits* on CD, my suggested initial order was about twenty-five thousand. We had one account that bought the entire twenty-five thousand. One account. Can you imagine that? Naturally, we made more." Whatever the case, when that false sense of security was lifted, a climate of anxiety crept in. Everywhere, Warner Bros. included, a bottom-line sensibility came down from above. The state of the industry was going to mess with Warners. Even if something, some creative spirit that still had meaning, was going to be more resilient than perhaps anyone knew, that didn't mean it was going to be pretty.

THE FIRST MOMENT OF A NEW MEDIA

Jeff Gold: "One day Howie Klein's secretary, Ilene, comes into my office and tells me that the new Depeche Mode album has leaked. At that time, the record companies were really concerned about records leaking before they hit radio. Ilene knows it's leaked because she's on CompuServe, this online service at the time, where all these kids are talking about the new Depeche Mode record and specific songs and the titles and what it sounds like. Now nobody at Warner Bros. is online except for Ilene and maybe Howie. I'm not. She was a bit panicky, like, 'Oh my God, this record's leaked, these kids are making tapes for each other, this is a horrible thing.' She's telling me this, and I'm thinking, 'Wait a minute, this is kind of good, isn't it? There are these fans talking about our record and getting excited'." If there were those who were exploring online possibilities before use of the Internet became commonplace, the largest part of the population drifted between a hopeful recognition of the new possibilities and a sense of the trouble that could come with it. Amidst the vacillations, artists nonetheless started to engage with their fanbases in new ways. **Jeff Gold:** "I remember we crashed AOL one day when we had Depeche Mode online with fans and another time with Perry Farrell. They were just getting thousands of people logging on and trying to submit questions. It was chaos, but the kind of chaos that a record company dreams about, and the artists were totally into it. Perry Farrell and Seal, I remember, were online at that time, and the fact that people could just send them questions and interact, it was just fantastic for us, fantastic for the artists, fantastic for the fans."

Experiments of that kind provided the basis for a new paradigm. Artists could participate directly, in fact they almost had to. **Dave Stein:** "We're all excited about the fact that the Internet, in many ways, means there's no more gatekeeper. We can find fans for our music easier. At the same time I'm sure we're frustrated by the fact that the audience attention span gets shorter and shorter. It's so much harder to keep track of the consumer. There's much more coming at them. It makes the story a little harder to stick."

BOB MORGADO, OR EVERY STORY HAS ONE

Adam Somers: "When I found myself in other settings, at other companies, I would instantly feel the difference of what's it like to be at a place where Mo is not the head guy. I can tell you, it's a whole different environment." **Diarmuid Quinn:** "You'd had Mo there for decades, a rock on the creative side and the business side. Any time you have that kind of long-term stability, and all of the sudden there's change, more change, change again, people are going to say, 'Wait, which way is up?' And, yes, they lost the plot."

Warner Bros. Records was always a business. And, since the entrance of Seven Arts and then Kinney National Services, its figureheads had reported to people outside the company. Steve Ross at Kinney had been Mo's boss for years. And by all accounts, Ross had given Mo the freedom he needed to build Warner Bros. Records as Mo deemed appropriate. Ross stayed out of the way until asked to back up his executives. By the early 1990s, however, things changed. Corporate restructuring, Ross's cancer diagnosis, unwanted power plays: It all challenged the framework of the label, until, finally, in 1994, Mo Ostin left the company.

In the early 1990s, Bob Morgado was changing the Warner Music Group. Mo Ostin had never been close to Bob Morgado. In style, Morgado was very different from Steve Ross. **Mo Ostin:** "If there was one thing I learned during my long tenure at Warners it was that creative freedom was absolutely necessary if you were going to be successful. A person who runs a company like Warner Bros. has to be empowered to make decisions and to take risks when necessary, to do whatever felt appropriate in terms of continuing and building the company. You could not suffer corporate interference, at least I couldn't. When things had changed to the extent that they did, I found that I couldn't live with it anymore. I decided that I would fulfill my contract until the end of its term, and then leave." A contract sat on his desk for months. That summer Warner Music International had scheduled an international convention in Montreux, Switzerland. Virtually every major company executive was there. **Mo Ostin:** "More than once during the convention, someone would come up to me and ask when I was going to sign my contract, I told them that I hadn't had a chance to deal with it properly and that my lawyers would look at it as soon as I got back to California."

Ostin, however, didn't head directly home. Before heading back to California, he stopped in London to check on business there. While in London, he got a call from Bob Krasnow, who told Ostin that Doug Morris, current head of Atlantic, had been named the head of the Warner American record companies. **Mo Ostin:** "I couldn't believe it. My contract clearly indicated that I reported directly to the chairman of the company. What Krasnow told me didn't necessarily mean that I had to report to Morris. However, what irked me was that I hadn't even been consulted." Ostin flew to New York and met with Morgado. **Mo Ostin:** "We discussed all kinds of issues, but he never once mentioned Morris and what Krasnow had told me. Finally he said, 'Oh, there's one more thing and I want to know what you think about it'." Morgado told Ostin that he was buried in responsibilities and work and that he needed help. He told Ostin that because of this overload, he was thinking about asking Doug Morris to run the US record companies. What, Morgado asked Ostin, did Mo think of the idea? Ostin said he'd get back to Morgado. Upon Mo's return to LA, his son Michael picked him up at the airport, asking if Mo had heard about Doug Morris.

Mo Ostin: "Before I left Morgado's office, he told me to keep his Morris idea quiet, which I did. But here was my son telling me about the decision, and he heard it from Irving Azoff. When we got to the house, I called Irving and asked him where he had heard about Morris' appointment. 'I heard it from David Geffen,' he said. So I called David, who said that he had heard it from Jim Fifield of EMI Records. That was it. Clearly the decision had been made to bring Doug Morris on—no matter what I thought about it. Half the music business knew it before I did. That was the last straw."

Ostin had been chief of Warner's music division for a quarter century. It was one of the lowest days of his life. **Mo Ostin:** "I had this incredible history with the company. I had the good fortune to be associated with some of the most amazing artists in the history of the business. I had employees that were outstanding and loyal to me and the company. It really hurt to make the decision to leave, but it was the only decision I could have made. I was done. I'd finish my contract, but I was done."

The Warner Bros. Records story is, in many ways, one of a great alliance between Mo Ostin and Steve Ross. The end of that alliance was not due to corporations getting involved. They already were. The end of that alliance came when the corporate relationship was no longer healthy, as it was for Ross and Ostin. But it had always been a business, and it had always involved corporate influences. Perhaps the remarkable part of the story is just how long those influences supported the label's artist-based approach. But it was a sorry end to Ostin's time at Warners. **Howie Klein:** "I can remember one time Mo calling Lenny in. I just happened to be with Lenny, so Mo brought us both in and had us sit down. He was on the phone and wanted us to see the way he handled some accountant type at Time/Warner who

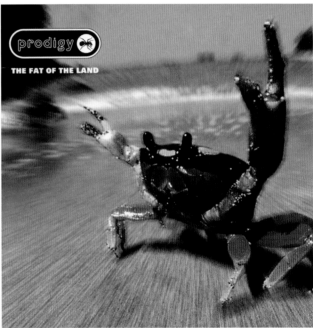

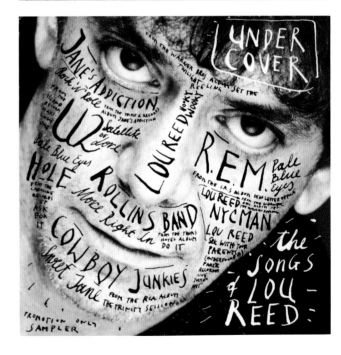

was telling him to drop Eric Clapton. That scene became so engrained in my head that I never forgot it. I'm sure this particular accountant never, ever brought up to Mo again that he should drop an artist—and here it was Eric Clapton. This was several months before that live record that sold ten million came out. So you have some fucking clueless accountant telling Mo Ostin, one of the most successful record executives in history, to drop one of the greatest artists in musical history, and Mo was thinking about this album that we're making with him, the *Unplugged* album, which went on to sell ten million records."

SUCCESSION AND MORE SUCCESSION

The rise of the Internet, the changing nature of the industry, Ostin's departure after so many years of productive and creative leadership: It all settled on the culture of Warner Bros. Records as a weight that would not immediately overwhelm the company but one which would continue to bear down on the organization. In Ostin's wake, presidents and chairmen came and went for several years. After consistency, flux.

Russ Thyret: "I gave an interview to somebody shortly after I was appointed chairman. They asked, 'You've been the third chairman in the last nine months, how does that make you feel?' And I said, 'I'm also the third chairman in the last thirty years, how does that make you feel? I'm defensive about it, how do you think I feel?' I loved Mo Ostin, didn't want to see him go."

Jeff Gold: "After Mo left, Lenny basically decided he wasn't going to stay. Then Danny Goldberg comes in, and I knew him and had worked with him, because he had a label at A&M. We got along fine. And then he got pushed out, and then Russ Thyret took over, and then Russ had some health problems and there was some thought that Russ was going to be pushed out. And then Phil Quartararo was brought in. So I was working for somebody five guys away from the guy who hired me. Remember, Mo had run this company for twenty-five years, and then in three or four years, you've got five different people essentially running this company? Then in terms of the music group, you had Bob, and he's forced out by Doug Morris, and Doug is forced out by Michael Fuchs, and Michael is forced out by . . . "

Eddie Rosenblatt: "Just a dreadful situation."

⬧ A man well-loved: Mo Ostin's last day at Warner Bros. Records, 1994.

PERRY FARRELL ON NOTHING'S SHOCKING

We were approached by companies other than Warner Bros.—one even offered us triple the money—but I'd heard so many great things about the label that I settled on the idea of going with what I thought was the best label in the world. I believed that at the time. And I feel I made the right decision. The fact that the people running Warner Bros. were involved in making records really made a difference to me. But we also knew that this was the home of Jimi Hendrix, the Talking Heads, the Ramones, Frank Sinatra. Persuasive stuff, right?

In the case of *Nothing's Shocking*, I feel like I definitely got the record I set out to make. I'd heard something in my head—and we got it on tape. In some respects that's not a big surprise, really. We'd played those songs live for a long time. A lot of times people go into the studio and then start making music—which can be an amazing way to make music, certainly fun and creative—but back then you typically had the songs in your set for a couple years before you entered the studio. I was using the vocal effects onstage. So much was in place that would define the record's character. We had the songs down, and then a great producer came along to capture the best sounds.

When it came to picking the producer for *Nothing's Shocking*, Dave Jerden's name came up. We'd heard that he worked with both the Rolling Stones and the Talking Heads, so that combination, I thought, would be fantastic for us. We were a very art-driven band, really knew where we wanted to go. When I met Dave Jerden, I found that he was a very strange but beautiful guy. I liked his intensity right away. He seemed to like music that was really over-the-top, heavy and strong. He had a thing he'd say whenever he felt the music was perfect: "It sounds like a Panzer division in your face."

Honestly? Most of us were junkies. So during the recording it was a matter of getting your dope, doing your dope, and playing your music. That leads not just to lots of pressure but complicated band dynamics. Not all of us took direction so well. It was intense between Dave and me, between Eric and me. We were young, didn't always trust people on the outside. This made things hard at times. A song like "Jane Says," for instance, was something that caused internal friction. I had this idea to add a steel drum, which Stephen Perkins played, but I got a lot of resistance from my group. They didn't want that song to have anything but an acoustic guitar. I felt like the steel drum became a hook, almost as much as the chorus. Oddly enough, when I went in to speak with the record company, they told me that the band was unhappy with how I was producing the song. That tells you something about the band's communication.

The artwork for *Nothing's Shocking*, which got a lot of attention, came from a dream I had of two women on a swing with their hair on fire. For the cover, I just did my best to re-create the dream. We made a bodycasting of my girlfriend at the time, and then made two molds. I was living in a storefront near Silverlake, so I had high ceilings and a big, square space to work in. A furniture store in the area created a custom chair that rocked side-to-side rather than front to back. The real trick, though, was to set the hair on fire—I think we used some kind of rubber glue—and take the picture right away. We didn't have too many chances. The heads started to get charred pretty quickly. We only took two or three pictures—but we got it. Everybody at Warners loved the artwork. But when we took it to retail, that's when we got resistance. The follow-up record, *Ritual De Lo Habitual*, had even more trouble, with some chains banning it altogether. Whether the ban helped—simply because of the publicity—would be hard to gauge.

In the end, being on a big label was, for us, a mixed blessing. We had freedom with Warner Bros. But money also came into the picture. Not surprisingly, it was when we got signed that things began to fall apart. Everybody in the band was pushing in a different direction. Actually, we were pushing in the same direction—we just weren't helping each other. There's always a lot of animosity when money comes into things, when business comes into things . . . and lawyers . . . things like that. But here's something that needs to be said: I keep saying that things were different then, right? Well, they were. And it's worth remembering just how that was so. In LA, for instance, there was an underground scene. You had bands putting their own shows on, throwing their own parties, creating their own art. And just like the kids, the record labels were going out to find this stuff. They weren't star-making—this wasn't *American Idol*. It wasn't about makeovers and turning what was happening in the clubs into product. We were part of an art scene, a music community. Within that community bands had their own styles, their own mannerisms, their own sounds. And that's what record companies were going out to find. Some good music got made that way.

PETER BUCK AND SCOTT LITT ON OUT OF TIME

PETER BUCK: Prior to recording *Out of Time* we'd been on the road for ten years, doing 150 shows and making a record most every year. So when the moment came to begin another recording, we went into our rehearsal studio and played electrically for about an hour before going, "Not that again." We'd been doing it that way for so long. So we started playing acoustic stuff.

I'd been playing with this folk music society in Athens, hanging around and learning about bluegrass and Irish music. But we were all feeling the need to do something different this time, to depart from our approach as a live band. On another level, we also perceived certain expectations in the air, like we were expected to do a "bigger," more commercial record. That didn't hold our interest. We turned our back on the expected path and tried just to follow whatever our inclinations were at the time.

SCOTT LITT: It was Peter's idea to make a record with strings and orchestral arrangements. And I truly believe that Mark Bingham's string arrangements made *Out of Time*. He came in, and in two days we put down all the string and woodwind ideas, crafting the sound for the album. He was really good—and his work laid a template for *Out of Time*. I believe that the depth of the recording was mostly achieved by those live strings on the songs—all the songs. Soundwise, it created a wide frequency bandwidth, which allowed room for everything else.

PETER BUCK: Mike, Bill, and I certainly listened to that ornate, 1960s pop, whether the Left Banke or Van Dyke Parks, and this could have influenced our thinking that adding string arrangements might be a way to go. We already had a vision for a more organic, less electric record. It was also something we hadn't done in the past. Mark Bingham, the arranger we used, was the friend of a friend. We'd heard some stuff he'd done, and he seemed like he'd be a nice guy to work with. We were also kind of afraid that if we hired the most famous string arranger in Hollywood we'd get the most famous string arrangement in Hollywood.

SCOTT LITT: "Losing My Religion" really feels like a song that came out just as it should.

PETER BUCK: "Losing My Religion" occurred in about a minute and a half. I'd just bought a mandolin, was trying to teach myself to play it, and would play into my tape player. Somewhere I had about twenty minutes of me fiddling around on mandolin, playing scales and so forth, and then "Losing My Religion" beginning to end, including the intro, followed by more scales. I thought it sounded kind of good, so I taught it to the guys. Within about two minutes we were playing it. Michael showed up to practice, sang it. The next day we had a recording. That song just came out whole, fully formed. We didn't need to try another version or add a heavier guitar. It was all there. It seldom goes that way.

SCOTT LITT: Speaking for myself, the music was a transition from *Green*. *Green* was extremely diverse—we tried a lot of stuff, and I think we "sharpened our palette" for future recordings. I love the feel of *Out of Time*—it's one that I engineered and mixed myself, because I thought *Green* wasn't completely realized and had gotten away from us a bit.

PETER BUCK: Nobody at that point had done much in the way of putting a rapper on a white record. When we had KRS-One record, it was remarkable how many people told us they thought we should take it off because, as they would tell us, "nobody likes rap." It was as if people who liked our records just wouldn't want that. But we thought it made musical sense. And rock & roll has always been about bringing different things together. Not to mention that it was totally cool. It was a great opener for *Out of Time*.

Radio people told us that having KRS-One on "Radio Song" was going to hurt our chances of having the song added at stations. It was hard to believe. But we weren't going to change it for that reason. What happened? We released it as a second or third single and . . . nobody added it. Those were different days. Hip-hop and rap were considered beyond the pale and "not really music." We didn't feel that way.

FLEA ON THE RED HOT CHILI PEPPERS SIGNING TO WARNER BROS. RECORDS

Our time at EMI was coming up. We'd been a band for going on ten years or so, and we were finally in a position to field some offers. It wasn't that we'd had a hit yet, but for some reason the industry felt that we were going to be something, that a breakthrough record would come and we'd be big. You could say the business world viewed us as a potentially profitable enterprise. So there we were, our contract at EMI complete, in a position to see what we could get. We met with all the record companies, and they all wanted to give us deals. Based on our experience, we thought, "Whoever gives us the most money is the one. Whoever we go with, it's not going to affect what we do—we're just going to make music like we always did." And the record company that offered the most money was Epic.

That part was easy. We said, "Done. Epic it is." We'd met with Geffen, Warners, Virgin, Island, I think, and some others. When we met with Mo and Lenny from Warner Bros. we really liked them. As human beings, they were the frontrunners—but we just wanted to get the most money we could get. So, we told Epic we were going to sign with them. We had a big signing party. We took pictures shaking hands with Epic executives over a big cake. The only thing we had not yet done was actually sign the contract.

Now, when it becomes public that we're going with Epic, all of the record label people we met with but turned down were furious at us. It was, "We took you out to dinner! We flew you on our private jet!" A lot of hostility. Except Mo Ostin. I got a call from Mo. He gets on the phone with me and says, "I just want to say that I wish you guys had signed with me, but I think you're a wonderful band and really wish you a great career. I enjoyed meeting all of you guys, no matter that it didn't work out."

The next day we had a rehearsal and I tell the other guys, "I got this incredible call from Mo Ostin. It was so sweet. He wasn't mad at all, totally understood." Then all the other guys say, "Yeah, he called me, too!" We'd always thought of labels as these evil things you simply had to deal with if you want to get a record out—but here's this real gentleman who seems to really care about the music and the people who make it. So, we're all standing there, feeling the same way, and we go, "Fuck it. Let's take less money and sign with Mo." We went with Warner Bros.

The choice began and ended with Mo, because we'd all fallen in love with him. But along the way we met great people. Lenny, of course, but also Steven Baker, who was always, time after time, a really solid guy for the band. Nobody pulled record company power bullshit on us. That era with Mo, Lenny, and Steven was really great for us.

The first record we made for Warners was produced by Rick Rubin. We'd met with Rick once before, but that was not a good meeting. He showed up at our rehearsal space with the Beastie Boys, who picked up our guitars and broke the strings—and we were a bunch of junkies and weirdoes. But what eventually came to pass was that in Rick we found a producer who could help us to find our strengths. And that's what Rick does, really. He only works with artists because he loves them, thinks there's something great about them. Then he just tries to bring out that thing in the artist he thinks makes them great. He doesn't have a formula—his approach changes contingent on what he sees as an artist's strength. With us, I think he views the interplay between the four of us as that thing. And then the individual contributions. He really brought out Anthony as a writer, making room for some vulnerability, and certainly made room for the genius of John Frusciante. He made a space in which we could all grow.

A lot of people, artists in particular, get Rick wrong. You'll be working in the studio or in the rehearsal room, and Rick will walk in, lie down on the couch, put his feet up, and either go to sleep or play two messages on his Blackberry. And you might be like, "What's he doing? We hired this fancy producer and he's . . ." But Rick's thing is that he tries to be as relaxed as possible. He knows, for himself, that to keep up with the amount of work he's doing, and to do it well, he needs to maintain that state. When he's relaxed, he can feel the music is flowing—and when it's not flowing, it disrupts that relaxation. Then he's up, and he's making changes to the music. He's on a spiritual path.

ICE-T ON "COP KILLER"

When we created the group Body Count, I was already on Warner Bros. as Ice-T. Seymour Stein signed me, and I'd put out three—actually four—albums. Body Count was a separate thing, though, and I never really thought it would be at Warner Bros. But as the group started to evolve people were saying, "You're on a rock label. You're on Sire. Take this to Sire." When I took it to Howie Klein he said, "We love it! This is what we do. Let's go."

You need to remember: at the time I was on Warner Bros., they were the home for anything that was aggressive and controversial. They had Prince, Madonna, Sam Kinison, most of Rick Rubin's label, which included Andrew Dice Clay. It was the place to be if you were on the edge. Who was more provocative than Madonna? And Sire also had Ministry, the Talking Heads. Warners had Geto Boys. It was kind of like that's where you wanted to be.

I always had a great relationship with Howie Klein and Seymour because they respected rap music but knew they weren't authorities. They gave me free rein. They were just like, "Yo. We don't know. So, if you say it's good it's good." And every record went gold, so . . . "Go for it!" And being a rock label, I think they were a little more open to some of the harsh stuff I was doing with hip-hop. When you compare what I was doing to what some hardcore rock was doing, it was nothing.

When we brought in an album called *Cop Killer*, it was no problem. Absolutely no problem. They put it out, and everybody was happy. The record was selling—and everybody was happy as hell. I was the number one rapper at the label. And now we were hitting with rock. So, I mean, I had the red carpet rolled out for me. They were treating me like . . . like Prince! I was cool with Mo Ostin, with Lenny Waronker. In the record business, if they invest money in you, and you bring them a return, you're golden.

So I'm walking around the bungalows over there at Warner Bros. I would come through, sit down. For me, it was the best time in music. See, there's a point in an artist's career when almost anything you say, people like. I'd just done *New Jack City*. Warner Bros. films liked me. It was a good time for Ice-T. The trouble started in Austin, Texas, with The Fraternal Order of Police.

We'd already been out performing the song "Cop Killer" for a year on the Lollapalooza tour. Nobody had said nothing. But what happened is that the police had started to go under siege. They'd killed somebody in, I think, Chicago or Detroit. LAPD was in trouble. And I think somebody, politically, said, "The best defense is an offense." Then somebody dug our record up and said, "Hey, look at this. This is a terrible record. This is a reaction to the Rodney King situation." Of course, *Cop Killer* had come out a year before Rodney King. But it didn't matter. It got political, and they started to attack. And when they attacked, they didn't attack me—they attacked Warner Bros. It was like, "We know Ice-T is mad, but how dare you give him a platform to speak."

Warners was like, "What the fuck is going on?" And every day it got more press and more press. I remember when somebody called me and said our nation's President was cussing me out on television. You gotta remember, this is a year after we put that record out. We're working on the next record. And there's the President saying my name on television, talking about *Cop Killer!*" The vibe from Warners was, maybe this will go away.

People have always asked me, "Hey, can you say something bad about Warner Bros.?" But, I mean, I was like the beginning of the end of Warner Music. I can remember sitting with all of them, with Lenny and all, and them saying, "This is a bad day. Because if we allow them to censor us, it will never end." Eventually they just kept chipping away at Warners, and it was the end.

But I was never blamed. I was never attacked by the label. No one ever reprimanded me. Of course, how are you gonna reprimand somebody you already partied about?! We'd just had the gold record party, with everybody tipping drinks and laughing. And then all of a sudden it was a problem. I respect Warner Bros. to this day. They did what they could. But at the end, when the shit just got out of hand, what happened was that I asked them for a release. We wrote a letter and said, "We've got a problem here. You guys are in trouble for what I did. You put out records—you shouldn't have to be politically connected to what I'm saying. But at this moment, my integrity is at stake. I can't change my tune—It'll end my career. You feel me? So I guess it's time we part ways." Everybody felt bad. Really, if Warner Bros. had fucked me, I'd tell you! But it wasn't like that.

↖ Sir Mix-A-Lot, 1992.
↑ Quincy Jones, 1989.
© Naughty By Nature, 1991.
← Al B. Sure!, 1988.

PRODUCER MITCHELL FROOM ON LOS LOBOS' *KIKO*

By the early 1990s Los Lobos had been a part of the roots rock scene for a while. I think they felt like they'd been down a well-worn path and it was time for some kind of change. It wasn't that this was articulated necessarily. But, remember, at the end of the 1980s there were critics and others asking whether rock music was dead. I remember Michael Penn's answer to this: "No, but it sure smells bad." Everything was feeling kind of worn out. I was feeling that way. Tchad [Blake, *Kiko* engineer and Froom collaborator] was feeling that way. And the band was feeling that way. For all of us, making *Kiko* was a nothing-to-lose scenario. Then, by the second track we all did together, something was clearly happening. It got very exciting, very quickly.

The band had started the record before Tchad and I got involved. I think there were five tracks that ended up making the record that they had either started or almost finished. They were recording with their friend Paul DuGre, who had a studio in this really rotten, rough part of LA. The guys in Los Lobos had to pay this homeless man to watch their cars while they were recording. Paul was a good engineer, but it was just a little home studio. And I think that felt good to the band, like they were starting over again—it was a total change of scene for them, and they wanted to build something new with this record.

When they played Lenny some tracks from those early sessions—and they had some very good stuff, "Peace," "Two Janes"—he suggested that they work with me, to see if they could take some things further. I'd worked with Los Lobos before, on *La Bamba* and a later track called "Angel Dance," that led Lenny to believe that maybe it would be a good combination. His idea was to just see what happens.

In my memory, the first thing we tried was the song called "Reva's House." It went well, and there were sections we started to experiment with. We were pretty happy with it. But after that we did "Angels with Dirty Faces" and "Kiko and the Lavender Moon." Then we were going. All of a sudden it all just opened

up. A number of factors converged that got us all excited, one of which was the sheer speed at which we were able to get things going. On "Angels with Dirty Faces," for instance, we used this optigon, this crazy optical keyboard, and turned one of its discs upside down, creating a rhythm pattern that had a backwards sound to it. Then Pete Thomas from the Attractions, the drummer on the record, played along with that loop. Suddenly it no longer felt necessary to have a band all playing live together in a room. It became about something else, like anything was possible.

Most of the tracks we recorded were started and finished in a day or two. With "Kiko and the Lavender Moon," it was the rough mix made at the end of the recording day that made the final record—that tells you something about the level of excitement. To begin a day with nothing and end with a track like that one is a very potent experience. Lenny was the guy who was really promoting the notion of a radical departure. So he was pleased with it.

Then, when the record came out, we just started hearing from people. I'll never forget it. It was a very big moment for me when both Elvis Costello and Tom Waits called me to say how much they liked *Kiko* . . . they'd never done that before . . . and I don't think they've done it since [laughs]. But I felt like we had really accomplished something in the moment. After *Kiko*—for me, for David Hidalgo, Tchad, Louis Perez—it was like there was energy left over. That was when David played us some other four-track demos he'd made at home. The demos had so much atmosphere to them that we thought there was no reason to re-record them. Once again, we went to Lenny to see if we could get a little money to play with this stuff. So we went right to work on it. Fourteen days later we were done and begged Lenny to put it out. I thought we'd made a David Hidalgo–Louis Perez record. But then I got a call telling me that I was a member of the Latin Playboys and our record was going to be released. That was one of the best days of my life.

↖ Cher, 1998.
↑ Enya, 2005.
☉ k.d. lang, 1998.
← Faith Hill, 1992.

↑ Barenaked Ladies, 1998.
↗ Alanis Morissette, late-1990s.
Ⓒ Goo Goo Dolls, 1998.

TOM PETTY ON WILDFLOWERS

When I was in the Traveling Wilburys we were on Warner Bros. Records. So it was around that time that I got to know Mo Ostin and Lenny Waronker. I was always impressed with them because they were approachable and they were music people. Mo had a great knowledge of the arts and really knew how to nurture a creative environment. Lenny was a guy . . . I still call Lenny from time to time if, say, I'm putting out a single, just to see what he thinks. Warner Bros. was quite the opposite environment from where I was at the time [MCA].

I was at Mo Ostin's house soon after *Full Moon Fever* had been rejected by my label. George [Harrison], Jeff [Lynne], and I would have these little picking parties, sitting around playing songs. And George would often play "Free Fallin'." It was a new song then, he had the record, and he liked it. So, in the midst of working up the Wilburys, we went to Mo's house for dinner. George was very close with Mo and had been for years. He loved Mo. Always did. After dinner we sat with Lenny, Mo, and Mo's wife Evelyn, and we thought, "Let's get the guitars out and strum a bit."

So we got our acoustics out and started singing. I remember Evelyn saying, "Mo, you've got to sign these guys up—listen to their vocal blend!" And we were trying to do just that, sing and get a good blend going between us. Then George said, "Play Lenny and Mo 'Free Fallin'." So I play it. And Lenny says, "That is an amazing song." I came back with, "Well, my record company just rejected it."

Lenny says, "Well, I'll tell you what. I'll sign you to Warner Bros. right now. Now." And Mo says, "Yes, we'll sign you right this minute, if that's what you want to do."

I told them that I had a year left on my contract. And it might have been longer than that. They said, "Let's just do the deal anyway. We won't say anything about it. And, when your deal runs out, you're on Warners." And that's exactly what I did. I made a deal with them, didn't say anything about it to anybody, and the amazing thing was that it didn't leak until right near the end of the MCA contract.

I remember one meeting in particular when Lenny came to my house and listened to every single thing we'd recorded for *Wildflowers*. We had so much music. What he did, which was great, was that he convinced us not to make it a double album, or double CD. We had two hours of music. Lenny talked us into cutting it back. And he was absolutely right. He saw it as too long, just too long, saying that we were wasting our material because no one will get to focus on it. He felt that there was so much there that the listener will start to take it for granted after an hour. That made perfect sense to me.

The history of the label and its people meant something to me. There were so many Warner Bros. artists that I admired. But, really, the first one I remember coming across was the Everly Brothers. I had this album called *A Date with the Everly Brothers*. I bought that when I was probably twelve years old and thought it was *the shit*. An amazing record. I still love it. It was on Warner Bros. Records. And when I made *Wildflowers*, I used the same style logo, the same label, that was on the Everly Brothers. I have always connected with the Everlys. In fact, there was a point when one of my daughters was going to the same school as one of Phil Everly's children. This meant Phil and I were two parents in the parking lot. I got to meet him. And, to me, these guys weren't even human—they were just too good. So I couldn't wait to get to school every day!

Son Volt

R.E.M.

GREEN

Alanis
Morissette

JANE'S ADDICTION

BEEN CAUGHT STEALING

THE FLAMING LIPS
ZAIREEKA
featuring the song
"The Big Ol' Bug Is The New Baby Now"
S-46004 #1

4 Compact Discs

WARNING: This is a unique recording. These eight compositions are to be played using as many as four compact disc players, and have synchronized portions. This recording also contains frequencies not normally heard or perceived recordings and on rare occasion has caused the listener to become disoriented.

eric clapton unplugged

around the fur

shove it

FILTER FILTER

300

PARENTAL
ADVISORY
EXPLICIT CONTENT

SALE OR OTHER TRANSFER

ADONNA
Confessions on a dance floor

IM SANDLER
Stan and Judy's Kid

Featuring 17 new skits and songs, including:
The Chanukah Song Part II
7 Foot Man
The Peeper
The Psychotic Legend Of Uncle Donnie
S-47629 (#1)

CHER

josh groban

A NEW ORDER RELEASE
Republic©
The limited run.

LIMP

GREEN
DAY
presents
american
idiot

Rich

arenaked ladies

stunt

a film by
JIM JARMUSCH
DEAD MAN

WANTED

RED

PEPPERS
MAGIK

CHAPTER EIGHT

CARRYING IT FORWARD

WHILE THE MUSIC BUSINESS CONTINUES TO BE BATTERED, WARNER BROS. RECORDS HAS MANAGED TO STAY CLOSE TO THE PHILOSOPHY THAT EARNED THE COMPANY ITS REPUTATION: MAKE IT ABOUT THE MUSIC AND ALL ELSE WILL FOLLOW.

REMEMBERING THE MACHINE SHOP

Amidst the madness, before, during, and after Mo Ostin's departure, music was released and new acts were signed. The B-52s had major hits, Tom Petty released *Wildflowers*, Madonna, now heading her own Warner affiliate, Maverick, remained at the front of whatever was happening, Rick Rubin's Def American joined the powerful roster of Warner affiliates, Al B. Sure! scored hits, longtime Warner acts including Neil Young and Rod Stewart remained locked into very productive album cycles, R.E.M. renewed their contract with the label for the kind of money that made the whole game seem strange, the Red Hot Chili Peppers broke wide open, Green Day did the same, releasing *Dookie*, Alanis Morissette had massive success with *Jagged Little Pill*, the Goo Goo Dolls found their way into the mainstream with movie placements playing a crucial role, Faith Hill would crossover with little trace of Nashville in tow . . . there was too much momentum to lose touch with the sheer force of the label's history. And if behind the scenes instability reigned, Warner Bros. Records was certainly not the only label feeling the discomfort. **Russ Thyret:** "The way that music was marketed and deals were made changed so much in the last five years, ten years, that all companies were going to change, Warners included, whether Mo left or not." Hallway conversations about the state of the industry were constant, never approached conclusion, and, finally, got monotonous.

Jeff Gold: "It's definitely harder to be a record company. It's not a business I'd want to be in right now." But with more listeners than ever before, just what the response to the situation should be was far from obvious. **Lenny Waronker:** "Along with Rick Rubin, I recently did a question-and-answer thing in Palm Springs with the international A&R staff. It was mostly Warner Bros. Records from LA along with the international people. The amount of enthusiasm that I felt as we were talking about the label's past was so real. I did feel like they wanted to hang onto some of that tradition. They were very earnest about it. It's not like it's all good guy/bad guy and the story is over with. That's not the case. People love music. So what do you do? Go and work for a record company. Unfortunately, the environment is not as much fun as it was thirty years ago."

Most significant to the last decade of the label's history has been the period of relative restabilization under Tom Whalley's leadership. **Mo Ostin:** "Tom has worked at a number of labels but really came up through Warner Bros. He started in the mailroom. I see him as a very good record man, a real record man with an A&R backbone." Among Whalley's challenges was the need to show long-term artists that continuity underpinned the label. Eric Clapton, Neil Young, Rod Stewart, Tom Petty, Mark Knopfler, the Red Hot Chili Peppers: All were acts brought in under Mo and Lenny's watch. **Tom Biery:** "I think the real restabilizing came with Tom Whalley. People who are so negative on big record companies and so on, if they could be a fly on the wall to see what goes on today, they'd be shocked. Yes, clearly, we're a corporation and need to sell records. But at the same time we're selling records, one of the goals is to cultivate the art. It's not like we're sitting around going, 'Oh, geez, these guys aren't making us any money.' We've never had a conversation like that, not in the rooms I've been in."

THE ARTIST'S LOT

Much of what has allowed Warner Bros. to recover its balance, despite the industry backdrop, has to do with the artists themselves. **Diarmuid Quinn:** "Tom Petty sent me the last song he added to the Mudcrutch record, 'Bootleg Flyer,' and I called him about it. He asks me, 'What if I come in and play the stuff for the company?' Sure enough, not even a week later, Petty comes in. He's hanging out, meeting people and talking about what we're going to do and how

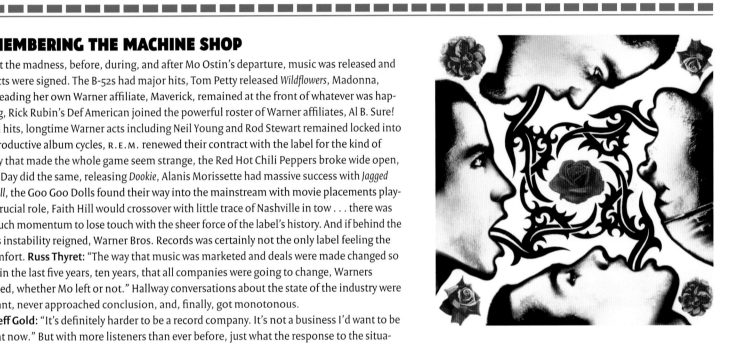

➍ Red Hot Chili Peppers, *Blood Sugar Sex Magik*, 1991. After moving over to Warner Bros. from EMI Records, the Chili Peppers would kick off a remarkable career run that continues to this day.

➍ Green Day, *American Idiot* era, 2005. With that album, their importance as an American rock & roll band would be confirmed *and* celebrated.

Opening spread: My Chemical Romance, *The Black Parade*, 2006.

we're going to market the Mudcrutch release. It was fantastic. I think that's sort of good for the soul, for him and *definitely* for us. It's a tougher road now, and it makes a huge difference when the artist participates. It's night and day. Artists participate, things happen. Direct cause and effect almost every time." With acts that are *looking* to break, active participation has become even more important. To remain aloof, as an artist, is less of an option than ever before. But, pointedly, Warners has made an effort to put together a stable of willing collaborators. **Tom Biery:** "The Disturbed fan base is hardcore. The band built serious loyalty among them. Touring. Touring, touring, touring and being so respectful of their fans. Last night at a benefit, Metallica did more meet-and-greets than most groups do in a month. I think this proactive approach is a thread through Metallica and Disturbed and My Chemical Romance and Linkin Park. Linkin Park does a fan club meet-and-greet every night. They care about their fans, and their fans know it."

Dave Stein: "To me, once an artist has recorded their music, they've done their job for us. But if they want to lend themselves to the process in a greater way, it's absolutely going to help. There is no doubt that in today's world, the more artists lend themselves to marketing, the greater the chance that the sales will be bigger and, as a result, their careers will be longer. And long careers have always been a Warner Bros. focus. I remember spending countless days on the road with the Goo Goo Dolls. They came in and did everything, met everybody, played anywhere. They were fantastic, and we started with them on Metal Blade Records, working Metal Blade into Warner Bros. Those guys knew how to not get in their own way. It made a difference."

A&R TODAY

In 1958, when Jim Conkling was named the first president of Warner Bros. Records, he carved out an area in which the label would focus: adult mainstream pop, with an emphasis on albums rather than singles. What saved Warner Bros. Records, eighteen months later, when Jack Warner was ready to bury the company in its own losses, was a new emphasis on roster diversity. Conkling made smart A&R decisions by signing a duo associated with rock & roll's young audience that charted pop, R&B, *and* country, the Everly Brothers, and Bob Newhart, a comedian. Those two acts brought the label enough stability to carry on. When in the singer-songwriter era Warner Bros. was launching superstars including James Taylor, Joni Mitchell, Neil Young, Van Morrison, and Gordon Lightfoot, they also brought in Deep Purple, Black Sabbath, Jethro Tull, and Alice Cooper. **Joe Smith:** "You had to have counterbalance. You had to cover everything. Reputation was one thing, our ability to make money and be respected as a record company was another. We had to be eclectic. And we had to be open to the next thing that came along." The diverse roster, as a practical strategy that has buoyed the company for decades, is another point of continuity at the label. **Craig Aaronson:** "You had that balance of Black Sabbath and Paul Simon. Now you've got Avenged Sevenfold and even Mastodon on one side, and on the other Josh Groban or Michael Bublé. Between them you can

find straightforward rock like Taking Back Sunday. We're active across the spectrum, looking for what's best in every area we can."

If any conspicuous difference marks the work of A&R then, in the years of Titelman, Waronker, Templeman, and others, and A&R now, it's the need to have A&R personnel of today follow their projects more aggressively from recording to release to the promotion and marketing. With the profusion of media outlets that exist and the increased competition for audience attention, it's no surprise that the A&R staff is no longer primarily made up of producers. **Craig Aaronson:** "I shepherd an artist through the company so the vision of who they are stays intact as the record is marketed. I stay very involved with everything, from the new media campaign to the marketing campaign, to when we go to radio and make videos. A&R is very much the main liaison between the business side and the creative side—but right in the middle of it all the time. It's not just about making the record and handing it over to the label. At least at this company." **Perry Watts-Russell:** "Tom Whalley has been adamant about his preference for A&R people who think comprehensively, who think like managers, who don't just make a record and hand it off to everybody else but come in and explain it to the company and to the individuals in the various departments . . . engage in a dialogue and present a vision."

If Whalley has used anything to restabilize Warner Bros. Records, it has been his effort to keep A&R at the center of everything and to follow through on Mo Ostin and Lenny Waronker's interest in empowering every department to share in that. **Dave Stein:** "Tom has kept that alive. Back then you could do it from any department in the building, and when I was still regional, you could do it from anywhere in the country. To give you an example: the BoDeans on Slash Records were strong in the Midwest, Chicago especially, which is where I was. They were the Beatles. It was unbelievable. I don't know what percentage of their records sold in Chicago, but it had to be extraordinarily high. Russ Thyret, Mo Ostin, and Lou Dennis gave us all the opportunity to not only maximize everything that was going on in that market for them but to spread the gospel throughout the company and throughout the country. You could jump on a conference call. Thyret and those guys never discouraged anybody from raving about whatever it was that had us excited. The word 'priority' was never used by these guys. I remember Tom Biery, in particular, being instrumental with The Flaming Lips, their song, 'She Don't Use Jelly,' taking that, from a band that was barely selling music at the time, getting a tremendous amount of critical review and year-end review, and then applying it to his market. All of the sudden 'Jelly' became a national record that came out of that our region."

Perry Watts-Russell: "Tom doesn't think that you have to be a senior person within the company to get behind something. If you have that level of passion and that level of vision and that level of commitment, he encourages people to identify that which excites them the

⬆ Linkin Park, *Hybrid Theory*, 2000. The band has sustained a long career in the face of remarkable flux, proving themselves a key act at Warner Bros.

⬆⬆ Green Day's monster record, *American Idiot*, 2005.

↖ *It's Time*, Michael Bublé, 2005. Harkening back to the era of Sinatra in which Warner/Reprise was born, Bublé found a wide audience.

most, and to then do something with it. He looks around him. As an example, I immediately believed that Damien Rice was a bona fide artist, the caliber of a Van Morrison or a Thom Yorke, and so immediately set about trying to bring him to the label. Tom asked me if I believed that on Damien's album there were big radio songs, songs that would cross formats at radio. My response was, 'No, I don't believe there are. I just believe that this is an amazing album.' But I said to Tom, 'If my impression of what you want to do with Warner Bros. is correct, then you want to be working with artists that people at this label are proud to work with. And I guarantee you that if we are able to work with Damien Rice, and a year from now you are to ask people at Warner Bros. who their favorite artists are, that the majority of them will include Damien as one of their favorite artists.' Tom said, 'Great, let's do the deal.' He actually came to me a few months after we'd done it and said, 'Well, it didn't take a year, did it? Everyone here is in love with Damien Rice.' So to me, that was a demonstration that Tom Whalley was responding to me and also to everyone else within the building."

365 DEALS

Dave Stein: "Regarding what are called—and I hate the name—360 degree deals, there's certainly a healthy dose of suspicion on the artist's side of things, which we all understand." In the name of survival, many record companies, Warner Bros. included, are beginning to locate the areas in which they can work with their artists to make the money that will cover their costs. If records aren't selling as they once were, merchandise is, tickets are. While there are those who remain skeptical, others, The Flaming Lips and Eric Clapton included, have found ways to expand the label's services. Gone are the days when Carl Scott and Bob Regehr used company money to support artists' tours and asked for nothing in return. At the time, they didn't need to, they'd get it back in sales. **Perry Watts-Russell:** "As Tom [Whalley] said, who on earth came up with the concept of, 'We're going to pour hundreds of thousands of dollars into your touring, we'll cover all the loss, and as soon as you start to make profits from your touring, we won't get any of it'? What genius came up with that business plan?" He actually went by two names, Carl Scott and Bob Regehr. But when they did it, it made sense. No more.

Perry Watts-Russell: "I've bought into Tom's philosophy. I point out to artists that 360 deals have been in operation ever since the industry started. Go back to Elvis Presley, for instance. What I mean by that is that managers sign 360 deals with their artists all the time— a manager gets a percentage of every single revenue stream generated by that artist, the argument being that the manager is overseeing the entire career. These deals will allow us to *develop* and follow artists in much the way it was once done with a Neil Young or an Eric Clapton or a Tom Petty. I have artists such as Matthew Bellamy from Muse and Damien Rice and Alex from the Arctic Monkeys—and one could hope that twenty years from now they would still be on Warner Bros., or if their bands have broken up they'll have solo careers. But these are the kinds of artists one wants to be engaged with over a long period. That's the aim."

Diarmuid Quinn: "You know all these 360 deals everybody's talking about? We like to call them 365 deals, because we'll work on your band 365 days a year. We don't just do it on an album cycle anymore. We do retail, e-commerce like crazy . . . we're just doing a lot more, building the brand and actually participating in the success of the brand on more levels than ever before."

✦ Muse stands as a great contemporary example of a band that built its career over time, refining its sound, exploring the sonic possibilities, and growing its audience. With Muse and others, the tradition of the long career carries on at Warner Bros. Records.

↗ Damien Rice, 2007. Working in the tradition of the singer-songwriters who helped put Warner Bros. Records on the map, Rice found a way to build a career through quality material, song placement in movies and television, and the sheer force of charismatic delivery.

STORIES WE COULD TELL

Lou Dennis: "I'm prejudiced, of course, but I think some of the best people ever in the music business were the ones who had the opportunity to work at Warner/Reprise."

Eddie Rosenblatt: "Anybody who could work with these people through that time was among the most fortunate ever in the music business. It was a great business."

Tom Biery: "It's an artist's label. Jack White came in and played us the White Stripes record. I mean the whole company. Not just senior executives or something. Everybody. They're all taking a cue from the master, Neil Young. Neil always comes in and delivers his record and plays it for the people who will bring it into the world."

Carl Scott: "I worked k.d. lang. Everybody laughed at her. Here's this big dyke wearing strange dresses, wearing cutoff cowboy boots. Nobody really got it except Seymour Stein and Carl Scott. And I just hammered. I believed in her. She was my child. And if it hadn't been for Seymour giving me some freedom, Mo allowing it to happen, and k.d. going along with it, she might never have happened. An amazing singer, and she never compromised herself. She could have been Celine Dion, but she would have had to compromise. I was willing to take her anywhere she wanted to go, because I believed in her—and that was what was going on at Warner Bros. through Madonna, through Van Halen, all the way back to fucking Peter, Paul & Mary. People believed in the music and the artist."

Adam Somers: "As far as the entertainment industry is concerned, it was probably the coolest ride that any group of people ever had."

David Berman: "We had so many great characters—Bob Krasnow, Seymour Stein, Bob Regehr . . . we truly had characters."

Jeff Gold: "I always thought that all things being equal, we had a competitive advantage because a kid could say, 'Hey, mom, I signed to Warner Bros., the label that has Frank Sinatra and Jimi Hendrix.' Rather than, 'Hey, mom, I signed to DGC, which is a division of Geffen records which is owned by David Geffen, who's . . .'"

Diarmuid Quinn: "This was the place I always wanted to work—because of the sort of legacy that Mo and Lenny laid down, that it was about artists and about art. Mo is the gold standard. He had the perfect balance of art and commerce."

Bob Merlis: "Obviously, Warner Bros. was a big, corporate record company, but it wasn't like . . . it had nothing in common with RCA, where I worked for a short period. When I was at RCA, I thought, 'I can't believe they ever have hits at this company.' It wasn't like Warner Bros, where everybody was on the inside of the thing, whatever it was. We knew we were at the best place. We always knew it. It was clear."

Dave Stein: "One thing that's consistent from the time that Mo was here to the present is that the job starts at signing great artists who are making great music. I would also say that we always took a great deal of pride in taking square pegs and putting them in round holes. I don't think anybody ever thought when they listened to Dire Straits' 'Sultans of Swing' that that was going to be a Top Forty record. But it became one. We had a lot of success in that time and took a lot of pride in—whether it was Laurie Anderson or whoever—going and getting it to the mainstream, breaking down those gatekeepers."

Craig Aaronson: "I saw My Chemical Romance play Madison Square Garden, headlining in front of fifteen thousand people. To be able to see that band, the same band I saw five years ago playing a small club in New York City for eighty people—there's something so powerful in that."

Liz Rosenberg: "It was the most beautiful thing. We were in this brownstone in New York for years, and no one wanted to leave work. No one wanted to go home. I remember all of us going out together, seeing an act and being thrilled . . . when we saw Rickie Lee Jones in the Village, and we just knew we were watching history. We knew we'd never forget that moment. Or the Sex Pistols, when they came into the office. Everyday was like that. It was stunning. I am so blessed to have been a part of that for so many years."

Russ Thyret: "I love this company, and I love everything that it has represented."

Mo Ostin: "This is the case of a company that really evolved and became, as far as I'm concerned, as good a company as there ever was in the history of the record business. And a lot of it was attributable to the fact that we had this incredible corporate support during the [Steve] Ross years, with minimal corporate interference. We were allowed to be entrepreneurial and take risks, and, because of this, we were able to empower our executives. Philosophically, we stayed close to our basic belief: that music was our highest priority, that we had to be an artist-oriented company, that whenever there was any conflict between art and commerce, the artist should prevail."

Howie Klein: "Can people still learn from it? I think it's the only way that a record company will ever be successful. I don't think it's possible for a record company to be successful any other way. I could be wrong. But someone would have to prove me wrong."

✦ Where it all began: the Warner Bros. Motion picture lot in Burbank under construction, 1930s.

The Flaming Lips, Steven Drozd, Wayne Coyne, Michael Ivins.

WAYNE COYNE ON THE SOFT BULLETIN

When we did *The Soft Bulletin*, there was some idea that this might be our last record. We go through these things every ten years or so where we think, "You know, I'm not sure that people really give a shit about what we're doing—and since no one really cares, why don't we just do what we like?" There is such an unplanned freedom to that. If people are paying attention, it can change the way you view your own creations. I think we were lucky to have placed ourselves in that void. So, *The Soft Bulletin* was really the combination of the songs we were writing, the sound that we were going for, and the mood we were in, based on the feeling that since there was no audience left for us anyway we may as well fucking become a new band or become a different band or just re-create ourselves however we please—because frankly no one gave a shit anyway.

Up to *The Soft Bulletin* we played like a standard—well, not *standard*, but standard enough—rock band. Then, suddenly, there were no rules anymore. We weren't playing at the same time, as a band, in the studio. We'd start with something as simple as a piano chord and build upon the mood of it. Steven [Drozd] played almost everything on this record. Michael [Ivins] plays some bass, and I play some guitar, but I mostly became a producer. The band became producers, working with this strange new group The Flaming Lips.

We started doing stuff that felt more like orchestration, using pianos and harmony vocals and just big, lush, emotional arrangements. We moved in that direction for a couple of years. Luckily for us, it came together at the right time. We wanted to write songs that weren't just a platform to say a bunch of freaky shit. These new songs—and the approach—were about something true, something internal about our own experiences.

Then we got lucky. Steven had the song "Race for the Prize," and I was able to put some lyrics to it. We started feeling like this could really be something. There was this emerging idea of humanity reaching. I had come up with "A Spoonful Weighs a Ton." The mood was futuristic, about death, about some epic realization that there was a little thing inside people that was a giant thing—weird ideas that, in the context of music, made us feel we could be utterly unrestricted. We had a sense that we could be dramatic, vulnerable, all these things. I didn't know if this was going to be a good thing for us, but as we made the record we realized that this was the kind of music we'd been longing to do.

With *Zaireeka*, which came out as four separate CDs meant to be played at the same time, we were asking a lot of the label. But our aim wasn't to pull a Lou

Reed *Metal Machine Music* on them. We really wanted to do that experimental type of record—and it wasn't necessarily saying fuck you to the commercial potential of The Flaming Lips. We thought it could be a part of what we do. The biggest dilemma for Warner Bros. would have been if it cost a half a million dollars to make it. But even by today's standards, we were making these recordings on small budgets. The money wasn't going for swimming pools and Cadillacs. The label knew they wouldn't be able to sell these records, but the idea was that if we didn't spend a lot of money, who cares? So often people think a major label is the enemy of the artistic approach I describe, but that hasn't been the case for us. And we've been on Warner Bros. since 1990. Almost twenty years. Of course, we never demanded that they give us a million dollars and put us on the cover of *Rolling Stone*. Our approach with the label has been this: "If you help us, we'll try to make some interesting, unique music. We're The Flaming Lips, we're from Oklahoma, and we'll do the best we can."

When we started to use computers on *The Soft Bulletin*, that was a big change from, say, even 1996. In a few short years we suddenly had a way to use this dense orchestration that would have been a much greater challenge just a few years earlier. We never knew that Steven was capable of, say, musical counterpoint and all that sort of bullshit that lends the arrangements an authenticity and emotion, but he really came to the fore at this time. The band was listening to John Coltrane—which we hadn't been able to wrap our brains around before—and Mahler, Stravinsky, things that seemed too abstract up to that point. At the same time we were listening to Aphex Twin, Fatboy Slim, more deejay-based things that were also new to us.

I remember playing early stuff from *The Soft Bulletin* for people and them going, "Gee, I don't know what you fellas are on about here." That reaction made us all the more interested in making it work. We all felt that way. It was a football-coach-at-halftime moment, with us really seeing that we wanted to follow this through. And, then, it was strange because a couple months after that it seemed like—I know it's silly to think these things are real—a zeitgeist shift took place, with people wanting something new out of rock. Something was happening *out there* that connected with what we were doing. It was the greatest thing when a year after that record had come out people viewed it as a classic album. But at the time of making *The Soft Bulletin*, it really felt like we were heading off to the gallows to hang ourselves.

↑ Red Hot Chili Peppers, 2006.
© Tegan and Sara, 2007.

JOSH GROBAN ON CLOSER AND THE WARNER BROS. LEGACY

I think the legacy Mo Ostin left behind is still the spirit of Warner Bros. Records. Even though things are tighter, the way of getting music out there has changed, the game is, as any executive or artist will tell you, in a growing pain kind of mode right now, the concept of artist development is alive and well at Warner Bros. Records. The label is still interested in building a career rather than building an immediate hit. My career is one example of that. The label appreciated what I had to offer, left me alone in the studio from day one, and when David Foster and I handed them the first product their response was—and this was when Phil Quartararo was there, and it holds for Tom Whalley: "This is not something that's necessarily 'in the box' for us, so to speak, but we think you're a unique artist, and we're going to find unique ways to promote you and build your career." From an artist standpoint, I can't tell you how much I appreciate that.

Over the course of my three or four albums I've learned a lot. For me, given where I was at when I got signed, the first learning curve came in making that debut album. Going into *Closer*, that's when I started developing my songwriting, that's when I started to spread out my sound a bit more. I realized I'd made the right steps with the first one, in kind of saying, "Hi, it's nice to meet you," but I hadn't done as much as I felt was possible in showing people the other side.

As a performer in a genre in which artists are always being clumped in with each other, I saw that with *Closer* I needed to show what was unique, to show the exploration—not just the beauty of sound and the singing. *Closer* was the first step in taking my fans to that new place. We took it even further with *Awake*, bringing in Herbie Hancock and Ladysmith Black Mambazo, bringing more of a World element into it.

With *Closer* David [Foster] and I certainly wanted to start where the last album had left off, wanted to continue to establish this sound that we had come up with on the first album—but it was very important to avoid the sophomore slump by showing something more. We didn't want it to just be, "Here are some of your favorite songs and here's a pretty voice and isn't that nice?" As I said, my own personal goal was that it had to include some songwriting of my own. And, of course, it's always nice when a song like "You Raise Me Up" lands on your doorstep. It was a combination of great A&R, finding great songs, not biting the hand that feeds you as far as your style goes, but recognizing that it's the artist's job to guide the fans, not the other way around.

Whenever you're the guy selling alone in the wilderness [Groban's last CD went four times platinum], the people who don't like your music are going to say, "See how horrible the music industry is? He's selling!" And the people who love you are saying, "See, good music can still sell!" You're either getting tomatoes thrown at you or you're being put on an even higher pedestal. So, it's somewhere in-between. I'm just happy that my fans are still buying records. But even in a climate of diminishing sales, what labels can do for artists—and Warner Bros. has done this for me—is invest in the long-term goal. Maybe it's not the first album, maybe it's not the first or second or third single. It's the development. That's how artists like Elton John and Madonna become what they are. Patience and guidance: that's what a company can give to an artist.

↑ Avenged Sevenfold, 2007.
↑→ Serge Tankian, 2007.
→ The Raconteurs, 2008.
© Taking Back Sunday, 2008.

MIKE SHINODA ON LINKIN PARK

In 1997 and 1998, Linkin Park showcased for every label in Los Angeles, more than once. All the big-name A&R guys heard us play and never called us back. We wound up on Warner Bros. by sneaking in through the back door. Someone the band knew and had been working with, had gotten a job in the Warner Bros. A&R office and sort of took us with him.

One of the first things that we did once we signed with Warner Bros. was to put out an e-mail saying that the band would be holding a meeting with the label's staff to introduce ourselves. We put the e-mail out to everyone at Warner Bros. The whole place was invited to come to this meeting. A lot of people at the label were intrigued by the invite. It wasn't something they got regularly from new acts that Warner Bros. had signed, especially an act that had only been signed for a week or two. So, on the day of the meeting, a lot of people showed up. If nothing else, they were curious about who we were and what was planned to happen at this meeting.

Once everyone was in the room, myself and the rest of the band pulled out all these charts and graphs snd outlines that explained to Warner Bros. the way in which we wanted to be treated and the way we wanted our fans to be treated. We also outlined a marketing plan and suggested ways the company might handle the marketing of our music. People from the marketing and promotions department were speechless. They had never seen such audacity. They had

never seen a brand-new act come to Warner Bros. and tell them how to do their jobs. And you know what? It was a crazy, audacious thing to do, but it got the message across. Linkin Park was intensely serious about its music, its fans, and its future at Warner Bros. We had done our homework, and we weren't kidding. That meeting became one of those events at Warner Bros. that people there have forever linked to the band and still talk about.

We would never have been able to do such a thing at any other record company. Things like this don't happen in the world of record companies. But Warner Bros. was an "artist-first" company. It's always been that kind of label. So we figured that the people there would take us seriously if we took ourselves seriously. We did, and after that meeting, they did.

Things were done with the band and with our fan club and street teams that had never been done before. For instance, we told Warner Bros. that we wanted to flood the street with cassette samplers of our music. This was 1999 and even though cassettes were definitely on their way out, our fans expected this of us. Music on the Internet was just beginning to happen; we didn't feel we could rely on it as a way of getting our music to our fans. So we put out massive amounts of cassette samplers. Warner Bros. didn't quite get what we were doing, but they trusted our judgment. That was the beginning of a great artist–record company relationship.

↖ Daniel Powter, 2005.
↑ Regina Spektor, 2007.
⊙ Deftones, mid-2000s.

GERARD WAY ON MY CHEMICAL ROMANCE

The first time we actually met Tom Whalley we had gotten this big break playing a gig opening up for Sparta at this place called Stingray's or something, in our home state. Then, literally an hour or two hours before we're supposed to go on, the pipes burst. All of the sudden, there are fire trucks pulling up. They had to evacuate the club, letting everyone know there wasn't going to be a show. And we knew Craig Aaronson from Warner Bros. A&R had come to see us. The label was courting us at the time.

This black sedan pulls up, and Craig is like, "Tom Whalley is here, came to see you guys tonight. Do you guys want to just go get something to eat?" We were like, "Wow, that's pretty cool, he came up to see us." So we said, "Sure, let's go to IHOP."

I think one of the things that Tom really liked about us is that we weren't interested in being wined and dined and having money thrown at us. We were very basic, simple guys, just liked playing. And, really, we were still at the point where we weren't even sure we needed a major label. We liked doing things on our own. But we were talking to them because we had finally started to feel like, maybe, we were ready. It was increasingly difficult for people to get our CDs because of the distribution factor.

So we're sitting at this IHOP with Tom in New Jersey, and it's pretty surreal. I don't know the last time Tom was in an IHOP. I could've guessed, though. We're talking about Primus and Tupac and Poison, all these artists he signed, and we're sitting there eating with him, and he says to us, "With all the artists that have ever really worked with me, it was a partnership. It wasn't anybody working for anybody—you don't work for the label and you don't do what we say. You do your thing, and we help make it happen." And we really got a sense for that right away.

But we met with Stacy Fass, our lawyer—and, at the time, it was basically me and Stacy taking all these phone calls from labels because the band had no management yet—and her amazing advice was this: "You guys are a band. Go be a band. You don't need this stuff right now." And that's exactly what we did. We turned down all the labels. We said, "If you still want us when we're ready, that's great, but right now, we're not ready. We're going to go be a band. We're going to go do this ourselves, see the world, get our own fans, sell our own t-shirts and CDs. We're going to do it all ourselves. This band is not ready for you—we just want to be really good."

We really did wait. I think it was over a year before we decided to take some flights out and meet some people. And in the end, I think we were always going to go with Warner Bros. I think there is such a confidence, not just in Tom or in Craig, but in the label itself. Each individual that we were about to work with was some kind of star. That's what it felt like. Like Brian Bumbery, our publicist—it felt like he was the best. Phil in radio—he was the best. Everybody was a perfect match for us. I don't know how they worked for other bands, but they were a perfect match for this band.

Jack and Meg White, The White Stripes, 2007.

TOM WHALLEY ON RECENT SIGNINGS AND LINKS TO THE FUTURE

We heard about this band in suburban New Jersey called My Chemical Romance, so Craig Aaronson of the A&R department and I went to see them. They were quite different from the bands I'd normally go after, but image-wise they were unique. They were coming out of this pop-punk, Warped Tour scene, but with an interesting, darker sensibility. From what I could tell, the sound of My Chemical Romance was something like pop-punk meets goth meets emo, which is a very interesting musical combination, to say the least.

At the time there were articles in the music press being written about how rock was dead or dying. But I had been seeing elements of an underground rock scene that was incredibly healthy and selling reasonable amounts of records. My strategy was to search out the best unsigned bands in this underground environment and turn them into arena bands. At least that was the goal.

My Chemical Romance was playing in an underage club that some parents had opened so that their daughter had a safe place to go on weekends. It was a rock club for kids where soda was served, very unglamorous for the type of band that My Chemical Romance is. So Craig and I watched the group with these young kids in the audience, all of whom went crazy for them.

Later that night we took members of the band to a New Jersey diner, staying until early in the morning, all the time trying to convince the band to sign with Warners. A few weeks later we brought My Chemical Romance to LA for further discussions, but now had competition from Interscope and a couple of other labels who had since heard about the band. I really wanted to sign My Chemical Romance, not just because they were a good band but because they were really young, and I still wanted to believe that, with time, you could let a talented band develop and grow into a creative force that would net great results—just like it used to happen in the past. Basically, my pitch to them was that they'd have to trust me and Warner Bros.' history in developing artists' careers. I had a vision for

the band and they had to believe me and the label to make it real. Ultimately, they signed with us.

The funny thing is that I'd thought it would take a few years for My Chemical Romance to develop. That obviously wasn't the case. They cut a demo before making their first album and played it to Craig, who got very excited about the songs. Craig played it for me and I felt the same way. We both thought the right thing to do was to get a top-line producer with a full budget and accelerate our plans with the band, which is what we did. As a result, My Chemical Romance cut this amazing debut record, which went platinum. There wasn't a whole lot of development going on in their case, which is sometimes the way it goes.

Jack White and the White Stripes was a case of a band being not only fully developed but at the top of their game when they became available to sign. Jack had this reputation of being an independent creative force who made great records but did things his way. The recordings the White Stripes had made were popular both with the difficult-to-please indie rock fans who loved the authenticity of what the band was all about *and* mainstream rock audiences.

Due to the death of the indie label that they had been with, the White Stripes were looking to sign to another label. Of course a lot of them were very interested. I immediately reached out to Jack White's management to set up a meeting, but we never could get it scheduled. Then one day out of the blue I got a call saying that Jack was available to talk if I could get to San Francisco. So very quickly, Craig Aaronson and I got on a plane out of LA and went to San Francisco to meet Jack for lunch. On the trip, I got sick on the plane—not the way you want to go into a meeting with an artist you think very highly of, who you believe ought to be on the Warner Bros. roster. I struggled to the restaurant where we were to have lunch. During our conversation, I had to get up and go to the restroom or step outside for some fresh air. I was miserable, but I tried to do everything I could to keep my poise and my stomach from just exploding because I knew this was my only chance of convincing Jack White that Warners was the right label for him. At the time I knew we were competing with Jimmy Iovine and other important names in the music business, and here I was completely out of it, figuring I didn't have a chance.

I tried to make some small talk at the table, hoping that I'd suddenly feel better and then be able to get down to the business of convincing Jack to sign with us. In the conversation, Jack remarked that he had come from a family of ten kids and had been raised Catholic. I told him that I had nine children. And that was it—we clicked. Suddenly there was a bridge between us that allowed us to connect, not on a professional level—at least not yet—but on a personal level. And with an artist like Jack, I think that's quite important to him.

For Jack, it was all about trust. He wanted to know that he could put his career into someone's hands and feel completely at ease with it. He wanted to be certain that he wasn't going to be forced to do things, musically, that he didn't want to do. That was easy for me to agree to because that was what Warner Bros. was always all about.

Despite hitting it off at lunch, I really didn't know what Jack's decision would be. I knew he'd make it when things felt right for him. I didn't meet with him again, nor did we have any future dialogue with him or his management. Finally, we heard that Jack wanted to be with Warner Bros. In the end, for Jack, it was mostly about the historical culture of Warner Bros. that traditionally gave artists all the room they needed to fulfill their musical visions. I think he saw me as the keeper of that culture. Because of who Jack White was—essentially a musician with a deep knowledge of American music history as well as someone with a great clarity of vision regarding the music he wanted to make—I came away from the White Stripes' signing with the sense that, above all other signings, this was the one in which I was able to link Warner Bros.' past with its present and future.

ACKNOWLEDGMENTS

From its conception to its realization, *Revolutions in Sound* has been a rigorously collaborative effort. Due to the nature of the Warner Bros. Records story, a story best captured through a multiplicity of viewpoints, the project called upon a multitude. Only a few of the many were involved in this project for the duration; others came in when the project needed their muscle. It was a bit like a barn raising. On behalf of everyone involved in *Revolutions in Sound*, I want to thank the artists themselves, many of whom gave their time to help tell the story. They are the story.

THE CREW: Steven Baker, A&R; Jeri Heiden, Ryan Corey, Art Direction and Design; Peter Fletcher, Project Manager; Warren Zanes, Author; John Heiden, Visual Research and Production; Julie Brunnick, Archivist; Jason Ware, Robert Mollet, Photography; Joyce Fletcher, Photo Clearance; Robert Santelli, Sidebar Contributions.

AT WARNER BROS. RECORDS: Tom Whalley, Diarmuid Quinn, Emio Zizza, Betsy Brown, Ellen Wakayama, Francesca Del Regno, Brigette Boyle, Greg Vineyard, Kathy Malloy, Charlie Springer, Liz Rosenberg, Tom Osborn, and Marcia Edelstein.

AT CHRONICLE BOOKS: Christine Carswell, Jay Schaefer, Brianna Smith, Jake Gardner, Jane Chinn, Laurel Leigh, Ken DellaPenta, and Dean Burrell.

SPECIAL ACKNOWLEDGMENTS: Jeff Ayeroff, Bob Merlis, Chris Steffen, Greg Geller, Don Fleming, Geoffrey Weiss, Lucian Zanes, Piero Zanes, Elinor Blake, Kendra Finn, and Finn Corey.

And, of course, thanks to Mo.

—Warren Zanes

PHOTO CREDITS

Richard E. Aaron – Bootsy Collins (p153)
Robert Alford – ZZ Top (p172)
© 1978 Ted Allan/mptv.net – Frank Sinatra (p53, 61)
Chris Anthony – My Chemical Romance (p216-217)
Martyn Atkins – Tom Petty and Rick Rubin (p213)
© 1978 Sid Avery/mptv.net – Allan Sherman (p38)
Chapman Baehler – Hot Hot Heat (p232)
Stephen Berkman – The Raconteurs (p228)
Andrea Bernstein – Nicolette Larson (p143)
Frank Bez – Little Feat (p104), Ry Cooder (p91)
Jay Blakesburg – Barenaked Ladies (p212)
Eric Blum – Devo (p160)
Kendall Bright – Sammy Davis, Jr. (p65)
Don Bronstein – Bob Newhart (p34)
Ed Caraeff – Tony Iommi (p106), Marc Bolan/T. Rex (p144)
© Andrew Catlin/www.andrewcatlin.com – New Order (p187)
Gavin Cochrane – Pretenders (p187)
© Anton Corbijn – Depeche Mode (p202), R.E.M. (p206)
© CSP Images – John Sebastian (p112)
Autumn DeWilde – Tegan And Sara (p226), The White Stripes (p234)
Henry Diltz – America (p114), Chris Isaak (p190), James Taylor (p89),
      Neil Young (p123)
Larry Dupont – Sparks (p141)
Nick Elgar – Paul Simon (p173)
Arthur Elgort – Steve Winwood (p149)
Glen Erler – k.d. lang (p211)
Kevin Estrada – Taking Back Sunday (p228)
Jonathan Exley – Dr. Demento (p98)
Perry Farrell – Jane's Addiction (p196-197)
© Barry Feinstein – Peter Paul & Mary (p30-31, 46), Gordon Lightfoot (p92)
Simon Fowler – Enya (p211)
Robbie Fry – Damien Rice (p222)
© Peter Gabriel Ltd. – Peter Gabriel (p176)
Elizabeth George – Little Feat (149)
Getty Images/Time & Life Pictures/Burton Berinsky – Atlantic Executives (p85)
Getty Images/Tom Copi – George Benson (p156)
Getty Images/David Corio – Ice-T (p208)
Getty Images/Richard Creamer – Sex Pistols (p159)
Getty Images/Michael Dobo – Emmylou Harris (p142)
Getty Images/Hulton Archive – Arlo Guthrie (p112), Roxy Music (p136), Jethro Tull (p134),
Getty Images/Metronome – Buddy Cole (p27)
Getty Images/Michael Ochs Archives – Allan Sherman (p47), Allman Brothers (p111), Badfinger (p105),
      The Beau Brummels (p77), David Byrne (p158), Deep Purple (p104),
      De La Soul (p170), Doobie Bros., Jimi Hendrix (p94), Ian Anderson (p104), Spike Jones (p35),
      The Kinks (p70), Jim Kweskin (p78), Van Dyke Parks (p112), Ramones (p159),
      Roxy Music/Bryan Ferry (p191), Rufus & Chaka Khan (p149), The Rutles (p160), Sandie Shaw (p66),
      Soft Cell (p168), Gary Wright (p154)
Getty Images/Terry O'Neill – Eric Clapton (p192), Elvis Costello (p189)
Getty Images/Time & Life Pictures/Alan Pappe – WEA Executives (p127)
Getty Images/Hulton Archive/Platt Collection – Neil Young (p122)
Getty Images/Time & Life Pictures/Ted Streshinsky – Tom Lehrer (p41)
Elliot Gilbert/Vistalux – Leo Sayer (p154)
Melodie Gimple – Mo Ostin and Lenny Waronker (p167)
David Goldman/www.davidgoldmanphoto.com – The Flaming Lips (p225)
© Lynn Goldsmith – B-52's (p164-165)
Don Graham – Tom Donahue (p57)
Dave Griffith – Alice Cooper (p124-125)
Michael Halsband/Landov – Rickie Lee Jones (p157)
James Hamilton – Donald Fagen (p187)
Mark Hanauer – Quincy Jones (p209), Sir Mix-A-Lot (p209)
Gary Heery – Paul Simon (p193)
Jeri Heiden – Howard Washington (p199)
Olaf Heine – Michael Bublé (p221), Josh Groban (p227)
Robin Hood – Randy Travis (p194)
Ellen Johnson – Stan Cornyn (p100)
Lloyd Johnson Photo – Norman Greenbaum (p111)
Dennis Keeley – Los Lobos (p210)
Gene Kornman – The Everly Brothers (p32)
Kristine Larsen – Naughty By Nature (p209)
© Laspata/DeCaro – Faith Hill (p211)
Michael Lavine – Cher (p211)
Joey Lawrence – Disturbed (p220)
Michele Laurita – Alanis Morissette (p212)
Jonathan Lennard – a-ha (p190)
Gary Leonard – The Blasters (p169)
© 1969 Linda Enterprises Ltd. Photographer: Linda McCartney – Jimi Hendrix Experience (p95)
Pamela Littky – Armor For Sleep (p232)
Wendy Lynch – Rilo Kiley (p232)
Clay Patrick McBride – Avenged Sevenfold (p228)
Philippe McClelland – Seal (p202)
Daragh McDonagh – Serj Tankian (p229)
Michael Maggid – Doobie Bros. (p105)

GERED MANKOWITZ copyright: BOWSTIR Ltd. 2008/mankowitz.com – Electric Prunes (p78)
Jim Marshall – The Grateful Dead (p93), Jimi Hendrix (p80-81)
Steven Meisel – Madonna (p179)
J. Michelle Martin-Coyne – The Flaming Lips (p224)
James Minchin III – Linkin Park (p221, 230)
Peter Darley Miller – Dwight Yoakam (p174)
Keith Morris – Richard Thompson (p110)
Deano Mueller – Al B. Sure! (p209)
Eva Mueller – Green Day (p218)
Michael Muller – Red Hot Chili Peppers (p226)
© Michael Muller/CORBIS – Deftones (p231)
Peter Nash – Quincy Jones (p169)
Melanie Nissen – The Goo Goo Dolls (p212)
Victoria Pearson – John Anderson (p195), k.d. lang (p195)
Harri Peccinotti – Steeleye Span (p110)
Perou – HIM (p232), Muse (p222)
Adria Petty & Christopher Frederick – Regina Spektor (p231)
Roger Prigent – Alice Cooper (p102)
Chuck Pulin – Randy Newman (p116)
Ken Regan/Camera5 – Fleetwood Mac (p144)
Herb Ritts – Don Henley (p192)
© Mick Rock 1977, 2008/www.mickrock.com – Talking Heads (p158)
Josh Rothstein – Daniel Powter (p231)
Todd Rundgren/James Lowe – Todd Rundgren (p140)
Mike Salisbury – Graham Central Station (p154)
Carl Samrock – Bob Seger (p143)
Courtesy Ed Sanders – The Fugs (p98)
John Scarpati – Jane's Addiction (p205)
Bonnie Schiffman – Dwight Yoakam (p195)
Robert Sebree – Tom Petty (p201)
© Norman Seeff 1977 – Steve Martin (p161)
Jim Shea – Hank Williams Jr. (p195)
© Kishin Shinoyama/Pacific Press Service – John Lennon and Yoko Ono (p192)
David Shore – Dean Martin (p64)
Jon Sievert – Youngbloods (p104)
David Steen – Rod Stewart (p155)
Phil Stern/CPi Syndication – Frank Sinatra (p50-51), Rat Pack (p60), Dean Martin (p64),
      Mo Ostin and Frank Sinatra (p54)
Yael Swerdlow – Mo Ostin's last day (p204)
© 1978 Ed Thrasher/mptv.net – The Association (p92), The Beau Brummels (p58), Petula Clark (p66),
      James Conkling (p17), Alice Cooper/School's Out Panty Party (p139), Sammy Davis Jr. (p65),
      Jimmy Durante (p41), Everly Brothers (p42), Harpers Bizarre (p59), Randy Newman (p91),
      Randy Newman and Lenny Waronker (p58), The Pentangle (p110),
      Kenny Rogers and the First Edition (p92), Frank Sinatra (p63), Nancy Sinatra (p62),
      Frank and Nancy Sinatra (p61), Don Rickles (p161), Lenny Waronker (p76), Mason Williams (p112)
Alberto Tolot – George Harrison (p192), Traveling Wilburys (p173)
© 1978 Gene Trindl/mptv.net – Allan Sherman and Warner Bros. executives (p40)
Pete Turner – Alice Cooper (p136)
Gus Van Sant – Red Hot Chili Peppers (p207)
Ben Watts/Kramer+Kramer – Naughty By Nature (p170)
Sherman Weisburd – Tiny Tim™ (p97)
George Whiteman – Flo & Eddie (p141)
Ginny Winn – Captain Beefheart (p141), Maria Muldaur (p143), Gram Parsons (p142),
      Bonnie Raitt (p143), Seals & Crofts (p114)
Neil Zlozower – Van Halen (p185)

COURTESY OF THE WARNER BROS. RECORDS ARCHIVES:

Beach Boys (p103), Tim Buckley (p102), Cheech & Chong (p161), Petula Clark and Tony Hatch (p68), George Clinton (p153), Bootsy Collins (p126), Alice Cooper's Debutante Ball (p128), Stan Cornyn (p101), The Dead Boys (p133), Deep Purple (p134), Dire Straits (p180), Earth Wind & Fire (p145), Faces (p145), Family (p97), Fleetwood Mac (p105), Gang Of Four (p175), The Grateful Dead with Joe Smith (p74-75), George Greeley (p26), Chico Hamilton (p26), Herbie Hancock, (p118), Harpers Bizarre (p79), Jimi Hendrix (p82, 84), The Kinks (p56, 71), Bob Krasnow (p67), Rod McKuen (p92), Bob Luman (p41), Mike Maitland (p36), The Mary Kaye Trio (p27), Dean Martin, Mo Ostin, Frank Sinatra and Sammy Davis Jr. (p60), The Meters (p136), The Music Man (p43), Napolean XIV (p78), Randy Newman, Lenny Waronker, Bob Regehr and Bob Merlis (p117), Evelyn Ostin (p200), Mo Ostin (p25, 135), Marty Paich (p41), Van Dyke Parks (p90), Pearls Before Swine (p97), Peter, Paul & Mary (p37), The Pretenders (p162, 163), Richard Pryor (p161), The Replacements (p180), The Routers (p40), Allan Sherman & Executives (p40), The Smart Set (p26), Connie Stevens (p26), Joe Smith (p36), James Taylor (p115), Russ Titleman (p148), Neil Young (p102), Warner Bros. Pictures Backlot (p10-11, 223), Warner Bros. Executives (p52, 101), Warner Bros. Offices (p166), Jack Warner (p12-13), Lenny Waronker (p28)

The publisher gratefully acknowledges the photographers who have provided for the reproduction of their work in this book. Every effort has been made to trace the ownership of all copyrighted material. Please contact the publisher about any inaccuracy or oversight and it will be corrected in subsequent printings.

INDEX